3—

D1454798

PRESIDENTS ON POLITICAL GROUND

PRESIDENTS ON POLITICAL GROUND

Leaders in Action and What They Face

Bruce Miroff

 University Press of Kansas

© 2016 by the University Press of Kansas
All rights reserved

Published by the University Press of Kansas (Lawrence, Kansas 66045), which was organized by the Kansas Board of Regents and is operated and funded by Emporia State University, Fort Hays State University, Kansas State University, Pittsburg State University, the University of Kansas, and Wichita State University

Library of Congress Cataloging-in-Publication Data

Names: Miroff, Bruce, author.
Title: Presidents on political ground : leaders in action and what they face / Bruce Miroff.
Description: Lawrence, Kansas : University Press of Kansas, 2016. | Includes bibliographical references and index.
Identifiers: LCCN 2016004960
ISBN 9780700622856 (cloth : alk. paper)
ISBN 9780700622863 (ebook)
Subjects: LCSH: Presidents—United States—Decision making. | Political leadership— United States. | Executive power—United States.
Classification: LCC JK516˙.M53 2016 | DDC 352.230973—dc23
LC record available at https://lccn.loc.gov/2016004960.

British Library Cataloguing-in-Publication Data is available.

Printed in the United States of America

10 9 8 7 6 5 4 3 2 1

The paper used in this publication is recycled and contains 30 percent postconsumer waste. It is acid free and meets the minimum requirements of the American National Standard for Permanence of Paper for Printed Library Materials Z39.48-1992.

For Nick, Anna, Joaquin, and Amalia

CONTENTS

PREFACE

Richard Nixon was in the White House when I began writing about the presidency. My first book, *Pragmatic Illusions: The Presidential Politics of John F. Kennedy*, was published in 1976. For four decades I have studied presidential politics; *Presidents on Political Ground* aims to distill much of what I have learned. My objective from the start has been to approach presidential leadership as the interplay of individual abilities and choices with the larger structures within which they have to operate. I have been associated in this respect with a subset of presidency scholars who emphasize *leadership in context*.

Although *Presidents on Political Ground* reflects a long career as a presidency scholar, it had a more immediate stimulus as well: the presidency of Barack Obama. Often during Obama's two terms I have been struck by analyses that ascribe his administration's course almost entirely to the president's personal strengths and weaknesses, with little regard for history and context. Obama has proven to be a prime illustration of the problem that motivated this book.

To be sure, some of the responsibility for the overly personalized explanations belongs to Obama himself. Elected at a moment of profound economic dislocation, Obama was drawn to the stories of past presidents who had turned grave crises into transformative moments in the history of the American republic. In the period between his election and his inauguration, he let it be known that he was reading books about Abraham Lincoln and especially Franklin D. Roosevelt. Obama tempted fate by suggesting analogies between their presidencies and his upcoming one. But once in office it did not take long for him to be disabused of this conceit. The wall of opposition he faced from congressional Republicans for his first major undertaking, a massive economic stimulus bill, swiftly demonstrated that he would be granted no Rooseveltian hundred days, indeed no opening for a historic transformation comparable to the New Deal.

Yet for many observers in the media, and especially for conservative and liberal political activists, the comparisons to FDR (and to other modern presidents at times) remained all too handy regardless of changed circumstances. To indignant conservatives, Obama has been seen as too much like FDR, whom they blame for the rise of big government, prone just like his progressive predecessor to executive power grabs and egregious violations of the Constitution. To disappointed liberals, Obama has been seen as a faint imitation of a progressive Roosevelt, too conciliatory and timorous to seize a rare opportunity for fundamental change. Another FDR in the White House would have radically transformed American health care into a "single payer" system and struck forcefully at Wall Street by breaking up the "too big to fail" banks and investment houses.

Amid the arguments over whether Obama has been dangerously strong or distressingly weak, the contextual frameworks that have shaped and circumscribed his administration have too often been obscured. The political ground over which he has traveled has been little charted. When Obama has resorted to executive orders as an alternative to legislative initiatives blocked in Congress, his unilateral actions have been seen as an unusually aggressive assertion of authority rather than a regular feature of every modern presidency. When Obama has suffered defeats in Congress, his modest legislative skills, falling well short of Roosevelt's masterful ways, have been regarded as the primary cause, leaving aside the fact that Roosevelt had overwhelming Democratic majorities in Congress for his first six years in office and did not have to face a Republican opposition that routinely sought to obstruct his every legislative move. Obama has operated in a different media environment, political economy, party system, and policy landscape than FDR encountered. Across the board his presidency has proceeded on a different, and for the most part more difficult, political ground.

President Obama is only one of the major figures in *Presidents on Political Ground*. While making references to presidents prior to the New Deal, the book is mainly concerned with the succession of presidents from FDR to Obama. The contextual understanding that I believe is needed to make sense of any of their presidencies provides me with my theme.

Large parts of *Presidents on Political Ground* were first formulated in response to two invitations for which I am very grateful. I was asked by Nigel Bowles and Alan Renwick to join a group of scholars developing a framework for the comparative study of political leadership. Two meetings of this group—at an American Political Science Association panel in Toronto and a workshop at the University of Oxford—drew me more deeply than before into an examination of presidents in the areas of coalition politics and domestic policy making. Subsequently, another project on comparative political leadership, organized by John Kane, Haig Patapan, and Ian Shapiro, led me to draft papers for meetings at Yale on the topics of "global leadership" and "good democratic leadership."

An ongoing politics and history group at the University at Albany, SUNY, provided me with a forum for extensive discussion of my paper on "Presidents and Economic Royalists." I thank my colleagues for the stimulating exchange.

Early versions of several chapters received helpful critical comments from a number of scholars. My thanks to Peter Breiner, Neil Chaturvedi, Brendan Doherty, Nan Keohane, the late Thomas Langston, Sid Milkis, and Mike Nelson.

Two anonymous readers for the University Press of Kansas were unusually supportive as well as thoughtful in their commentary. For his insightful reading of the entire manuscript, I am especially grateful to Steve Skowronek. The late James MacGregor Burns was an inspiration for my work on leadership and a good friend.

My association with the University Press of Kansas has long been a pleasure. Fred Woodward, by now an old friend, worked with me once again on developing the book project, and Chuck Myers has skillfully brought it to completion. Carol Kennedy and Larisa Martin have brought their skills to copyediting and production, respectively.

I have been blessed by my children's love but also have benefited by their career choices that connect me to political environs relatively distant from my academic position. Nick, a journalist who reports on Latin American politics and culture, and Anna, who has worked in political fundraising and strategic communications, have plenty to teach their father.

My wife, Melinda Lawson, a historian, has been the best of partners in every regard. We talked about Abraham Lincoln on the night we met in 1984, and our shared passion for history and politics has never flagged. Neither has the love and understanding that she has always given me.

PRESIDENTS ON POLITICAL GROUND

Introduction

A MACHIAVELLIAN METAPHOR

The prince, Machiavelli writes, must always keep his mind on war. While hunting in the countryside, hardening his body for the physical rigors of war, he must also study the landscape for prospective fields of battle. The prince needs to "learn the nature of the terrain, and know how mountains slope, how valleys open, how plains lie, and understand the nature of rivers and swamps." Machiavelli cites a historical model for training the military mind in this manner. When Philopoemen, an Achaean general, traveled through the countryside with his companions, he quizzed them: "If the enemy were on that hilltop and we were here with our army, which of the two of us would have the advantage? How could we attack them without breaking formation? If we wanted to retreat, how could we do this? And if they were to retreat, how could we pursue them?'" Even in peacetime, Philopoemen sought to comprehend "all the contingencies that can occur in an army."[1]

My subject in this book is presidents and not princes, politics and not warfare. But I employ Machiavelli's discussion in chapter 14 of *The Prince* as the source of the master metaphor for this study of presidents on the ground of political struggle. Presidents are not likely to win major battles or to avoid damaging defeats if they are not attuned to the shifting terrains upon which their political contests will be decided. They require something akin to what Joseph Nye calls "contextual intelligence"—the capacity to examine in advance the distinctive characteristics of each ground upon which they hope to advance or might have to retreat.[2]

Unlike Machiavelli, I do not presume that any insights I glean from this study will be taken up by leaders themselves. The audience for whom I write contains anyone who tries to understand presidential action: political scientists, historians, journalists, and ordinary citizens. My target is the all-too-common tendency to evaluate presidents without sufficient attention to context, to focus on the dramatic figure in the foreground and leave indistinct the terrain upon which the action unfolds. Without understanding the ground of presidential politics, evaluations are bound to be distorted, whether in the form of too much praise or, more often, too much blame.

In studying presidents on political ground, Machiavelli is a valuable guide for more than his landscape metaphor. The Machiavellian perspective I adopt in this book draws less from the notorious proponent of deception or violence than from the pathbreaking analyst of politics as a dynamic field of struggle. By alerting

1

readers to the flux and contingency of politics, the author of *The Prince* cautions against idealized formulas or pat generalizations about leadership. In Machiavelli's world, so much is always in play for the person at the top that success remains tenuous and failure is never far away. Yet his cold-eyed vision is not meant to discourage action; on the contrary, it is when political leaders know the ground over which they must proceed that sometimes mastery becomes possible and great ends can be achieved.

The shape of conflict, Machiavelli suggests in chapter 14 of *The Prince*, changes with each terrain. The contours of battlefields will look quite different depending on whether they are located in the mountains, in the valleys, or on the plains. Some terrains will be advantageous, favoring an offensive strategy; other terrains will be daunting, with prudence warning of the likelihood of retreat. In many instances the terrain appears neutral, and victory goes to the side that makes the smarter maneuvers on the field of battle. The variability of political ground and of the conflicts that are fought on it is a core proposition of this study of presidents. Presidential action is hardly all of a piece; each ground upon which it proceeds must be understood through its own distinctive features.

Even solid knowledge of each distinct ground for political conflict is not a surefire aid to the actor or guide to the analyst. As Machiavelli famously teaches, it is the unpredictable that ultimately haunts political action: "Fortune is the arbiter of one half of our actions."[3] In his most biting example of Fortune in *The Prince*, Cesare Borgia made every right move to gain power, only to fall when he became gravely ill at the worst possible moment. One does not have to look far to see the role of Fortune in the careers of recent presidents, whose original agendas were dramatically altered by events they could not have anticipated. In his first year in office, George H. W. Bush's administration was blindsided by the remarkably swift collapse of the Soviet empire in Eastern Europe. In his son's first year in office, the terrorist attacks of September 11, 2001, transformed a domestic presidency for a time of peace into a presidency that assumed a global wartime footing. Barack Obama campaigned for the presidency with a long list of domestic reforms in mind, only to have them overshadowed by a financial collapse less than two months prior to his electoral victory. Political ground, then, is not only variable depending on the topography of the terrain; it can also be unstable, subject to earthquakes of greater or lesser magnitudes.

Taking into account all of the factors that contribute to the uncertainties facing a prince, Machiavelli might have been expected to present a pessimistic account of political leadership. On the contrary, for him it is the hardships of political action that test the mettle of leaders and the barriers to success that evoke the creativity of the best among them. "Without a doubt," he writes, princes become great when they overcome difficulties and obstacles that are imposed on them; and therefore Fortune, especially when she wishes to increase the reputation of a new prince, who has a greater need to acquire prestige than a hereditary prince does, creates enemies for him and has them take action against him so that he will have the chance to overcome them and to climb higher up the ladder his enemies have brought him.[4]

Machiavelli's view that dangerous times are fertile ground for great leadership has become familiar to Americans in accounts of the most storied presidents, like Abraham Lincoln and Franklin D. Roosevelt, who led the nation through its most perilous crises.

To understand the leadership of princes amid variability, flux, and contingency, Machiavelli turned to history. His approach recommends itself to a study of presidential leadership on political ground. To the extent that we can discover patterns in presidential actions—patterns that might be different on each distinct political ground—we are most likely to find them through historical investigations. Single-factor explanations for presidential performance, as widely disparate as personality, rational action, or political economy, invariably leave too much in the shadows. Rather than narrowing the angle of vision, a historical approach offers a wide array of cases to review. The trick is to make sense of them by discerning the essential configurations into which most fall. That is the task set for this book.

FIVE POLITICAL GROUNDS

One of the unique features of the contemporary American presidency is that chief executives are, unlike any other political officials, expected to be active across the board. They are judged by how well they navigate their way across a plethora of political terrains. This book does not attempt to provide a comprehensive study of these terrains. Rather, it focuses on five political grounds, chosen not only for their intrinsic importance but for the relative paucity of our knowledge about them.

The chapters that follow explore political terrains that differ considerably from one another. Chapter 1 examines the ground of media. Chapter 2 switches the focus to the ground of political economy. Chapter 3 sets out to map the ground of coalition politics. Chapter 4 studies the politics of domestic policy making. Chapter 5 covers recent developments that have shifted the political ground for presidential leadership in foreign policy.

It will be readily apparent that I have omitted some of the most important grounds for presidential leadership, especially Congress and public opinion. These two terrains have been extensively charted by leading presidency scholars, such as George Edwards III, Jon Bond and Richard Fleisher, Charles Jones, and Mark Peterson in the case of Congress, and Jeffrey Cohen, George Edwards III, Samuel Kernell, Larry Jacobs, and B. Dan Wood in the case of public opinion. They are domains of presidential activity that have lent themselves to impressive quantitative analyses, with historical cases playing only a secondary role. Interestingly, these studies of Congress and of public opinion mostly conclude that the ground for presidential advances is rockier than conventional wisdom would have it. The titles of two books by Edwards—*At the Margins* with respect to presidential influence in Congress and *On Deaf Ears* with respect to presidential efforts to change public opinion—sum up how legislative and public opinion contexts often impede and frustrate leadership.[5]

PRESIDENTIAL LEADERSHIP IN CONTEXT

To highlight the grounds and delineate the contexts for presidential action is to raise the issue of determinism. I want to address this issue up front. To do so will require a brief excursus into competing frameworks for understanding the presidency.

Broadly speaking, presidential studies fall into two categories, with their placement depending on the relative explanatory balance that authors establish between individual agency and structural context. For some scholars, the individual actor is the center of attention, with context noted but seldom elaborated. For other scholars, structures are placed at the fore, with the actor's choices and their outcomes heavily influenced by contextual factors. The individual actor perspective is common in many areas of presidential studies, and it is overwhelmingly favored by journalists and citizens. Challenging what is typically conventional wisdom has been the task of the alternative approach, which argues, as George Edwards III puts it, that "we should focus less exclusively on the president and devote more attention to the context in which the president seeks to lead."[6]

The most famous study of the presidency, Richard E. Neustadt's *Presidential Power*, presents the classic account of individual agency in the White House. Neustadt begins with a structural observation: there is a substantial gap between the high expectations surrounding presidential leadership and the limited constitutional powers of the executive in a system of "separated institutions *sharing* powers."[7] But *Presidential Power* has little further to add about the contextual parameters for executive actions. Rather, Neustadt's concern is how an individual president can close the gap, maximizing limited resources through attentiveness to power stakes and skill at persuading other elite actors. Talent and temperament are his ultimate answers to the puzzle of powerful presidential leadership.

Rational choice scholars, seemingly at an opposite pole from Neustadt in their approach to presidential leadership, share his fundamental emphasis on individual agency. For those in the rational choice camp, the personal qualities of a president can be ignored, at least for the purpose of generating testable hypotheses. As William Howell writes in *Power without Persuasion*, "Rational choice emphasizes the things that all presidents have in common. It treats presidents as generic types, intentional actors who seek policy objectives within well-defined institutional settings."[8] More than Neustadt, rational choice scholars specify the contexts within which presidential actions take place; with their roots in game theory, they are attentive to the institutional parameters and rules that advantage or disadvantage the players. Yet as the name of this approach suggests, the reigning assumption is that any president will be a rational actor who will aim to maximize power wherever the opportunity arises.[9] Moreover, as a unitary actor, the president will be able to move more single-mindedly and coherently than a collective decision making body like the Congress.[10] For all of their theoretical and methodological differences with Neustadt, rational choice scholars share with him an optimistic assumption that power-seeking presidents can prevail over the forces that constrain them.

As is the case with presidential studies that privilege individual agency, contextual approaches appear in very different forms. Two are highlighted here because they are the ones most relevant to this book: the behavioralist approach and the historical-institutional approach. Behavioralist scholars apply statistical methods to large data sets, which in the case of the presidency include congressional roll call votes on presidential proposals, time-series of presidential approval scores, and polling data on responses to presidential efforts at changing public opinion on policy issues. Perhaps the most prominent scholar in these areas, the aforementioned George Edwards III, has repeatedly demonstrated that contextual factors, such as the partisan distribution of seats in Congress or the low level of public interest in politics, explain a great deal more about the fate of presidential ventures than do variations in presidential talent or temperament. Yet if Edwards's work is less sanguine about the prospects for presidential success than are the studies from Neustadt or the rational choice camp, he still leaves space for effective presidential agency. Edwards doubts that presidents can transform the critical contexts for their leadership, but a president who recognizes the opportunities as well as the obstacles that contexts present, and who moves prudently to exploit these opportunities, can achieve a great deal in the office.[11]

Even more central to this book than the contextual approach of behavioral-ists is the historical-institutional approach to the presidency. The most prominent historical-institutional work on the presidency, Stephen Skowronek's *The Politics Presidents Make*, sweeps over the whole history of the institution to uncover a remarkably persistent set of patterns. Skowronek divides the history of the presidency into a series of partisan regimes, each of which dominates the office for a generation or more. Within these regimes, four types of presidents are characterized, depending on whether they found the regime, maintain it, are caught in its collapse, or oppose it without the ability to overthrow it. For Skowronek, presidential success or failure is not, in a fundamental sense, attributable to individual ability or rationality; they are recurrent features of when and where presidents fall in the life span of a regime. Great success is reserved for founders of regimes; presidents in the middle years of a regime produce ambivalent results; presidents left holding the bag for regimes that are breaking down are saddled with a reputation for personal ineptitude. Structure is foremost for Skowronek, but like Edwards, he is hardly unconcerned about opportunities for agency. The great irony in his work is that all presidents disrupt the larger political system in the drive for accomplishments, but more often than not the disruptions end up exploding in their faces.[12]

This study of presidents on political ground has clear affinities with the scholarship of Edwards and Skowronek. Indeed, I have long admired their work and draw many insights from it. Skowronek's scholarship, in particular, plays a prominent role in this book, especially in chapter 3. Yet the political grounds I study here have only a modest amount of shared territory with the political grounds that they have explored. Edwards's studies have concentrated primarily on legislative politics and public opinion; I concentrate on political grounds beyond these two. Skowronek develops a macro-historical theory of presidential leadership; I operate closer to the ground in my explorations into presidential history and discern patterns that are more diverse than the ones he has highlighted.

Siding with Edwards and Skowronek, as opposed to the theoreticians of individual agency, in emphasizing context, I share with them a concern not to devalue the efforts and accomplishments of individual presidents. In each chapter that follows, context represents the political ground, but the stories of presidents as they venture across that ground occupy the larger part of the text. A contextual approach does not imply that presidential acts or fates are predetermined. On the contrary, elaborating the circumstances in any field of action is a prerequisite to assessing the intentions, strategies, and records of presidents in that field. Sometimes accused of advancing a deterministic theory of presidential politics, Skowronek supplies a rejoinder with which I concur: "I believe that understanding leadership contexts ultimately enhances our appreciation of human agency, that we end up with a truer measure of each individual effort—of its novelty and of the broader significance of that novelty—when we take into account basic differences in the way the leadership problem gets configured and understand what is entailed in trying to master each configuration."[13]

A PREVIEW

Each of the five chapters that follow explores a different political ground for presidential action. All combine conceptual analysis with historical cases. Yet the form of analysis and the kinds of cases considered vary with each new political ground.

"Media and the Presidential Spectacle" covers the ground on which a president's identity is established and contested. The contemporary ground for presidential appearances is visual as much as verbal, shaped by television and social media as much as by traditional print media. This is unstable ground: presidents were first advantaged by the rise of network television, then diminished with a profusion of visual choices and a proliferation of platforms for criticism of presidential performances. Yet in the modern era there has been an unchanging expectation for presidents to appear as larger-than-life figures, mounting winning dramas that will impress the mass public. Modern media is the ground for the presidential spectacle: the presentation of character and the deployment of gestures that claim, in defiance of critics, to demonstrate presidential virtue. Five case studies in this chapter—of Kennedy, Reagan, Clinton, the second Bush, and Obama—illustrate the possibilities and pitfalls of these presidential spectacles on media ground.

"Presidents and Economic Royalists" switches the focus from identity to power. Charged with the duty of managing the American economy, presidents have to cope with the pressures from and the resources of powerful actors in the corporate and financial sectors. The recent experience of the Obama presidency amid the Great Recession suggests the pitfalls in neglecting to chart this ground. This chapter focuses in particular on Democratic presidents from FDR to Obama. Elected primarily by constituencies other than the rich and powerful, Democratic presidents tend to have tense and tangled relationships with those that Roosevelt dubbed "economic royalists." Case studies of Roosevelt, Kennedy, Clinton, and Obama display a pattern in these relationships: Democratic presidents need cooperation from business, eventually find themselves in confrontation with the rich and powerful, but ultimately back away from forceful, much less radical, actions and underwrite corporate and financial profits in the service of economic growth.

"Presidents and Coalition Politics" takes presidents onto the ground where followers and foes collide. Presidential rhetoric is typically high-minded, presenting leaders who represent and serve the entire nation. Presidential practice involves grubbier political tasks, necessitating services to some groups and interests while neglecting (or punishing) others. Regardless of their agendas or parties, presidents have to grapple with the imperatives of building, maintaining, and fending off threats to their political coalitions. Strong coalitions are central to electoral prospects, legislative accomplishments, and long-term legacies. Considering presidents from FDR to the present, this chapter maps the terrain of coalitional politics. It attempts to catch presidents in the acts of coalitional politics, placating groups traditionally allied with their parties, scrambling customary alliances when policy objectives cut across established cleavages, poaching among the rival party's supporters, and warding off the potential disaster of coalitional collapse.

"Tough Terrain" studies presidents making domestic policy on political ground. Domestic policy making has proven to be dangerous ground for recent presidents, with signature policy initiatives resulting in devastating electoral consequences. Even when the electoral fallout is less extensive, the politics of domestic policy presents numerous difficulties for presidents. The conventional method of scoring victories and defeats—whether presidential proposals are enacted into law—fails to capture the variety of battles that presidents fight on this ground. I distinguish in this chapter between three kinds of domestic policy making that reflect the dynamic features of the context within which presidents have to act. In situations where the political ground is favorable, presidents can act as policy entrepreneurs, initiating programs that they personally prefer. In other instances, presidents' supporters press hard for bolder measures than presidents have planned to advance. Where rivals threaten to take over an important piece of political ground, presidents may have to outflank their adversaries with policy proposals that run counter to their past stances and actual preferences.

"Foreign Policy Making on Partisan Ground" highlights a recent heightening of political conflict on the ground where presidents are supposed to encounter the fewest political problems. Partisan polarization now infects foreign policy making as much as it does domestic policy making. This chapter traces the growing divergence between Republicans and Democrats in worldviews, showing how opposing perspectives on national security, first articulated by landslide losers Barry Goldwater and George McGovern, eventually came to be partisan orthodoxies. The impact of polar orthodoxies on presidents from Reagan through Obama has been paradoxical. On the one hand, in the field of foreign policy and defense presidents now face greater resistance from the opposing party in Congress and through the media, along with stronger demands for fidelity to party doctrine from their own supporters. On the other hand, presidents today have more maneuverability to zigzag across the lines of partisan cleavage in the name of global realism than they did during the era of a rigid Cold War consensus.

All five of these chapters originated as essays in edited volumes or as conference papers.[14] All have been substantially revised, expanded, and updated; all have been reframed through the Machiavellian metaphor of political ground. Any of the chapters can be read as an independent essay. But only when taken as a whole can they illustrate this book's larger theme: the importance of understanding the disparate and shifting terrains upon which presidents have to operate as political actors.

1. Media and the Presidential Spectacle

Machiavelli depicts a prince who is a tough-minded warrior, astute in the calculated deployment of violence. Yet his prince is also a talented actor, skilled in the manipulation of appearances. While doing whatever it takes to gain and maintain power, the prince "should appear, upon seeing and hearing him, to be all mercy, all faithfulness, all integrity, all kindness, all religion. . . . [F]or ordinary people are always deceived by appearances and by the outcome of a thing."[1] The politics of appearances is just as relevant for presidents as it once was for princes, but the critics of presidential performances today are now more likely to sniff out deception, even when it is not really there.

From the now numerous and scattered precincts of the American media, the observers of presidents' performances speculate about their hidden motives and judge their visible talents. Presidents have had to cope with media coverage since the beginnings of the American republic. They have always used the media to communicate with the public and seek its support, and in turn they have provided rich fare for political partisans and commercial promoters alike. From the early days of a localized partisan press, through the emergence of a national web of magazines and leading newspapers, to the birth of electronic media with radio, presidents increasingly took center stage in a national political drama. But the full force of presidential performances did not emerge until the coming of television. Television brought the essential visual quality of a presidential persona into everyday sight. Ordinary citizens no longer had to imagine how presidents talked, moved, or emoted, how graceful or stiffly they acted, how intimate or how distant they seemed; all that was (or so it appeared) right before their eyes. Television, supplemented now by the Internet and social media, created a new political ground for presidents. It made possible, indeed necessary, what is the subject of this chapter: the presidential spectacle.

Although television became the ground for the presidential spectacles of modern times, that ground has been shifting in recent decades. At first, essentially from John F. Kennedy to Ronald Reagan, television was smooth ground, providing presidents with political advantages that their predecessors might well have envied. As Matthew Baum and Samuel Kernell have written, this was the "golden age of presidential television." Three national networks—CBS, NBC, and ABC—dominated the new medium, capturing about 90 percent of the viewing audience (local channels accounted for the remainder). When the White House asked for prime air time for a major address, all three of the networks honored the request, setting aside their regular programming. With nothing else to watch while the president was speaking, even viewers with little interest in politics tended to stay tuned in.[2] During this period, George Edwards observes, "presidential speeches routinely attracted more than 80 percent of those watching television."[3] Not only did presidents command huge audiences on the occasions when they chose to address the general public, but they were regularly seen and heard on nightly network news programs that drew a large viewership. Snippets or "sound bites" from presidents' minor addresses and press conferences averaged forty-two seconds in 1968 (a figure that would fall to fewer than seven seconds three decades later).[4]

Over the last three decades, however, the "golden age of presidential television" has become only a memory. Regardless of their personalities, party, or media skills, presidents today no longer encounter visual media that favor their capacity to reach a mass audience on their own terms. Cable was the initial culprit in doing away with the "golden age," providing television watchers with numerous alternatives to presidential addresses.[5] According to Edwards, "by the late 1990s, the president was attracting less than a third of homes to watch even his State of the Union message."[6] But cable was only the beginning of a transformed media environment offering an enormous number of options *not to watch* a president. Today, television is a platform for viewing not only hundreds of channels but also DVDs or streaming videos, while laptops, tablets, and smart phones duplicate most of those choices while adding some of their own. Presidents no longer rely as much as in the past on major broadcast speeches because they know that their audience has shrunk. The remnant of the public that does tune in to a president appears to be composed of the most politically attentive citizens—and in an era of partisan polarization, a sizable share of that audience is already inclined to boo rather than to cheer.

The demise of the "golden age of presidential television" has been accompanied by the demise of what might be called the "golden age of presidential news coverage." Through quantitative analysis, Jeffrey Cohen uncovers the shift in coverage of presidents from predominantly favorable to predominantly unfavorable. As a consequence of growing competition among diverse media, "soft news" about celebrities or human interest stories has increased at the expense of "hard news" about politics; excepting niche political shows or websites that generally attract small audiences, news media devote less space to presidents and their activities than they did decades ago. The tone of presidential coverage has become more negative; especially compared to how journalists wrote about presidents such as Eisenhower and Kennedy, today's White House reporters are predisposed to be less deferential and more skeptical. Journalists' stories are also a conduit for increasingly media-savvy opponents, who let almost no presidential message pass through to the public without disparagement.[7] And the explosion of ways to reach the public outside of the "mainstream media" has presented adversaries of the president with vehicles for vehement critiques that would hardly have been heard when presidents commanded the airwaves.

So if presidents, like princes, have always had to act their parts, the number and nature of their critics have magnified the harshness of the reviews. Worse yet for an actor, journalists have found ways to go backstage and reveal presidents without the protection of their official costumes. An intrusive media is no longer inclined to cut presidents slack by staying silent about the secrets that presidents wish to conceal.[8] Franklin D. Roosevelt could keep the extent of his physical handicap out of public photos; John F. Kennedy conducted his sexual affairs with only a wink from knowing reporters. That sphere of presidential privacy has shrunk. There is no parallel from the "golden age of presidential news coverage" to the sex scandal that left the Clinton presidency dead in the water for over a year amid a drumbeat of sensational media revelations leading to impeachment and trial.

Although presidents today have lost much of their earlier edge over the traditional media, they now derive some compensation from new social media. Through a rapidly proliferating array of channels, including Facebook, Twitter, Instagram, and YouTube, the White House can circumvent reporters in communicating its preferred messages and images. The Obama presidency has been a pioneer in the deployment of social media: as of 2015, a White House Office of Digital Strategy numbered fourteen young staffers, slightly exceeding the number of personnel in the Office of the Press Secretary at the beginning of the administration. In May 2015, Obama became the first president to Tweet (with the handle of @POTUS). Yet while social media offer presidents the chance to communicate free of criticisms from skeptical journalists or carping from partisan opponents, their reach is largely limited to existing supporters. Social media targets—and at times can energize—the president's base, especially youthful followers, but it seldom reverberates among a wide audience. In the annals of presidential media, it is unlikely that Obama on Twitter will rank with FDR's Fireside Chats or Kennedy's press conferences.[9]

To map today's rougher media terrain for contemporary presidential performances is not, however, to assume that the critics always occupy the commanding heights. Presidents have a large number of helpers in coping with the media: more members of the White House staff work directly or indirectly on public communications than on any other presidential function.[10] Presidents play the lead role in the dramatic productions that each modern White House mounts, but these are complex productions that require many kinds of talents. Moreover, presidential drama is not limited to televised speeches or other public appearances. Much of what the modern presidency does, in fact, involves the projection of images whose purpose is to shape public understanding and garner public appreciation. Leadership in the modern presidency is often enacted as a spectacle.

THE PRESIDENCY AS SPECTACLE

Examination of the presidency as a spectacle involves asking how a president seeks to appear, but also what the public actually sees. We are accustomed to gauging the public's responses to a president with polls that measure approval and disapproval of overall performance in office and effectiveness in managing the economy and foreign policy. Yet the pollsters' categories say more about the kind of information that politicians, journalists, or academic researchers want than about the terms through which most members of a president's audience judge the president. A public that is presented with presidential spectacles will not ignore questions of effectiveness, but its judgments will be colored by the terms of the spectacle.

A spectacle is a kind of symbolic event, one in which particular details stand for broader and deeper meanings. What differentiates a spectacle from other kinds of symbolic events is the centrality of character and action. A spectacle presents intriguing and often dominating characters not in static poses but through actions that establish their public identities.

Spectacle implies a clear division between actors and spectators. As Daniel Dayan and Elihu Katz have noted, a spectacle possesses "a narrowness of focus, a limited set of appropriate responses, and . . . a minimal level of interaction. What there is to see is very clearly exhibited; spectacle implies a distinction between the roles of performers and audience."[11] A spectacle does not permit the audience to interrupt the action and redirect its meaning. Spectators can become absorbed in a spectacle or can find it unconvincing, but they cannot become performers. A spectacle is not designed for mass participation; it is not a democratic event.

Perhaps the most distinctive characteristic of a spectacle is that the actions that constitute it are meaningful not for what they achieve but for what they signify. Actions in a spectacle are gestures rather than means to an end. What is important is that they be understandable and impressive to the spectators. Roland Barthes illustrates this distinction between gestures and means in his classic discussion of professional wrestling as a spectacle. Barthes shows that professional wrestling is completely unlike professional boxing. Boxing is a form of competition, a contest of skill in a situation of uncertainty. What matters is the outcome, and because that is in doubt, we can wager on it. But in professional wrestling, the outcome is preordained; it would be senseless to bet on who is going to win. What matters in professional wrestling are the gestures made during the match, gestures by performers portraying distinctive characters, gestures that carry moral significance. In a typical match, an evil character threatens a good character, knocks him down on the canvas, abuses him with dirty tricks, but ultimately loses when the good character rises up to exact a just revenge.[12]

It may seem odd to approach the presidency through an analogy with boxing and wrestling—but let us pursue it for a moment. Much of what presidents do is analogous to what boxers do: they engage in contests of power and policy with other political actors, contests in which the outcomes are uncertain. But a growing amount of presidential activity is akin to pro wrestling. The contemporary presidency is presented by the White House as a series of spectacles in which a larger-than-life main character and a supporting team engage in emblematic bouts with immoral or dangerous adversaries.

Facilitated by the emergence of visual media, spectacle has also been fostered by the president's rise to primacy in the American political system. A political order originally centered on institutions has given way, especially in the public mind, to a political order that centers on the person of the president. Theodore Lowi wrote, "Since the president has become the embodiment of government, it seems perfectly normal for millions upon millions of Americans to concentrate their hopes and fears directly and personally upon him."[13] The "personal president" that Lowi describes is the object of popular expectations that are both excessive and contradictory.[14] The president must attempt to satisfy the public by delivering tangible benefits, such as economic growth, but these will almost never be enough. Not surprisingly, then, presidents turn to the gestures of the spectacle to satisfy their audience.

To understand the modern presidency as a form of spectacle, we must consider the presentation of presidents as spectacular characters, the role of their teams as supporting performers, and the arrangement of gestures that convey the meaning of their actions to the audience.

A contemporary president is, to borrow a phrase from Guy Debord, "the spectacular representation of a living human being."[15] An enormous amount of attention is paid to the president as a public character; every deed, quality, and even foible is regarded as fascinating and important. The American public may not learn the details of policy formulation, but they know that Gerald Ford bumps his head on helicopter door frames, that Ronald Reagan likes jellybeans, and that Bill Clinton enjoys hanging out with Hollywood celebrities. In a spectacle, a president's character possesses intrinsic as well as symbolic value; it is to be appreciated for its own sake. The spectators do not press presidents to specify what economic or social benefits they are providing; nor do they closely inquire into the truthfulness of the claims presidents make. (To the extent that they do evaluate the president in such terms, they step outside the terms of the spectacle.) The president's featured qualities are presented as benefits in themselves. Thus John Kennedy's glamour casts his whole era in a romanticized glow, and Reagan's amiability relieves the grim national mood that had developed under his predecessors.

The president's character must be not only appealing in itself but also magnified by the spectacle. The spectacle makes the president appear exceptionally decisive, tough, courageous, prescient, or prudent. Whether the president is in fact all or any of these things is obscured. What matters is that he or she is presented as having these qualities, in magnitudes far beyond what ordinary citizens can imagine themselves to possess. The president must appear confident and masterful before spectators whose very position, as onlookers, denies them the possibility of mastery.[16]

The presidential qualities most likely to be magnified will be those that contrast dramatically with the attributes that drew criticism to the previous president. Reagan, following a president perceived as weak, was featured in spectacles that highlighted his potency. The elder Bush, succeeding a president notorious for his disengagement from the workings of his own administration, was featured in spectacles of hands-on management. Clinton, supplanting a president who seemed disengaged from the economic problems of ordinary Americans, began his administration with spectacles of populist intimacy. The younger Bush, replacing a president notorious for personal indiscipline and staff disorder, presented a corporate-style White House where meetings ran on time and proper business attire was required in the Oval Office. Obama, coming after a president widely disparaged as intellectually incurious and ideologically stubborn, emphasizes his openness to dialogue and pragmatism.

Presidents are the principal figures in presidential spectacles, but they have the help of aides and advisers. The star performer is surrounded by a team. Members of the president's team can, through the supporting parts they play, enhance or detract from the spectacle's effect on the audience. For a president's team to enhance the spectacle, its members should project attractive qualities that either resemble the featured attributes of the president or make up for the president's perceived deficiencies. A team will diminish presidential spectacles if its members project qualities that underscore the president's weaknesses.

A performance team, Erving Goffman has shown, contains "a set of individuals whose intimate cooperation is required if a given projected definition of the situation is to be maintained."[17] The team can disrupt presidential spectacles in a number of ways. A member of the team can call too much attention to himself or herself, upstaging the president. This was one of the disruptive practices that made the Reagan White House eager to be rid of Secretary of State Alexander Haig. A team member can give away important secrets to the audience; Budget Director David Stockman's famous confessions about supply-side economics to a reporter for the *Atlantic* jeopardized the mystique of economic innovation that the Reagan administration had created in 1981. Worst of all, a member of the team can, perhaps inadvertently, discredit the central meanings that a presidential spectacle has been designed to establish. The revelations of Budget Director Bert Lance's questionable banking practices deflated the lofty moral tone established at the beginning of the Carter presidency.

The audience watching a presidential spectacle, the White House hopes, is as impressed by gestures as by results. Indeed, the gestures are sometimes preferable to the results. Thus, a "show" of force by the president is preferable to the death and destruction that are the results of force. The ways in which the invasion of Grenada in 1983, the bombing of Libya in 1986, and the seizing of the Panamanian dictator Manuel Noriega in 1990 were portrayed to the American public suggest an eagerness in the White House to present the image of military toughness but not the casualties from military conflict—even when they are the enemy's casualties.

Gestures overshadow results in a presidential spectacle. They also overshadow facts. But facts are not obliterated. They remain present; they are needed, in a sense, to nurture the gestures. Without real events, presidential spectacles would not be impressive; they would seem contrived, mere pseudoevents. Some of the facts that emerge in the course of an event, however, might discredit its presentation as spectacle. Therefore, a successful spectacle, such as Reagan's "liberation" of Grenada, must be more powerful than any of the facts on which it draws. Rising above contradictory or disconfirming details, the spectacle must transfigure the more pliant facts and make them carriers of its most spectacular gestures.

Presidential spectacles are seldom pure spectacles in the sense that a wrestling match can be a pure spectacle. Although they may involve a good deal of advance planning and careful calculation of gestures, they cannot be completely scripted in advance. Unpredictable events will occur during a presidential spectacle. If the White House is fortunate and skillful, it can capitalize on some of those events by using them to enhance the spectacle. If the White House is not so lucky or talented, such events can detract from, or even subvert, the spectacle.

Also unlike wrestling or other pure spectacles, the presidential variety often has more than one audience. Its primary purpose is to construct meanings for the American public. But it also can direct messages to those whom the White House has identified as its foes or the sources of its problems. In 1981, when Reagan fired the air traffic controllers of the Professional Air Traffic Controllers Organization (PATCO) because they engaged in an illegal strike, he presented to the public the spectacle of a tough, determined president who would uphold the law and, unlike his predecessor, would not be pushed around by grasping interest groups. The spectacle also conveyed to organized labor that the White House knew how to stoke popular skepticism about unions and could make life unpleasant for a labor movement that became too assertive.

As the PATCO firing shows, some presidential spectacles are intertwined with policy objectives. Spectacle production and policy production are fundamentally different: spectacle deploys gestures to burnish the identity of the president; policy production employs means to solve problems affecting others. In practice, however, the world of politics often throws spectacle together with public policy. Spectacle can operate as a handmaiden to policy promotion, as when Barack Obama hiked to a receding Alaskan glacier to dramatize his agenda on climate change. Alternatively, policy can operate as a handmaiden to spectacle, as when George H. W. Bush proposed a ban on flag burning to cast himself as a superpatriot or Bill Clinton called for school uniforms to present himself as a stern father rather than a serial philanderer.

Compared to the serious stakes in policy making, presidential spectacles sometimes can appear trivial. Presidents are supposed to be working hard for the American public, not strutting a stage to impress their audience. Yet on today's media ground, presidents cannot dispense with spectacle if they hope to be effective as policy makers. As we will see in the case of Barack Obama, good policy by itself is not enough in the age of spectacle.

WHAT SPECTACLE COMMUNICATES

Spectacle is a quintessentially modern form of presidential communication with the public. But it needs to be distinguished from two more familiar forms of presidential communication that have been widely studied: rhetoric (as a genre) and White House campaigns to increase public support for presidential proposals before Congress. Presidential rhetoric attracts researchers from the fields of political science and communication. Armed with ancient rhetorical categories derived from Aristotle and contemporary analytical frames from scholarship on speech and literature, scholars pore over the structure, substance, and tropes of presidential addresses to explore their overt and subtle messages. Landmark presidential speeches are now deemed worthy of entire volumes.[18]

The quest for public backing of presidential proposals attracts a different breed of scholars, whose methodology is primarily statistical and whose concern is with measuring influence. While rhetorical scholars presume that strong speeches have a potent impact on their intended audience, behavioralist scholars mostly produce skeptical findings calling into question the familiar conceit that presidents have at their disposal a "bully pulpit." Even the most talented public communicators in the presidency, George Edwards demonstrates with a mass of empirical evidence, "find it very difficult to move the public. Usually they fail."[19] Lawrence Jacobs observes that "research on a wide range of cases of presidents making public appeals and attempting to trade on their popularity consistently demonstrates little effect on public opinion or congressional success."[20]

Rhetoric is sometimes part of a presidential spectacle, but usually only a small part. Spectacle revolves around an ensemble of gestures, only some of which are rhetorical. Indeed, the visual is typically as prominent in spectacle as the verbal. Even in the case of presidential speeches, spectacle involves the physical setting and its symbolism, the president's physical appearance and the impressions it conveys, the visible reactions of the spectators and the emotions they display. Apart from speech making, the contemporary White House produces a stream of presidential photos and videos and stages an array of presidential tableaux. Outside of White House control, the actions and gestures of others, supportive or hostile, reinforce or undermine the spectacle. None of this can be captured by the tools of rhetorical analysis.

The debunking of the "bully pulpit" conceit through careful quantitative studies might, at first glance, raise doubt about the effectiveness of presidential spectacles. Yet if spectacle is not reducible to rhetoric, neither is it primarily about "persuasion" in the traditional sense of changing minds on the issues. Their effectiveness measured by tracking polling data over time, brief but intensive presidential campaigns to boost support for priority proposals in such areas as tax policy or health policy usually produce modest and sometimes counterproductive results. Instrumental communication of this sort can also play a part in the presidential spectacle, but spectacle in the main is a more continuous and pervasive feature of the contemporary presidency.

So if spectacle is not to be equated with rhetoric or with presidential persuasion on the issues, what is it good for? Drawing on a term from sociology, spectacle can be understood as a form of "impression management." Since everyone, according to Erving Goffman, engages in impression management in daily life, the presidential spectacle might be called "spectacular impression management." It aims to craft public impressions of the president's identity as a leader, especially his/her virtues and strengths. Most members of the public, even those in the minority that listen to or read presidential speeches, will not parse their meanings with the analytical bent of pundits, much less rhetorical scholars. The number of citizens open to changing their minds on controversial proposals because of what presidents say is also small. But almost anyone who pays at least minimal attention to the news will have an impression of the president, the best-known figure in all of American life and the sole political leader who can claim to represent the entire nation. For a mass audience that does not pay close attention to political issues and that does not analyze the import of a president's words, spectacle is a bid, almost always a contested one, to define in shining terms who the president is.

With impressions of the president's identity at stake in spectacle, this form of communication functions simultaneously for offense and defense. On the positive side, effective presidential spectacles buttress favorable public impressions formed during the original quest for the office and carry forward their promise. They secure general support that can survive the ups and downs of particular political contests. They frame the personal contrasts that will be central in the campaign for reelection. And they provide presidents with a reserve of good will that can survive even grave threats to their political fortunes. Presidents who have achieved an appealing identity through spectacle, such as Ronald Reagan and Bill Clinton, have bounced back from scandals and finished their administrations high in the polls, while presidents untouched by personal disgrace but lacking the identity of an effective leader, such as Jimmy Carter and George H. W. Bush, have seen their popularity plummet by the end of their time in office.[21]

Spectacle is about defense as well as offense. The image of the "bully pulpit" may have been more applicable in earlier presidential days. Perhaps, however, it was always a misleading trope: presidents never occupied a sanctified elevation from which they spoke to congregants who would not dare to dispute their sermons. Partisan foes and media critics were, from the beginning of the Republic, poised to contradict their words and challenge their purposes. I noted at the beginning of this chapter that on the political ground of the contemporary media, the foes are more amplified and the critics are noisier than ever before. So presidents now stand more exposed than before, with challengers constantly seeking to strip them of virtue and deny their capacity—or even their right—to govern. No wonder that spectacle, as contrived and manipulative as it may seem, can appear to presidents as indispensable armor.

PRECURSORS OF THE PRESIDENTIAL SPECTACLE

Visual as well as verbal, accessible at once to every American, the presidential spectacle is distinctively modern. But presidential image making is as old as the Republic. It is possible to trace the precursors to the presidential spectacle—a prehistory so to speak. There is not space here for that full-blown prehistory. But it is worth briefly observing a few of the significant signposts on the way to spectacle.

George Washington was as self-conscious of his image as any contemporary president. In an age fascinated by the idea of fame as an Enlightenment substitute for the immortality of the soul, Washington was the most famous American before he became president, and he was intent on keeping public admiration intact as he became the nation's first chief executive.[22] But the transition from the traditional pageantry of royal rule in Britain to the novel public enactment of republican executive authority in America was uncertain, and Washington's inclinations leaned toward the traditional. When the president greeted respectable visitors at a weekly levee, he dressed in black velvet, his hair powdered, with an ornamental sword symbolizing his power. When he set out on a tour of the southern states, he rode in an elegant coach, decorated with his personal coat-of-arms, and was accompanied by four servants in colorful livery. Unlike his successors in the presidency, Washington was personally unassailable, but by his later presidential years there were growing rumblings among Jeffersonian republicans that their rival Federalists were all too eager to emulate monarchical symbols.[23]

When the Jeffersonians came to power in 1801, they deliberately substituted home-grown republican gestures for ancestral British rituals. Thomas Jefferson walked from his boardinghouse to his first presidential inauguration. The first Jeffersonian president to tour the states, James Monroe, avoided any traces of British traditions. As Richard J. Ellis writes, "Monroe eschewed the elaborately decorated, privately owned carriage that had transported President Washington. Instead, Monroe rode in public stagecoaches or on horseback. . . . [Observers praised] Monroe's plain republican appearance and his much-publicized desire to avoid processions and parades."[24]

Once democracy replaced republicanism as the dominant American conception of self-government, presidential symbolism oscillated between the heroic and the humble. Andrew Jackson, self-made, willful, and fierce, became an emblem for a brash and prideful new nation. The alternative to Jackson was democratic modesty. In his gestures and even in his physical appearance, Abraham Lincoln became the embodiment of what he called "the plain people" of America.

With the rise of national media—popular magazines and a Washington press corps—in an America robust with industrial and military power at the end of the nineteenth century, a different possibility for presidential image making emerged: the president as the country's chief celebrity. This possibility was brilliantly exploited by Theodore Roosevelt, a genius at self-promotion. Roosevelt's rise to the presidency owed as much to his skill at using media as to his physical courage: his dramatic heroics in Cuba would not have so fully captivated the country had he not brought along reporters and photographers to record his deeds and arranged for an advance contract so that soon he could embellish his own adventure in a thrilling magazine serial and book. Once in the White House, he invited in the press, establishing quarters for reporters on the premises and handing out major presidential news himself. His administration was a parade of flattering images of the president as "the steward of the people"—Roosevelt as "trust buster" (though

William Howard Taft busted more trusts) or Roosevelt as scourge of the "male-factors of great wealth" (though the majority of his campaign funds in 1904 came from wealthy businessmen and he struck up a cozy entente with the House of Morgan). Long before John F. Kennedy's metaphorical New Frontier, Roosevelt brought the iconic symbolism of the Wild West to the White House: the author of "The Strenuous Life" embodied his own preaching as presidential bear-hunter.[25]

The creation of radio, the first medium capable of reaching all Americans at the same time and in their own residences, shifted the ground of presidential im-age making once again. Histrionic gestures and bellowed speeches in the style of Theodore Roosevelt were no longer required; a president now could approach the public in a quieter way and with a smoother voice. Franklin Roosevelt's radio talks were quickly dubbed "Fireside Chats" because they made the president sound as if he was in the same room with his listeners. Through the electronic magic of radio, the president claimed a personal bond with many millions of followers. The Hudson River patrician could not embody "the plain people" as Lincoln had, but in his radio talks he could welcome them as "my friends" and picture them as "the workmen in the mills, the mines, the factories; the girl behind the counter; the small shopkeeper; the farmer doing his spring plowing; the widows and the old men wondering about their life's savings."[26] Now simultaneously celebrity for the people and intimate of the people, Roosevelt pioneered the image of the "personal president." All that remained for the emergence of the modern spectacle was that a president be seen in action as well as heard in speech.

THE EMERGENCE OF TELEVISION AND THE PROMISE OF SPECTACLE: JOHN F. KENNEDY

The promise of spectacle as presented on television was first explored by the ad-ministration of John F. Kennedy. The vast majority of American homes contained a TV set by the beginning of the 1960s, and television became for the purposes of spectacle Kennedy's real New Frontier. To be sure, the possibilities of spectacle were too novel, and the pull of grave Cold War issues too strong, for spectacle to be at the center of the most important events during the Kennedy presidency. None-theless, spectacle was present even in those events—and was still more prominent in secondary undertakings.

During the course of his brief presidency, Kennedy became a remarkable spectacle character. His candidacy had been hindered by critics' skepticism about his age, experience, and political accomplishments. But seeming flaws were soon transmuted into virtues. His would be a presidency that projected youth, vigor, and novelty, that recast the institution itself as a headquarters for intelligence and masterful will. Qualities that signified strength were supplemented by qualities—wealth, physical attractiveness, and wit—that evoked glamour. Kennedy's character was portrayed by the media as pleasurable in its own right. But it also carried larger symbolic meanings, representing, on the surface, the American aspiration to excellence, and, at a deeper level, the nation's excitement with its status as a democratic empire.

Although some of the glitter of Kennedy's character has been rubbed off by later revelations, his winning attributes became a model for many of his successors. Even if they could not hope to emulate all of his appealing qualities, they could strive for that grace in being president that was Kennedy's ultimate hallmark. Richard Nixon had some talent at staging spectacles—witness the shrewd handling of his 1972 trip to China—but he could never come close to matching Kennedy's grace. For example, Nixon and his advisers recognized the impact of pictures of Kennedy walking along the beach or sailing at Hyannis Port on Cape Cod. But their attempt to project the same relaxed charm produced farce rather than spectacle. When news photographers were alerted to shoot pictures of the president walking by the Pacific near his vacation home at San Clemente, they discovered Nixon "traipsing along the beach in an ill-fitting windbreaker, a pair of dress trousers, and *street* shoes."[27]

Kennedy's team also received exceptional media coverage, demonstrating that the people surrounding a president could contribute their own spectacle value. Members of Kennedy's staff and cabinet were portrayed as a "ministry of talent," a constellation of uncommonly intelligent and able men revolving around a brilliant star. Even more engaging was the image, favored by Kennedy himself, of his team as a "band of brothers." In reality, Patrick Anderson showed, Kennedy's staff "hummed with an undercurrent of jealousy, rivalry, and friction."[28] What the public saw, though, was a corps of youthful and impressive aides bound together by their dedication to an equally youthful and impressive leader. Kennedy's team thus served in his spectacle as an extension of its head, magnifying his qualities to add to his luster.

Intelligence and toughness were particularly featured in the area of foreign policy. With McGeorge Bundy as the president's special assistant for national security affairs and Robert McNamara as the secretary of defense, Kennedy had members of his team who underscored his own claim to foreign policy mastery. McNamara became legendary for his analytical sharpness, while Bundy, the former Harvard dean, came across, in the words of David Halberstam, as "the sharpest intellect of a generation, a repository of national intelligence."[29] Projecting unflagging drive and steely determination, both men served as emblems of a forceful foreign policy that could repel communist aggression in an era of heightened Cold War peril.

An even more direct extension of the president's persona was his brother, the attorney general. Not only did Robert Kennedy's intelligence and drive recall those of the president; his closeness to his brother made their strengths appear intertwined. Robert Kennedy still was burdened during this period with a reputation for ruthlessness that contrasted uncomfortably with John Kennedy's charm. Yet the president was not tarnished by his brother or any other aide, both because of his own self-deprecating wit and because his team included an unusually good-humored member in press secretary Pierre Salinger. Salinger became one of the best known of Kennedy's "New Frontiersmen" not because he shared their much-vaunted strengths but because he supplied comic leavening. As Patrick Anderson observed, Salinger "was Kennedy's Falstaff and he made the most of the role."[30]

The most dramatic actions of the Kennedy presidency aimed to produce results rather than to showcase gestures; the modern presidential spectacle had not yet fully come into its own. Yet even in such critical moments as the steel crisis of 1962, the civil rights struggle of 1963, and the recurring Berlin and Cuban crises, the Kennedy White House provided spectacular images that would impress its successors and help to shape future media expectations. Sometimes it was photographic images of the president at the center of a White House command post, cool and deliberate in the heat of crisis. Sometimes it was the image of the president on television as the voice of a righteous nation, denouncing the greed of steel company executives and pronouncing the moral imperative of civil-rights progress.

Where spectacle predominated on the New Frontier was in secondary areas. The space race was rich in spectacle value: Kennedy's public pledge to send a man to the moon had less to do with scientific advancement than with demonstrating the superiority of America's (and the president's) undaunted spirit in the face of the Soviets' head start in space. Physical fitness was a minor spectacle (and a subtle distraction from the president's health issues), as highly publicized fifty-mile hikes by New Frontiersmen highlighted the theme of restoring vigor to American life. The presidential press conference was adapted to the purposes of spectacle and became a venue for some of Kennedy's most popular performances. As the first chief executive to permit live television coverage of his press conferences, Kennedy used this forum to demonstrate to the public his mastery of information, quick intellect, and pointed humor. The substance of his remarks was less important than his appealing way of speaking, while an appreciative corps of reporters served as a stand-in for an admiring public. As much as his dramatic national addresses during prime time, his press conferences vividly manifested the promise of spectacle. Kennedy was television's president, and every one of his successors in the office would be challenged to live up to the standard for spectacle that he first set.

THE TRIUMPH OF SPECTACLE: RONALD REAGAN

The Reagan presidency was a triumph of spectacle. In the realm of substantive policy, it was marked by striking failures as well as significant successes. But even the most egregious of the failures—public exposure of the disastrous covert policy of selling arms to Iran and diverting some of the profits to the Nicaraguan contras—proved to be only a temporary blow to the political fortunes of the most spectacular president since Kennedy. With the help of two heartwarming summits with Soviet leader Mikhail Gorbachev, Reagan recovered from the Iran-contra debacle and left office near the peak of his popularity. His presidency, for the most part, floated above its flawed processes and failed policies, secure in the arresting visual images at the core of its successful spectacle.

The basis of this success was the character of Ronald Reagan. His previous career in movies and television made him comfortable with and adept at spectacles; he moved easily from one kind to another.[31] Reagan presented to his audience a multifaceted character, funny yet powerful, ordinary yet heroic, individual yet representative. His was a character richer even than Kennedy's in mythic resonance.

Coming into office after Jimmy Carter, a president who was widely perceived as weak, Reagan as a spectacle character projected potency. His administration featured a number of spectacles in which Reagan displayed his decisiveness, forcefulness, and will to prevail. The image of masculine toughness was played up repeatedly. The American people repeatedly viewed images of a president who, even though in his seventies, rode horses and exercised vigorously, a president who liked to quote (and thereby identify himself with) movie tough guys such as Clint Eastwood and Sylvester Stallone. Yet Reagan's strength was balanced nicely by his amiability; his aggressiveness was rendered benign by his characteristic one-line quips. The warm grin took the edge off the toughness, removed any intimations of callousness or violence.

Quickly dubbed "the Great Communicator," Reagan presented his character not through eloquent rhetoric but through storytelling. As Paul Erickson has demonstrated, Reagan liked to tell tales of "stock symbolic characters," figures whose values and behavior were "heavily colored with Reagan's ideological and emotional principles."[32] Although the villains in these tales ranged from Washington bureaucrats to Marxist dictators, the heroes, whether ordinary people or inspirational figures like Knute Rockne, shared a belief in America. Examined more closely, these heroes turned out to resemble Reagan himself. Praising the heroism of Americans, Reagan, as the representative American, praised himself.

The power of Reagan's character rested not only on its intrinsic attractiveness but also on its symbolic appeal. The spectacle specialists who worked for Reagan seized on the idea of making him an emblem for the American identity. In a June 1984 memo, White House aide Richard Darman sketched a reelection strategy that revolved around the president's mythic role: "Paint RR as the personification of all that is right with or heroized by America. Leave Mondale in a position where an attack on Reagan is tantamount to an attack on America's idealized image of itself."[33] Having come into office at a time of considerable anxiety, with many Americans uncertain about the economy, their future, and the country itself, Reagan was an immensely reassuring character. He had not been marked by the shocks of recent U.S. history—and he denied that those shocks had meaning. He told Americans that the Vietnam War was noble rather than appalling, that Watergate was forgotten, that racial conflict was a thing of the distant past, and that the U.S. economy still offered the American dream to any aspiring individual. Reagan (the character) and America (the country) were presented in the spectacles of the Reagan presidency as timeless, above the decay of aging and the difficulties of history.

The Reagan team assumed special importance because Reagan ran what Lou Cannon has called "the delegated presidency."[34] As the public knew, Reagan's team members carried on most of the business of the executive branch; his own work habits were decidedly relaxed. Reagan's team did not contain many performers who reinforced the president's character, as Kennedy's youthful, energetic New Frontiersmen had. But it featured several figures whose spectacle role was to compensate for Reagan's deficiencies or to carry on his mission with a greater air of vigor than the amiable president usually conveyed.

David Stockman was the most publicized supporting player in the first months of 1981. His image in the media was formidable. *Newsweek*, for example, marveled at how "his buzz-saw intellect has helped him stage a series of bravura performances before Congress" and acclaimed him "the Reagan Administration's boy wonder."[35] There was spectacle appeal in the sight of the nation's youngest budget director serving as the right arm of the nation's oldest chief executive. More important, Stockman's appearance as the master of budget numbers compensated for a president who was notoriously uninterested in data. Stockman faded in spectacle value after his disastrous confession in fall 1981 that budget numbers had been doctored to show the results the administration wanted.

As Reagan's longtime aide, Edwin Meese III was one of the most prominent members of the president's team. Meese's principal spectacle role was not as a White House manager but as a cop. Even before he moved from the White House to the Justice Department, Meese became the voice and the symbol of the administration's tough stance on law-and-order issues. Although the president sometimes spoke about law and order, Meese took on the issue with a vigor that his more benign boss could not convey.

Secretary of Defense Caspar Weinberger became the administration's most visible cold war hard-liner. As the tireless spokesperson and unbudging champion of a soaring defense budget, he was a handy symbol for the Reagan military buildup. Nicholas Lemann noted that although "Weinberger's predecessor, Harold Brown, devoted himself almost completely to management, Weinberger . . . operated more and more on the theatrical side."[36] His grim, hawk-like visage was as much a reminder of the Soviet threat as the alarming, book-length reports on the Russian behemoth that his Defense Department issued every year.

The Reagan presidency benefited not only from a spectacular main character and a useful team but also from talent and good fortune in enacting spectacle gestures. The Reagan years were sprinkled with events—the PATCO strike, the Geneva summit, the Libyan bombing, and others—whose significance lay primarily in their spectacle value. The most striking Reagan spectacle of all was the invasion of Grenada. As an archetypal presidential spectacle, Grenada deserves a close look.

Reagan ordered American forces to invade the island of Grenada in October 1983. Relations had become tense between the Reagan administration and the Marxist regime of Grenada's Maurice Bishop. When Bishop was overthrown and murdered by a clique of more militant Marxists, the Reagan administration began to consider military action. It was urged to invade by the Organization of Eastern Caribbean States, composed of Grenada's island neighbors. And it had a pretext for action in ensuring the safety of the Americans—most of them medical students—on the island. Once the decision to invade was made, U.S. troops landed in force, evacuated most of the students, and seized the island after encountering brief but unexpectedly stiff resistance. Reagan administration officials announced that in the course of securing the island, U.S. forces had discovered large caches of military supplies and documents indicating that Cuba planned to turn Grenada into a base for the export of communist revolution and terror.

The details that eventually came to light cast doubt on the Reagan administration's claims of a threat to the American students and a buildup of "sophisticated" Cuban weaponry in Grenada. Beyond such details, there was the sheer incongruity between the importance bestowed on Grenada by the Reagan administration and the insignificance of the danger it posed. Grenada is a tiny island, with a population of 100,000, a land area of 133 square miles, and an economy whose exports totaled $19 million in 1981.[37] That U.S. troops could secure it was never in question; as Richard Gabriel has noted, "In terms of actual combat forces, the U.S. outnumbered the island's defenders approximately ten to one."[38] Grenada's importance did not derive from the military, political, and economic implications of America's actions, but from its value as a spectacle.

What was this spectacle about? Its meaning was articulated by a triumphant President Reagan: "Our days of weakness are over. Our military forces are back on their feet and standing tall."³⁹ Reagan, even more than the American military, came across in the media as "standing tall" in Grenada.

The spectacle actually began with the president on a weekend golfing vacation in Augusta, Georgia. His vacation was interrupted first by planning for an invasion of Grenada and then by news that the U.S. Marine barracks in Beirut had been bombed. Once the news of the Grenada landings replaced the tragedy in Beirut on the front page and television screen, the golfing angle proved to be an apt beginning for a spectacle. It was used to dramatize the ability of a relaxed and genial president to rise to a grave challenge. And it supplied the White House with an unusual backdrop to present the president in charge, with members of his team by his side. As Francis X. Clines reported in the *New York Times*,

> The White House offered the public some graphic tableaux, snapped by the White House photographer over the weekend, depicting the President at the center of various conferences. He is seen in bathrobe and slippers being briefed by Mr. Shultz and Mr. McFarlane, then out on the Augusta fairway, pausing at the wheel of his golf cart as he receives another dispatch. Mr. Shultz is getting the latest word in another, holding the special security phone with a golf glove on.⁴⁰

Visuals of the president as decision maker were particularly effective because pictures from Grenada itself were lacking; the Reagan administration had barred the American press from covering the invasion. This move outraged the press but was extremely useful to the spectacle, which would have been subverted by pictures of dead bodies or civilian casualties or by independent sources of information with which congressional critics could raise unpleasant questions.

The initial meaning of the Grenada spectacle was established by Reagan in his announcement of the invasion. The enemy was suitably evil: "a brutal group of leftist thugs." America's objectives were purely moral: to protect the lives of innocent people on the island, namely American medical students, and to restore democracy to the people of Grenada. And the actions taken were unmistakably forceful: "The United States had no choice but to act strongly and decisively."⁴¹

But the spectacle of Grenada soon expanded beyond this initial definition. The evacuation of the medical students provided one of those unanticipated occurrences that heighten the power of spectacle. When several of the students kissed the airport tarmac to express their relief and joy at returning to American soil, the resulting pictures on television and in the newspapers were better than anything the administration could have orchestrated. They provided the spectacle with historical as well as emotional resonance. Here was a second hostage crisis—but where Carter had been helpless to release captive Americans from Iran, Reagan had swiftly come to the rescue.

Rescue of the students quickly took second place, however, to a new theme: the claim that U.S. forces had uncovered and uprooted a hidden Soviet-Cuban base for adventurism and terrorism. In his nationally televised address, Reagan did not ignore the Iran analogy: "The nightmare of our hostages in Iran must never be repeated." But he stressed the greater drama of defeating a sinister communist plot. "Grenada, we were told, was a friendly island paradise for tourism. Well, it wasn't. It was a Soviet-Cuban colony being readied as a major military bastion to export terror and undermine democracy. We got there just in time."[42] Grenada was turning out to be an even better spectacle for Reagan: He had rescued not only the students but the people of all the Americas as well.

As the spectacle expanded and grew more heroic, public approval increased. The president's standing in the polls went up. *Time* reported that "a post-invasion poll taken by the *Washington Post* and ABC News showed that 63% of Americans approve the way Reagan is handling the presidency, the highest level in two years, and attributed his gain largely to the Grenada intervention."[43] Congressional critics, although skeptical of many of the claims the administration made, began to stifle their doubts and chime in with endorsements in accordance with the polls. An unnamed White House aide, quoted in *Newsweek*, drew the obvious lesson: "You can scream and shout and gnash your teeth all you want, but the folks out there like it. It was done right and done with dispatch."[44]

In its final gestures, the Grenada spectacle actually commemorated itself. Reagan invited the medical students to the White House and, predictably, basked in their praise and cheers. The Pentagon contributed its symbolic share, awarding some 8,000 medals for the Grenada operation—more than the number of American troops that had set foot on the island. In actuality, Gabriel has shown, "the operation was marred by a number of military failures."[45] Yet these were obscured by the triumphant appearances of the spectacle.

That the spectacle of Grenada was more potent and would prove more lasting in its effects than any disconfirming facts was observed at the time by Anthony Lewis. Reagan "knew the facts would come out eventually," wrote Lewis. "But if that day could be postponed, it might make a great political difference. People would be left with their first impression that this was a decisive President fighting communism."[46] Grenada became for most Americans a highlight of Reagan's first term. Insignificant in military or diplomatic terms, as spectacle it was one of the most successful acts of the Reagan presidency.

A POSTMODERN SPECTACLE: BILL CLINTON

Reagan's successor, George H. W. Bush, had two disparate spectacles: a masterful spectacle in global affairs, an inept spectacle on the home front. The man who defeated him, Bill Clinton, had many more than two, for Clinton's was a post-modern spectacle. A postmodern spectacle, previously more familiar in popular culture than in presidential politics, features fleeting images and fractured conti-nuity, surfaces without depths, personae rather than personalities. Characters in a postmodern spectacle succeed not by capturing the lasting admiration or trust of their audience but by artfully personifying the changing fashions that fascinate it.

Depictions of Clinton by close observers in the media tended to agree on his shape-shifting presidential performance but to differ about whether it should evoke moral indignation or neutral evaluation. One caustic Clinton watcher, *New York Times* columnist Maureen Dowd, called the president "the man of a thousand faces."[47] Other commentators preferred cool, postmodern terms such as *makeover* and *reinvention,* the same words used to describe a diva of contemporary pop culture, Madonna.[48]

Clinton's presidency had important elements of constancy, including the suc-cessful economic course he first charted in 1993 and his underlying attachment to government as a potentially positive force in society. The frequent changes of course during Clinton's two terms owed as much to the formidable political constraints he faced as to the opportunities for spectacle he seized.[49] Moreover, historical precedents for Clinton's "mongrel politics" may be found in the admin-istrations of presidents such as Woodrow Wilson and Richard Nixon, who also were accused of opportunistic borrowing from ideological adversaries in eras when the opposition party set the reigning terms of political discourse.[50] None-theless, Clinton's repeated redefinitions of himself and his presidency made these predecessors seem almost static by comparison. Sometimes awkwardly, sometimes nimbly, Clinton pirouetted across the presidential stage as no one before him.

Clinton's first two years in office were largely a failure of spectacle. The prom-ising populist intimacy he displayed in the 1992 campaign quickly gave way to a spectacle of Washington elitism: social life among the rich and famous (including an infamous $200 haircut by a Beverly Hills stylist) and politics among the en-trenched and arrogant (the cozy alliance with the Democratic congressional lead-ership). The new president seemed simultaneously immature (the undisciplined decision delayer aided by a youthful and inexperienced White House staff) and old-fashioned (the big-government liberal with his bureaucratic scheme to reform the health care system). The crushing rebukes that Clinton suffered in 1994—the failure of his health care plan even to reach the floor of the House or Senate, and the Republican takeover of both houses in the midterm elections—showed how little he had impressed his audience. Yet a postmodern irony was at work for Clinton—his defeats freed him. Not having to implement a large-scale health care plan, Clinton was able to dance away from the liberal label. Not having to tie himself to his party's congressional leadership in a bid for legislative achievement, he was able to shift his policy stances opportunely to capitalize on the excesses of the new Republican agenda.

In his first two years, Clinton lacked an important ingredient of many presidential spectacles: a dramatic foil. George H. W. Bush had Manuel Noriega and Saddam Hussein, but the post–Cold War world was too uninteresting to most Americans to supply foreign leaders ripe for demonization. (That would change after September 11, 2001.) The hidden blessing of the 1994 elections for Clinton was that they provided him with a domestic foil of suitably dramatic proportions: Speaker of the House Newt Gingrich. Gingrich was often compared to Clinton—and the comparison worked mostly in Clinton's favor. Shedding the taint of liberalism, Clinton pronounced himself a nonideological centrist saving the country from Gingrich's conservative extremism. Before, Clinton had talked and shown off too much in public; now, in comparison to the grandiose garrulousness of Gingrich, he seemed almost reticent—and certainly more mature. Attacked as too soft in his first two years, Clinton could turn the image of compassion into a strength by attacking a foil who proposed to reduce spending for seniors on Medicare and to place the children of welfare mothers in orphanages. Lampooned as spineless in his first two years, Clinton could display his backbone by winning the budget showdown with Gingrich and the Republicans in the winter of 1995–1996.[51]

In a postmodern spectacle, a president can try on a variety of styles without being committed to any one of them. As the 1996 election season commenced (and as Gingrich fled the spotlight after his budget defeat), Clinton executed another nimble pirouette by emulating the patron saint of modern Republicans, Ronald Reagan. Clinton's advisers had him watch Reagan videotapes to study "the Gipper's bearing, his aura of command."[52] His campaign team found a model for 1996 in the 1984 Reagan theme of "Morning in America," in which a sunny president capitalized on peace and prosperity while floating serenely above divisive issues. Like Reagan in 1984, Clinton presented himself in 1996 as the benevolent manager of economic growth, the patriotic commander in chief, and the good father devoted to family values. Unlike Reagan, he added the images of the good son protecting seniors and the good steward protecting the environment. Clinton's postmodern appropriation of Reagan imagery helped to block the Republicans from achieving their goal of a unified party government fulfilling Reagan's ideological dreams.

Clinton's postmodern spectacle shaped the public's impressions of his team. With a man of uncertain character in the White House, strong women in the cabinet drew special attention: Attorney General Janet Reno at the outset of his first term, Secretary of State Madeleine Albright at the outset of his second. But no members of Clinton's cabinet or staff played as important a supporting role in his spectacle as his wife, Hillary, and his vice president, Al Gore. Hillary Rodham Clinton appeared as an updated, postfeminist version of Eleanor Roosevelt, a principled liberal goad pressing against her husband's pragmatic instincts. Like Eleanor, she was a hero to the liberal Democratic faithful and a despised symbol of radicalism to conservative Republican foes. Al Gore's spectacle role was to be the stable and stolid sidekick to the quicksilver president. Even his much-satirized reputation as boring was reassuring when counterpoised to a president who sometimes appeared all too eager to charm and seduce his audience.

A postmodern spectacle is best crafted by postmodern spectacle specialists. When Clinton's presidential image began taking a beating, he turned for help to image makers who previously had worked for Republicans but who were as ideologically unanchored as he was. In 1993 Clinton responded to plunging poll ratings by hiring David Gergen, the White House communications chief during Reagan's first term. But the amiable Gergen was unable to reposition Clinton as a centrist nearly so effectively as Dick Morris, Clinton's image consultant after the 1994 electoral debacle. Morris had worked before for Clinton but also for conservative Republicans such as Senate majority leader Trent Lott. As a *Newsweek* story described him, Morris "was a classic mercenary—demonic, brilliant, principle-free."[53] It was Morris's insight, as much as Clinton's, that rhetoric and gesture, supported by the power of the veto, could turn a presidency seemingly moribund after 1994 into a triumphant one in 1996.

The remarkable prosperity the nation enjoyed during Clinton's second term purchased an unusual stretch of calm (some called it lethargy) for his administration—until the Monica Lewinsky storm threatened to wreck it in early 1998. Numerous Americans of all political persuasions were appalled by Clinton's sexual escapades and dishonest explanations in the Lewinsky affair. But for Clinton-haters on the right, long infuriated by the successful spectacles of a character who symbolized (for them) the 1960s culture they despised, the Lewinsky scandal produced a thrill of self-confirmation. See, they proclaimed, his soul *is* the moral wasteland we always said it was. The unwillingness of most Americans to concur with conservative Republicans that Clinton's moral failures necessitated his ouster from the presidency only made his impeachment and conviction more urgent for the right. If strong support for Clinton in the polls indicated that the public was following him down the path toward moral hollowness, then removing him became a crusade for the nation's soul, an exorcism of the moral rot jeopardizing the meaning of the Republic.

But the moralistic fulminations of the right were no match for the power of spectacle. It was not spectacle alone that saved the Clinton presidency. Clinton was protected by prosperity and by Americans' preference for his centrist policies over the conservative alternatives. He was aided, too, by the inclination of most Americans to draw a line between public rectitude and private freedom. Nonetheless, Clinton's eventual acquittal by the Senate owed much to spectacle. To be sure, his own spectacle performance in the Year of Lewinsky was hardly his best. Perhaps no role suited Clinton so little as that of repentant sinner. But he was blessed by even worse performances from his adversaries. Just as Newt Gingrich had been necessary to resuscitate Clinton from the political disaster of 1994, so was Kenneth Starr, the independent counsel in hot pursuit of the president, essential to his rescue from the personal disaster of 1998. Starr's self-righteous moralism disturbed most Americans more than Clinton's self-serving narcissism.

In the end, the shallowness of the postmodern spectacle that had characterized the Clinton presidency from the start supplied an ironic benefit in the Lewinsky scandal. Had Clinton possessed a stable, respected character, revelations of secret behavior that violated that character might have startled the public and shrunk its approval of his performance in office. His standing in the polls might have plummeted, as President Reagan's did after the disclosure that his administration was selling arms to terrorists. But because a majority of Americans had long believed, according to the polls, that Clinton was not very honest or trustworthy, his misbehavior in the Lewinsky affair came as less of a shock and was diluted quickly by frequent reminders of his administration's popular achievements and agenda. Postmodern spectacle is not about character, at least not in a traditional sense; it is about delivering what the audience desires at the moment. Personality, political talent, and a keen instinct for survival made Bill Clinton the master of postmodern spectacle.

Postmodern spectacle may be shallow, but in Clinton's hands it became quite effective. Neither of the two presidents who succeeded him have been inclined to his postmodern approach—George W. Bush because he was too ideological and Barack Obama became he is too focused on addressing policy problems to pay much attention to gestures. Neither has been as successful at spectacle as was Clinton.

THE SOURING OF SPECTACLE: GEORGE W. BUSH

George W. Bush scored the highest Gallup approval rating in history after the terrorist attacks on September 11, 2001—and the highest Gallup disapproval rating ever during his final year in office. Bush's was a spectacle that soared briefly, then soured worse than that of even his most beleaguered predecessors in the White House.[54]

Although Bush promised the novelty of "compassionate conservatism" during the 2000 campaign, his administration's original agenda mainly followed the familiar priorities of the Republican right. But Bush's conservatism ran deeper than his policy prescriptions. In its characters, its styles, and its gestures, the Bush administration was determined to reach back past the postmodern spectacle of Bill Clinton and restore the faded glories of contemporary conservatism.

One fund of recycled images and themes upon which Bush drew was the Reagan spectacle. As a presidential character, Bush enjoyed many affinities with Reagan. He presented himself as a Reagan-style nonpolitician whose optimism and bonhomie would brighten a harsh and demoralizing political environment. His principal policy prescriptions for the nation also recycled Reaganesque themes and gestures. Like Reagan, Bush rapidly pushed through Congress a massive tax cut that favored the wealthy in the guise of an economic stimulus, using "fuzzy math" to promise Americans the pleasure of prosperity without the pain of federal deficits. Like Reagan, too, Bush promoted a national missile defense system that would use cutting-edge (and still nonexistent) technology to restore the ancient dream of an innocent America invulnerable to the violent quarrels that beset the rest of the world. Even the Bush administration's most politically costly stance in its early months, presidential decisions favoring private interests over environmental protection, was couched in the Reagan-style claim of protecting the pocketbooks of ordinary citizens. Revising a Clinton rule that would have mandated higher efficiency for central air conditioners, Bush's secretary of energy, Spencer Abraham, indicated that his goal was to save low-income consumers from having to pay more to cool their homes or trailers.[55]

Recycled images and themes from his father's administration were equally evident in the early months of Bush's presidency. They were especially useful as emblems of the new president's "compassionate" side. Like his father, "W" trumpeted his conciliatory stance toward congressional opponents and set out to be an "education president." Bush's recycling of paternal gestures also was apparent in his meetings with representatives of the groups that had opposed his election most strongly. Just as the father had met with Jesse Jackson after winning the White House, the son invited the Congressional Black Caucus. Neither Bush expected to win over African American voters through these gestures. Instead, each hoped to signal to moderate whites that he was a "kinder, gentler" (George H. W. Bush) or "compassionate" (George W. Bush) conservative who exuded tolerance and goodwill.

On September 11, 2001, when al-Qaida terrorists killed thousands of Americans in a twisted spectacle of their own by piloting hijacked airliners into the World Trade Center and the Pentagon, Bush was given the chance to stage a more politically potent spectacle. The recycled conservative became the warrior president. Clumsy in his first public responses to the horror of September 11, 2001, Bush quickly hit his stride in what would be the most effective spectacle gesture of his entire presidency. On September 14, he visited Ground Zero, the scene of devastation at the World Trade Center. Standing on a pile of Trade Center rubble, with his arm around a retired fireman, Bush spoke through a bullhorn to mourn the loss of lives and express gratitude to the assembled firefighters, police, and first responders. When someone in the crowd shouted that he couldn't hear the president, Bush replied: "I can hear you! The rest of the world hears you! And the people—and the people who knocked these buildings down will hear all of us soon!" In response, the assemblage began chanting: "U.S.A., U.S.A." Riveting visually as well as verbally, and expressing in very few words the deep emotions of a nation in shock, the bullhorn episode made Bush into an icon of American solidarity, pride, and defiance.[56]

The president's speech to Congress on September 20, combining a forceful response to terrorism, a compassionate response to tragedy, and a teaching of tolerance toward followers of the Islamic faith, struck a careful balance. However, after the initial success of the military campaign against al-Qaida and the Taliban regime that harbored it in Afghanistan, the balance in Bush's original approach to September 11 gave way to a consistently martial tone. Paced by Secretary of Defense Donald Rumsfeld, the Bush administration began to feature a spectacle of muscular globalism. In his State of the Union address in January 2002, the commander in chief previewed an expansion of the war on terror to combat an "axis of evil," composed of North Korea, Iran, and especially Iraq.[57] Bush's dramatic phrase, which made headlines around the world, rhetorically invoked both the nation's Axis enemies in World War II and the Soviet "evil empire" of the Cold War to amplify the peril posed by new adversaries in the Middle East and Asia. In its emphasis on eliminating the regime of Saddam Hussein in Iraq, the phrase gestured toward the spectacular completion by the son of the mission in which the father, it now seemed, had sadly fallen short. The speech began the buildup to the war against Iraq that was launched a year later, as the Bush administration mustered its political and rhetorical resources to portray Saddam's regime, with its alleged weapons of mass destruction and ties to al-Qaida, as a sinister threat to American security.

The war in Iraq was far more serious and deadly than Reagan's invasion of Grenada, and Bush's spectacle specialists were on the lookout for even more gripping gestures that would display a president "standing tall." As Elisabeth Bumiller noted in the New York Times, "The Bush administration, going far beyond the foundations in stagecraft set by the Reagan White House, is using the powers of television and technology like never before."[58]

Copiloting an S-3B Viking onto the deck of the aircraft carrier *Abraham Lincoln* on May 1, 2003, President Bush starred in what was instantly recognized as a new classic of presidential spectacles; the press quickly dubbed it Bush's *Top Gun* affair, recalling the Tom Cruise movie. The White House used the carrier as its stage to announce that major combat operations in Iraq were over; a banner over the president's head was emblazoned, "Mission Accomplished." Every detail of the event was meticulously planned for how it would look on television and in newspaper photos. The landing of the Viking at sea highlighted the degree of risk, with the fighter jet brought to a halt by the last of the four cables that catch planes on the carrier deck. Members of the *Lincoln* crew were garbed in varied but coordinated shirt colors as they surrounded the president—reminiscent of a football halftime ceremony. At the center of this massive stage was President Bush, who played his part with evident relish. *New York Times* columnist Maureen Dowd described the moment: "He flashed that famous all-American grin as he swaggered around the deck of the aircraft carrier in his olive flight suit, ejection harness between his legs, helmet tucked under his arm, awe-struck crew crowding around."[59]

Through these gestures, Bush's spectacle specialists implanted his image as a warrior president while eliding the realities on the ground in Iraq. Adhering to the tradition of civilian control of the military, Bush's predecessors had generally eschewed military garb. But his choice of martial clothing on the *Abraham Lincoln* and at subsequent appearances with soldiers deployed to Iraq played up his oneness with the American armed forces. The tailhook landing on the carrier suggested that Bush, as copilot, was willing to share some of the risks to which his decisions as commander in chief exposed American troops. No matter how controversial the war in Iraq might be, the one aspect of it that aroused consensus among Americans was the steadfast courage of the armed forces. Amalgamating himself with the troops through warrior spectacles, Bush signified that this virtue was his, too.

Subsequent media inquiries unearthed details that called into question this signification. Viewers of Bush's dramatic flight to the *Abraham Lincoln* had witnessed what appeared to be a risky jet landing at sea. Later it was revealed by the press that the aircraft carrier was close to San Diego and could have been reached by helicopter; in fact, the ship had sailed a bit further out into the Pacific so that the California coastline would not be visible on television.[60] The president also was derided later on for the "Mission Accomplished" banner, whose sentiment turned out to be wildly premature.

Although the premises with which Bush had taken the nation to war in Iraq were soon shown to be false, his 9/11 image as America's protector against terrorists and his identification through spectacle with American troops were formidable assets when he faced the voters in 2004. At the hands of the president's campaign managers (some of whom had designed his Iraq spectacles), John Kerry, a decorated war hero in Vietnam, was re-created as a foreign-policy weakling compared with George W. Bush, who had avoided Vietnam but had become a spectacle warrior.

Yet if Bush's spectacle specialists had hoped to portray the invasion and occupation of Iraq as an adventure tale, by the time of Bush's reelection, it was beginning to turn into a horror story instead. The "bad guys" in Iraq, with their suicide bombings and beheadings, perpetrated such sickening violence that Americans began to wonder what had happened to the Bush administration's prediction that Iraqis would greet U.S. forces as liberators. Even worse for the Bush spectacle was horror on the American side. American guards at the Abu Ghraib prison abused and sexually humiliated Iraqi prisoners. Meanwhile, American troops, many left poorly protected due to insufficient armor, were subjected to grievous wounds from insurgent explosive devices in Iraq, and when they were shipped home, they were housed in shabby medical facilities. Most Americans continued to perceive the troops as virtuous, but it was increasingly difficult to find virtue in the civilian leaders who had sent them into such a hell.

September 11, 2001, was an unexpected event that allowed Bush's spectacle to soar. Hurricane Katrina in 2005 was an equally unexpected event that compounded Bush's failures in Iraq and soured his presidency for the remainder of his term. The hurricane that devastated New Orleans and the Gulf Coast was among the worst natural disasters in American history. But it was also a political disaster for the Bush presidency. Television, the tool of presidential spectacle, now savagely undermined it. Heart-wrenching pictures of hurricane victims, most of them poor and black, were powerful as well for what was absent: the federal rescue effort that could have saved many. Irate media commentators suggested that the president had abandoned his people.

President Bush's personal role in the Hurricane Katrina story contributed to that message. On vacation when the hurricane struck the Gulf Coast, Bush was urged by his top political adviser, Karl Rove, to fly over New Orleans and survey the damage. But unlike his "Mission Accomplished" landing, this was no *Top Gun* immersion in the thick of action. Photos of Bush soaring high above New Orleans in the comfort and safety of *Air Force One*, his press secretary Scott McClellan later observed, fostered "an image of a callous, unconcerned president."[61] Accompanying stories of incompetence on the part of Bush's subordinates in response to the hurricane, the pictures suggested a president who poorly comprehended what was happening either at home or abroad.

Bush's team made its own contributions to the souring of his spectacle. The hapless supporting player in the Hurricane Katrina story was Michael Brown, the lightweight head of the Federal Emergency Management Agency. Leading roles in the Iraq fiasco were played by administration heavyweights, especially Vice President Dick Cheney and Secretary of Defense Donald Rumsfeld. Both Cheney and Rumsfeld became notorious in the media for the arrogance with which they wielded power and dismissed criticism. Cheney was prone to cheery pronouncements about Iraq that had no connection to events on the ground, as when he proclaimed that the insurgency was in its "last throes" just before it reached new depths of violence. Rumsfeld was inclined to downplay discontent in the military's ranks, replying to one soldier who bemoaned the lack of armor for trucks: "You go to war with the army you have, not the army you might want."[62] Bush eventually dumped Rumsfeld, but he could not fire the vice president, whom critics dubbed the Darth Vader of American politics.

Changes in the media also played a part in the souring of the Bush spectacle. President Bush did have help from FOX News, a cheerleader for Republicans and a scourge of Democrats. But on the other side of the ledger were numerous cable (and Internet) commentators who picked apart all of the Bush administration's flaws. Perhaps the deadliest deconstruction of Bush and his team was the work of Comedy Central's satirists of spectacle, Jon Stewart and Stephen Colbert.

By his final months in office, Bush's spectacle had become so sour that the president was nearly ignored by the media. As the extraordinary election contest between Barack Obama and John McCain took center stage in 2008, Bush seemed more spectator than performer. A small and unexpected occurrence during the president's last visit to Iraq in December 2008 marked the finale of his spectacle. Infuriated by what had happened to his country after Bush invaded it, an Iraqi journalist threw both of his shoes (a gesture of extreme contempt in his culture) at the American president during a news conference.[63]

Four spectacle moments encapsulated the downward arc of Bush's presidential image. At Ground Zero, he had become an icon for a courageous American response to September 11. On the aircraft carrier *Abraham Lincoln*, he had starred in the part of triumphant warrior president, only to have the contrived gestures of that spectacle later exploded by grim realities on the ground in Iraq. After his ill-fated flyover of New Orleans in the wake of Hurricane Katrina, an image of indifference to suffering had been added to an image of incompetence in performance. Bush had wanted to emulate Reagan in "standing tall." In Baghdad at the end of his presidency, he was reduced to ducking footwear.

SPECTACLE AND RATIONALITY:
BARACK OBAMA

Shortly after President Barack Obama and the Democratic Party took a "shel-lacking" in the 2010 congressional elections, Obama told a journalist that he had been too preoccupied with enacting legislation at the expense of connecting to the American public: "the symbols and gestures—what people see coming out of this office—are at least as important as the policies we put forward."[64] A year and a half later, amid the 2012 campaign, he returned to the theme in a television interview: "The mistake of my first term . . . was thinking that this job was just about getting the policy right. And that's important. But the nature of this office is also to tell a story to the American people that gives them a sense of unity and purpose and optimism, especially during tough times."[65] Obama's words are unusual in a dual sense: seldom before has a president openly acknowledged the power of specta-cle—and seldom before has a president candidly acknowledged his own shortfall in using this power.

Anyone witnessing Obama's remarkable campaign for the presidency in 2008 would never have predicted this shortfall. Obama's was one of the most spectac-ular runs for the presidency in American history. The historic audacity of a black man in aiming for and then capturing the White House was a spectacle all by itself. But Obama's rhetorical gifts and golden smile captivated and energized millions, as vast throngs assembled along the campaign trail to be energized by his message of hope and change. Of what other presidential candidate could it be said that his campaign oratory could be remixed as song: when will.i.am of the Black Eyed Peas assembled an all-star cast of musicians and actors to transform Obama's "Yes We Can" speech in an early primary into a music video, it swiftly went viral and became an anthem for the candidate's young supporters.

The first great spectacle of the nation's first black chief executive came on in-auguration day in 2009, as a crowd record-breaking in both numbers and diversity assembled on the National Mall in the freezing cold to hear Obama's first words as president. Yet his speech proved to be less a carryover of the campaign's excitement than a harbinger of the letdown to follow. Obama's inaugural address was more sober than uplifting. Quoting Scriptures, the new president said that the time had come "to set aside childish things." His reference was to the preceding years of "petty grievances . . . and worn-out dogmas." Yet his words might as well have referred to the staging of spectacle as one of those "childish things."[66]

In place of the power of spectacle, the Obama White House focused intently on the power of policy. Situating himself, as Stephen Skowronek has observed, in the Progressive tradition, the new president operated under the assumption that "good policy" alone could transform the nation.[67] Bill Clinton had demonstrated that small-bore policy could make for smart symbolic politics. But Obama was after large-scale legislative victories in economic recovery, financial regulatory reform, health-care reform, and alternative energy.

The hallmark of Obama's approach to his job was rationality and expertise applied to problem solving. His was a serious and substantive politics—but one that cut against the requirements of spectacle. The protracted, unseemly process of congressional action and the complex, highly technical details of the legislation that resulted were so often arcane that few outside the Washington elite could follow the action. In the midst of shepherding several history-making bills to passage, Obama was unable to communicate their public meaning. Spectacle thrives on narrative simplicity—and Obama's rational style of policy making was anything but simple.

Obama's critics flooded into this vacuum of narrative simplicity, enacting potent spectacle gestures of condemnation. Eschewing the "policy-wonk" discourse of the president and his administration's technocrats, Obama's opponents seized on elemental motifs of birth and death. A bizarre "birther" meme spread through the Internet, and subsequently received extensive coverage in the "mainstream media," to the effect that Obama was an illegitimate president because he had not definitively proved that he had been born in the United States. A small clause in the president's vast health-care bill providing for physician recommendations on end-of-life care was turned by former vice-presidential candidate Sarah Palin into the chilling claim that "Obamacare" would create "death panels," with government bureaucrats deciding whether elderly patients with serious illnesses would be allowed to live.[68] The most important counter-spectacle to the Obama presidency was the Tea Party movement that emerged only a few months into his administration. If Obama's presidency suggested that the United States had passed a tipping point and become a multiracial and multicultural nation nurtured by supportive public policies, the Tea Party harked back to a mythical founding in which all of the Founders were of native stock and individual liberty, rather than any Progressive version of active government, was the nation's true creed.[69]

There was an opening in Obama's first term for counter-spectacles to his left as well as to his right. Obama's policies shied away from any explicit statement that an important aim of theirs was to halt a decades-long march toward greater economic inequality. The "Occupy" movement that erupted on Wall Street in fall 2011, and then spread to many other cities, cut through the obfuscation with the simple slogan of the "99%" versus the "1%." Although the movement proved to be short-lived, the dramas of resistance to finance capital that it staged thrust the subject of economic inequality onto the public agenda as Obama had never managed to do. Unlike the counter-spectacles to his right, this one, although critical of the president, encouraged him, well into his third year in office, at last to try on the mantle of economic populism.

The one arena of presidential spectacle in which Obama clearly prevailed during his first term was international affairs. As his secretary of state, the president had the assistance of the most respected and popular member of his team, erstwhile rival Hillary Rodham Clinton. The most satisfying moment of spectacle in Obama's first term was undeniably the killing of Osama bin Laden in his Pakistani hideout by Navy Seals. By contrast to the byzantine Washington processes through which a policy-oriented president had to navigate his way, here was direct, forceful, decisive executive action, carried out in the name of justice but with a strong emotional edge of righteous revenge. Unfortunately for Obama, the gains he reaped in the polls from bin Laden's death were short-lived; the public's attention soon shifted back to the grim economic crisis at home, in which the president's current actions hardly appeared so successful.

Against this bleak domestic backdrop, observers began to view Obama as a spectacle character in terms radically at odds with his campaign image in 2008. Many journalists, who had been fascinated by Obama's electrifying persona during the campaign, now depicted the president as a cold, aloof figure, unable to stir public excitement because he had become so "professorial." Taken aback by the diminution of "hope" and the halting progress in "change," many of the president's ardent supporters became dejected and failed to turn out for the off-year congressional elections that dealt a terrible blow to his legislative prospects. Only Obama's most strident opponents continued to perceive him in the White House just as they had characterized him during the campaign: as an alien figure, more socialist than liberal, more European than American, more of a threat to than an embodiment of the American Dream.

Periodically, the Obama White House attempted to shed the image of a disconnected president and recapture some of the magic of the 2008 campaign through gestures of intimacy or folksiness. Campaigning for Democratic candidates in 2010, Obama appeared in "backyard conversations," talking with a small crowd of "neighbors" seated on plastic chairs on the lawn of a presidential supporter.[70] On the campaign trail in 2012, while running against a teetotaler and struggling to attract the support of white working-class men, Obama enthused about his love for drinking beer and his introduction of a home brew to the White House. This latter gesture elicited some enthusiastic chants of "four more beers."[71] But in general, gestures of this kind were too small and wan to reestablish the impression of a leader at one with followers.

If it proved difficult for Obama to alter the impression of coldness on his own, he was the beneficiary of reflected warmth from those close to him. Most important in this regard was the glow of his family, especially his wife, Michelle. Considerably more popular than her husband according to the polls, Michelle Obama tackled everyday problems, from childhood obesity to the travails of military families, with energy and charm. A more subtle contributor to the task of lightening up the president's image was Vice President Joe Biden. With his notorious penchant for verbal gaffes, Biden generally failed to gain the appreciation that he deserved as one of the president's most seasoned and savvy advisers. Although the criticisms that circulated about Biden drove down his public approval ratings, the vice president's unvarnished persona brought a down-to-earth touch to an administration otherwise prone to lofty atmospherics. No one accused Joe Biden, with his working-class roots and associations, of acting like a haughty lecturer talking down to his students. Biden was the perfect companion for the president in an early photo-op outing to Ray's Hell Burger, a small DC-area eatery.[72]

Even had Obama enacted warmer and more winning spectacle gestures during his first term, the depth and persistence of the economic crisis would have remained an enormous obstacle to public approval. Unrelenting statistics—and images—of joblessness and home foreclosures haunted the White House, as a large majority of Americans repeatedly told pollsters that the country was heading in the wrong direction. George W. Bush continued to receive more of the blame for economic bad news than Obama, but a cheerless nation could hardly be expected to be enthusiastic about reelecting its president. Entering the 2012 campaign season, Republicans, who had effectively contributed to Obama's feckless reputation as economic manager by obstructing most of his proposals to Congress for recovery, understandably entertained high hopes of making him a one-term president.

The elections of 2012 proved to be a rude awakening for the GOP. During his first three years in office, the president, in his successes and especially his shortfalls, had commanded most of the attention, while his Republican adversaries had been seen only out of the corner of the public's eye. Now, much like Bill Clinton once he was handed Newt Gingrich as a foil, Barack Obama looked a lot better to many of his doubters when he was sized up against Mitt Romney. It is hard to imagine a rival who had less of a chance to draw support away from Obama's base of women, minorities, and young voters. In the simple terms of spectacle, Romney was squarely of the rich, making Obama, despite his own actual affluence, symbolically middle class. With his fixation on the "job creators" at the top of the economic ladder, Romney turned the president into the champion of a vast majority who are not employers, especially the 47 percent that Romney famously disparaged. If the Obama of his first three White House years was criticized as distant and chilly, Romney came across as so sober and stiff that by contrast the president appeared positively on fire.

However, Obama's surprisingly comfortable margin of victory owed as much to his renewed energy and passion as to his rival's abundant shortcomings. Once more in a campaign context (and not a policy-making context), he found his groove again. Some of the magical appeal of 2008 returned to the Obama spectacle: if his original supporters were not so starry-eyed this election season, they proved no less ready to donate their money and volunteer their time. The president adopted a more combative persona than four years earlier, as the earnest rhetoric of unity and bipartisanship gave way to the feisty phrases of a populist and partisan. The Obama of 2012 was a fighter for his endangered followers, defending women's reproductive rights, rescuing young undocumented immigrants from deportation, and holding open a door to opportunity to many other Americans threatened by Republican calls to slash federal spending. Momentarily, the remote and wordy Obama of the first three years reappeared in near-disastrous fashion in the first debate with Romney. But the president battled back in the second and third debates, taking the fight to an opponent with flashes of aggressiveness that had seldom been seen in his White House career.

Obama's second inaugural address, unlike his first, was uplifting and even visionary. Yet before long his presidency was again mired in stalemate and tumbling back down in public approval surveys. Republicans had not defeated Obama on Election Day, but they were increasingly effective in frustrating his legislative agenda on a day-to-day basis. Despite pleas from Republican strategists that the party needed for its own future prospects in presidential elections to support comprehensive immigration reform, House Republicans denied the president any success on his top domestic priority for his second term. Even greater blows to Obama's image came in foreign affairs, the one bright spot for spectacle in his first term. In 2013, when Obama backed down from a threatened use of air power to blunt the brutality of the Assad regime in Syria's civil war, he was widely portrayed as a weak commander in chief. The following year, the astounding victories of the Islamic State in Syria and especially Iraq carried still greater spectacle consequences for the president. Grisly executions by the would-be caliphate, carefully staged and globally disseminated as a spectacle of extremist fury, deflated Obama's past claims of progress in the struggle against terrorism and evoked uncomfortable parallels with the souring of George W. Bush's spectacle in the cauldron of the Iraq War.

Late in 2014, after a second Democratic drubbing in midterm elections, the Obama of the 2012 campaign—a fighter for his followers and a challenger to outdated norms—reappeared. Accepting the futility of pressing his agenda before Republican congressional majorities dead set on rejecting it, the president adopted a new governing strategy that presented a provocative brand of presidential leadership. Circumventing Congress, he acted unilaterally on an array of controversial issues: ordering a halt to the deportation of millions of undocumented immigrants, restoring diplomatic relations with Castro's Cuba, moving forcefully to lead the international community in the battle against climate change. Boosted by indicators of a gradually accelerating economic recovery and impressive numbers in signups under the Affordable Care Act, and buoyed by liberal enthusiasm that the long-delayed promise of "hope" and "change" was at last at hand, the president exuded a renewed self-confidence.

Yet in his second term Obama remained resolutely a rationalist, only intermittently attentive to the media demand for spectacle. He happily promoted his hip image among his young followers, making a number of appearances on Jon Stewart's *Daily Show* and humorously promoting signups for the Affordable Care Act on Zach Galifianakis's online interview show, "Between Two Ferns." Obama appeared uncomfortable, however, with traditional media gestures. When a flood of migrant children from Central America crossed into Texas in the summer of 2014, creating a sudden "crisis" at the border, a presidential inspection of the "disaster area" was the expected response. But Obama balked at this convention. "I'm not interested in photo ops," he told the press. "I'm interested in solving the problem. There is nothing taking place down there that I am not intimately aware of and briefed on." The president was no doubt correct within the framework of policy making. But by rejecting the terms of the spectacle, he opened himself up to criticism that he was uncaring in the face of suffering. With predictable hyperbole, Republicans pounced, declaring this to be Obama's "Katrina moment." For their part, journalists were puzzled that the "photo op," a standard gesture in the White House media playbook, was so abruptly discarded.[73]

CONCLUSION

It is tempting to blame the growth of spectacle on individual presidents and the calculating spectacle specialists with which they now surround themselves. What happened—or more precisely didn't happen—at the Texas border in 2014 suggests that we resist the temptation and recognize how institutionalized the media's expectation of presidential spectacle has become. The growth of spectacle reflects structural developments in American politics: the extreme personalization of the modern presidency, the excessive expectations of the president that most Americans have, and above all the media coverage, less friendly now than during the "golden age of presidential television," that fixes on presidents and treats American national politics largely as a narrative of their adventures and misadventures. Whether presidents advance successfully across the ground of media, in the fashion of Kennedy and Reagan, or suffer political wounds as they come under fire, in the manner of the second Bush and Obama, they will be viewed through the standards of the spectacle.

Judged by a very different standard—that of America's traditional democratic values—the promotion of gesture over accomplishment, the obfuscation of exec-

utive responsibility, and the encouragement to citizens' passivity that have typi-
fied many past presidential spectacles are troubling. Yet spectacles have become
so much a part of the modern presidency that they cannot be neglected even in
the communication of high-minded goals. Rational discourse about the complex
issues facing the American people may match up better with civic ideals, but the
"symbols and gestures" of spectacle are what the media and the public have come
to expect and can more easily understand. Spectacle appears to be inescapable
today whether a president is seeking to manipulate or simply to lead.

2. Presidents and Economic Royalists

The fiercest antibusiness tirade in the history of the modern presidency was launched at the 1936 Democratic convention in Philadelphia. Drawing on the imagery of the American Revolution, Franklin D. Roosevelt depicted a commonwealth in renewed danger and summoned his followers to take up the struggle against modern oppressors. "It was to win freedom from the tyranny of political autocracy that the American Revolution was fought," he observed. But the economic and technological developments that defined industrial America had allowed "economic royalists" to carve out "new dynasties." Ordinary Americans still possessed their political rights, but they were no longer free in the economic sphere: "The hours men and women worked, the wages they received, the conditions of their labor—these had passed beyond the control of the people, and were imposed by this new industrial dictatorship." In this class-divided nation, "the political equality we once had won was meaningless in the face of economic inequality." In thunderous language that inevitably drew charges of demagoguery, FDR threw down the gauntlet: "These economic royalists complain that we seek to overthrow the institutions of America. What they really complain of is that we seek to take away their power. Our allegiance to American institutions requires the overthrow of this kind of power."[1]

This speech's theme was prefigured, albeit in more calculating fashion, by Machiavelli, who advised his prince to defend the common people against oppression by the *grandi*, the arrogant and domineering few. A prince who allied himself with the rich and powerful nobles could be little better than their instrument. But a prince who opposed them with the support of the many could aspire to great achievements.[2] Renaissance Florence was a world apart from America circa 1936, but FDR staked his leadership on the same premise as Machiavelli's.

Roosevelt could strike some damaging blows against the "economic royalists," but he could not overthrow their power. Indeed, since his death the revolutionary rhetoric of 1936 has not been emulated by his successors. Nonetheless, conflict between presidents and corporate and financial elites has been a recurrent feature of modern American politics. Particularly for Democrats in the White House, carried into office largely by middle- and lower-class voters, relationships between the presidency and the reigning powers of the political economy are bound to display tensions and sometimes boil over into direct conflict. At the same time, those same powers so shape economic life in the United States that no president can govern without their cooperation. Given the expectation that presidents are responsible for effective management of the American economy, the interaction of executive and private power is critical for understanding the contemporary presidency.

This chapter takes us onto the ground of political economy. The terrain upon which presidents confront wealthy political adversaries has little in common with the terrain upon which they act out spectacles before the media. At the core of spectacle is a struggle over the president's identity. On the ground of political economy, the struggle between presidents and "economic royalists" is over money and power. Perhaps the most striking difference between these two fields of political contestation is that the ground of political economy is much more uneven. When presidents come into conflict with economic elites, the latter typically have more of the weapons that determine the outcome of the contest. Here, presidential retreats are more likely than advances.

Curiously, if we turn to the literature on the presidency, we find scant attention paid to the interaction of executive and private power. There is an abundance of books, articles, and papers on presidential relations with the executive branch, Congress, the courts, and the public. Only a handful of political scientists have written about the interaction between presidents and economic elites.[3]

Neglect of this interaction leads to a short-sighted view of what drives presidential appointments and policy making. The choices that presidents do or don't make on economic matters are abstracted from the political-economic landscape within which they must maneuver. Presidents are ascribed greater freedom of action than they actually (and often correctly) perceive, and are assigned greater blame for failing to take bold steps that are in large measure beyond their capacity. In this regard, liberal complaints that President Obama has been too soft on the big banks have a familiar ring if we look back to the criticisms leveled against previous Democrats in the White House. Indeed, such criticisms once were leveled at FDR himself, for his confrontational stance against the "economic royalists" was neither the initial nor the ultimate hallmark of his interaction with private economic power.

The focus of this chapter is on the relationship between presidents and "economic royalists," starting with FDR. I concentrate on Democrats in the White House for a simple reason: because Republican presidents have been, except for a few tiffs, in agreement with the principles and priorities of the business community. It is when and where potential conflicts are most likely—with Democratic presidents—that the power of private economic forces to affect and circumscribe executive decision making is more significantly manifested.

The chapter proceeds in three stages. First is an analytical survey of an array of factors that delineate the political-economic ground upon which Democratic presidents interact with the business community. Second, I present short case studies of four Democratic presidents on this ground: Franklin D. Roosevelt, John F. Kennedy, Bill Clinton, and Barack Obama. Drawing on the first two parts, the conclusion describes characteristic patterns in the interactions between Democratic presidents and the reigning elites of American capitalism.

PRIVATE POWER AND THE FIELD OF ECONOMIC POLICY MAKING

Several decades ago, during a brief heyday of interest in the workings of the capitalist state, a heated theoretical debate pitted "instrumentalists" against "structuralists." Instrumentalists argued that capital exercised direct influence on government through campaign contributions, lobbying, and the penetration of key governmental hierarchies by personnel drawn from the corporate world. Structuralists downplayed direct influence; they suggested that the essential role of capital in the modern economy biased policy making in a corporate-friendly manner regardless of the ideology of executives or the political activities of businesspeople.

I have no interest in taking sides in a largely forgotten debate. Rather, my approach is an all-of-the-above account of the political-economic field. I briefly sketch six features of this field. The first two—economic structure and economic ideology—form the fundamental context within which presidents and the business community interact. The remaining four—state personnel, the political economy of the party system, business organization and lobbying, and campaign money—involve the political forces directly at play in these interactions. Together, these six generally tilt the field in favor of business and pose formidable obstacles to presidents whose agenda aims to correct that tilt.

My focus in both the analytical and historical sections of the chapter is on macroeconomic management, a responsibility that every president has faced since FDR. It is not on cases in which presidents come into conflict with a few firms rather than with the business community at large. When a president can deal with one part of the private economy in relative isolation from the rest, or even better can exploit divisions between different sectors, the odds of success will be greater than when business as a whole objects to White House words or actions.

Economic Structure

In understanding the field of action for presidential management of the economy, a consideration of economic structure is indispensable. As both non-Marxist and neo-Marxist social scientists have explained, an economy in which productive assets are privately owned profoundly limits the room for maneuver of government officials. They are the ones held responsible for overall economic performance, yet they cannot command owners of capital to invest it or to maintain, much less expand, employment. As Fred Block has written:

[T]hose who manage the state apparatus—regardless of their own political ideology—are dependent on the maintenance of some reasonable level of economic activity. This is true for two reasons. First, the capacity of the state to finance itself through taxation or borrowing depends on the state of the economy. . . . Second, public support for a regime will decline sharply if the regime presides over a serious drop in the level of economic activity, with a parallel rise in unemployment and shortages of key goods. Such a drop in support increases the likelihood that the state managers will be removed from power one way or another.[4]

Charles Lindblom famously describes this structural situation as "the privileged position of business." To miss the importance of economic structure is to mistakenly treat business as just another interest group in a pluralistic system. To Lindblom, business executives alone wield influence on a scale comparable to government officials. Though business cannot dictate to government, neither can government dictate to business. On the contrary, government officials ordinarily pursue business-friendly policies to induce private investment and employment. Even more important, they avoid unfriendly policies that shake "business confidence" and set into motion an "automatic punishing recoil" in the form of reduced investment and employment. Lindblom's metaphor for the political-economic context of presidential policy making is grim: "the market as prison."[5]

For both Block and Lindblom, writing in the 1970s and 1980s, that investment decisions are in private hands is the key to the structural advantages of capital in its relationship to the state. Their focus on investment, while still important, bespeaks a theoretical analysis rooted in the era of industrial capitalism. But capitalism has always been dynamic, and in the last three decades industrial capitalism has increasingly been overshadowed by finance capitalism in the United States. What presidents have needed—or feared—from capital has changed as power has shifted in the private economy. In the era of industrial capitalism, as the following case studies will show, FDR needed industry to ramp up production and JFK needed industry to accelerate economic growth while maintaining price stability. In contemporary finance capitalism, Clinton needed the bond market to lower interest rates and Obama has needed Wall Street to unfreeze credit markets.

A handy indicator of the shifting relationship between the presidency and capital is the capacity of presidents to affect private management. FDR could challenge "economic royalists" and Kennedy could face down the top executives of "Big Steel," but neither had any say over industrial management. By the time of Clinton and Obama, however, no one still spoke with awe about "Big Steel" or "Big Auto." In the context of the Great Recession, the Obama administration could fire the CEO of General Motors, Rick Wagoner, in exchange for saving the corporation from demise. Yet Obama has had to remain solicitous toward the new financial titans, such as Lloyd Blankfein of Goldman Sachs and Jamie Dimon of JPMorgan Chase.

Economic Ideology

The decline of Keynesian economic thought in the United States (at least until the Great Recession), and the concomitant rise of monetarism and supply-side economics beginning in the 1980s, is a familiar story. Yet any assumption that this trajectory involves a transformation from antibusiness to probusiness policy prescriptions is simplistic. Even though market-fundamentalist ideas have favored business and finance more than their neo-Keynesian predecessors, the latter were practically attuned to the role of capital in macroeconomic policy making.

When Keynesian ideas first achieved prominence in the United States in the late 1930s and early 1940s, Alan Brinkley has argued, they represented something of a retreat from earlier New Deal approaches to taming the power of capital. Rather than intervening directly in the private economy through planning or antimonopoly measures, many New Deal Democrats began to favor fiscal policy that would stimulate demand and generate growth without touching corporate prerogatives. By contrast to later neo-Keynesianism, however, the original American Keynesians appear as social democrats. Under the aegis of FDR, their brand of fiscal policy favored public investment and social welfare spending, not tax cutting, as the means to a mass-consumption and full-employment economy.[6]

With conservative interests on the rebound during World War II and its aftermath, the original American Keynesians were unable to translate their ideology into public policy save for the watered-down Employment Act of 1946. Neo-Keynesian ideas became ascendant and gained the sanction of official policy only during the Kennedy-Johnson years. And when they did so, they looked quite different than the ideas of the New Dealers. Economic historian Robert Lekachman describes Kennedy-Johnson policies as "commercial Keynesianism." With "commercial Keynesianism," tax cutting became the preferred approach, with many alterations in the tax code designed to induce greater business investment. To hold down the size of deficits, the growth of domestic spending was curtailed. At first skeptical of neo-Keynesian ideas because of the sanctity of a balanced budget, businessmen were won over by Kennedy's portrayal of the benefits to be reaped. Writing in the mid-1960s, Lekachman observed that "Keynesian prescriptions, the monopoly of reformers and radicals during the 1930s and 1940s, have very nearly become the favorite medicines of the established, propertied interests in the community."[7]

Once the "stagflation" of the 1970s settled in, the American business community no longer seemed to like the taste of neo-Keynesian remedies. Corporate and financial leaders increasingly gravitated to market-centered ideas honed in conservative think tanks and embraced by the New Right leadership of the Republican Party. With the Reagan Revolution, the ideas of Milton Friedman and supply-side tax cutters were heralded as the only path to prosperity. What political scientist Mark A. Smith calls "right talk" about liberating the free market came to dominate economic thinking, becoming so pervasive that even the Great Recession of 2008 could only dent, but not dislodge, its hold over macroeconomic policy. Embraced ever more zealously by Republicans, free-market ideas played a significant role for Democrats as well, most notably in the Clinton presidency and in a more abashed form in the Obama presidency.[8]

State Personnel

During the Cold War years, elite theorists such as C. Wright Mills, Gabriel Kolko, and G. William Domhoff pointed out the preponderance of former corporate and banking executives at the highest reaches of the national security state. As Richard Barnet summed up the evidence in *Roots of War*, "If we look at the men who have held the very top positions, the Secretaries and Under Secretaries of State and Defense, the Secretaries of the three services, the Chairman of the Atomic Energy Commission, and the Director of the CIA, we find that out of ninety-one individuals who held these offices between 1940 and 1967, seventy of them were from the ranks of big business or high finance." In the post–Cold War era, this account of the national security state no longer holds true. Since the second term of Bill Clinton, the Department of State has been headed by three women, two African Americans, and a long-time legislator who was an antiwar activist as a young man; none came from big business or high finance. At the top of the Department of Defense, white men still have held the monopoly, but at least in Democratic administrations the preference has been for former members of Congress (Les Aspin, William Cohen, Leon Panetta, and Chuck Hagel) rather than corporate or financial alumni.[9]

Once we turn from national security to economic management, however, we find continuity rather than change in the backgrounds of high-level state personnel. At the Department of the Treasury, secretaries in Democratic as well as Republican administrations almost all come from corporate or Wall Street boardrooms. Consider the three postwar Democratic presidents examined later in this chapter. Kennedy's secretary of the treasury, C. Douglas Dillon, was a Republican from a Wall Street investment firm. Clinton's secretaries of the treasury were a wealthy, conservative senator from Texas, Lloyd Bentsen; the top executive at Goldman Sachs, Robert Rubin; and Rubin's protégé, economist Lawrence Summers. Obama's appointments to head Treasury have been Timothy Geithner, another Rubin protégé and man of Wall Street (though from the Federal Reserve Bank of New York rather than an investment firm or hedge fund), and Jacob Lew, who followed his years in the Clinton administration with a profitable stint at Citigroup.

We cannot, of course, infer policy positions directly from policy makers' previous experiences. Nonetheless, the pattern of appointments at Treasury suggests two conclusions important for an understanding of the political-economic ground upon which presidents must act. First, Democratic presidents all seemingly have operated on the premise that top economic appointees must be welcomed by the business and financial communities. Second, state personnel with high-level business backgrounds are more likely than personnel from other backgrounds to know and sympathize with the perspective of the corporate and financial world.

Unlike Republican administrations, Democratic administrations tend to include at least a few progressive economists who are critical of the probusiness tilt in public policy. John F. Kennedy had a John Kenneth Galbraith; Bill Clinton had a Joseph Stiglitz; and Barack Obama had a Jared Bernstein (in his first term). Yet if Democrats in the White House keep some liberal economic gadflies on the premises, these critical voices sound off only on the margins of economic debate. Their arguments typically do not win out when presidents finalize their policy choices.

The Political Economy of the Party System

The unique features of the American party system stand out as another landmark on the political-economic field. In broad terms, the American political system has always contained a probusiness party but has never contained a true labor party. As John Gerring's *Party Ideologies in America* has shown, strong support for business interests has persisted through the rise and fall of parties, from the Federalists to the Whigs to the Republicans. Labor has not enjoyed comparable support from Democrats save for a few brief eras (e.g., Jacksonian Democracy and the Wilson administration). Labor's greatest period of political influence was short, lasting from the mid-1930s only into the late 1940s. After Truman's victory in 1948, Gerring observes, Democrats displayed a "declining enthusiasm for labor." While organized labor has remained allied with the Democratic Party since the New Deal, labor's policy victories during Democratic administrations have become increasingly scarce. The latest example is the failure of labor's top legislative priority at the beginning of the Obama administration—a "card-check" system to give unions a better shot at winning certification in the face of management advantages—to gain a hearing in a Democratic Congress.[10]

Republicans have supported business interests against Democratic presidents for a long time, but the level of probusiness sentiment has only risen with the demise of Republican progressives and moderates. As Thomas Edsall writes, recent years have witnessed "the *merger* of the Republican Party, the conservative movement, and American business. More than ever before, business, from Main Street to Wall Street, has been fully integrated into the Republican Party structure." As labor's clout (and numbers) has declined, business's successes in Congress have mounted. Advancing business interests during GOP administrations, Republicans in Congress fiercely defend them when Democrats are in power.[11]

While Republican presidents can usually count on strong support for business within their party's ranks, Democratic presidents who might want to correct a probusiness tilt in policy have a less reliable party base. Between the second New Deal and the 1970s, the powerful southern wing of the Democratic Party, fearing the disruption of its racialized labor markets, rejected liberal economics and allied with business interests in a cross-party conservative coalition.[12] As the Democratic Party began to shrink in the South after the civil rights revolution of the 1960s, southern Democratic officials attempted to hold on by countering northern liberalism with a more business-friendly party faction anchored in the Democratic Leadership Council. Outside of the South, moderate Democrats, especially from swing districts, have been the target of substantial business campaign donations, especially when they occupy committee chairs important to business interests.[13]

On questions of economic legislation, Democratic presidents cannot even be sure of the votes of liberal Democrats. If the legislation at issue is seen as injurious to business interests, congressional liberals from affected states are prone to defect. Known as an antiwar liberal, Senator Alan Cranston was also a defender of California's aerospace industry. Senator Charles Schumer is a reliable and highly active liberal except when New York's dependence on Wall Street is involved. Jacob Hacker and Paul Pierson call defectors like these "Republicans for a Day."[14]

Business Organization and Lobbying

Save for a handful of highly publicized issues, presidents and Congress feel pressure from organized interests far more than from voters. And in what Hacker and Pierson dub "organized combat" over economic legislation, business interests ordinarily muster more firepower than their adversaries. One can point to periods—the 1930s or the late 1960s/early 1970s—in which other organized interests successfully mobilized and won policy victories at the expense of business or finance. Yet these periods were followed by business counter-mobilization in the late 1930s/early 1940s and mid-1970s that restored an imbalance of power. In the latter period, for example, the business community reacted to recent environmental and worker-safety legislation that raised the costs of production by an energetic political campaign to regain the upper hand. Big businesses were more effectively organized for political influence through the formation of the Business Roundtable, while the clout of small businesses was enhanced through a revitalization of the U.S. Chamber of Commerce. Both the Roundtable and the Chamber remain important fixtures of "organized combat" today.[15]

The chief weapons in "organized combat" are lobbying and campaign contributions. The business community, of course, has more money than any other interests to spend on both. Lobbying by individual businesses, trade associations, and peak business groups exceeds their spending on campaigns. As a prominent study of lobbying by Frank Baumgartner et al., *Lobbying and Policy Change*, demonstrates, "the richest side does not always win" when seeking policy change. Yet businesses are more likely than other interests to have "friends in high places." These friends are particularly helpful when the objective of business lobbyists is to block rather than to foster changes in the law. To the extent that corporations and financial institutions already enjoy a "privileged position" in both the economy and existing law, by preserving the status quo they "usually get what they want." The satisfaction of business interests through obstruction is simultaneously a source of frustration for a president wishing to push pro-consumer or pro-worker legislation through Congress.[16]

Counting wins and losses in the case of lobbying does not tell the whole story. As the example of the financial regulatory reform law sponsored by President Obama, known as Dodd-Frank, illustrates, what appears on the surface as a failure of business lobbyists actually demonstrates how lobbying pays off. Amid widespread public anger at Wall Street, held responsible for crashing the American economy through its reckless and immensely profitable behavior, financial regulatory reform could not be derailed. Yet as the complex legislation proceeded through the House and Senate, banking lobbyists and their friends in high places were successful in watering down a number of its key provisions. And even after passage, banking industry lobbyists remained highly active in both pressuring regulatory agencies drafting rules to implement Dodd-Frank and working closely with probusiness legislators in both parties to soften the impact of the law on their employers.[17]

Campaign Money

Money has always mattered in American electoral politics, but with the decline of local party organizations and the rise of expensive consultant-run and television-heavy political campaigns, it has come to matter even more in the last forty or fifty years than before. The superior resources that business interests bring to campaign giving affect Democratic presidents in both indirect and direct fashion. Indirectly, business money affects the composition and policy bent of Congress. The preponderance of business donations go to the more business-friendly party, especially when Democrats lack majority status and do not chair the key economic committees. Republican challengers in particular are more likely to secure significant funding than Democratic ones. But plenty of Democratic members of Congress also rely on campaign contributions from wealthy business donors, and with that money comes the incentive to keep the cash flowing by avoiding votes that might offend benefactors. Long before the *Citizens' United* decision in 2010, Thomas Edsall pointed out that the "pattern of campaign contributions . . . works to provide a clear mandate in favor of business and conservative interests, while encouraging legislative divisiveness and inaction within the Democratic Party."[18]

The direct impact of money on Democratic presidents is evident in their fund-raising trips.[19] Since the advent of the Internet, Democratic presidential candidates have been better positioned to turn to small donors to match or even surpass Republican money. Yet when they travel to meet the well-heeled, they make plain that a significant portion of the funds they need for their campaigns will still come from the wealthy. Many affluent Democratic donors—for example, Hollywood celebrities or trial lawyers—are typically not enamored of corporate or financial interests. Nonetheless, the important role of Wall Street elites in financing Democratic presidential candidates presents a different picture. Many Wall Streeters seem to prefer the more cosmopolitan Democratic Party to the Republican Party of heartland cultural and religious conservatives—that is, so long as the Democrats don't threaten their core economic interests.

Wall Street contributions to Barack Obama are revealing of the incentives and disincentives that they represent for Democratic presidential candidates. Many big donors from Wall Street responded to the same magical appeal in Obama during the 2008 campaign as other starry-eyed supporters. For example, employees of Goldman Sachs contributed approximately $1 million to Obama that year, about four times as much as they gave to John McCain.[20] But four years later, a number of those donors had become disenchanted, not so much because Obama was earthbound as because he had cost them money with Dodd-Frank and made some unflattering remarks about the rich. With Mitt Romney, a proud alumnus of the financial sector, as Obama's challenger, Goldman Sachs employees shifted their money to the Republicans, giving Romney about twice as much in 2012 as Obama had received in 2008.[21] Obama's rocky relationship with the financial community will be discussed later in the chapter. The point of this excursion into his campaign finances is that just as Democratic legislators are likely to see business donations drop if they vote contrary to business interests, so can Democratic presidential candidates expect Wall Street funding to decline if their words or actions incur the displeasure of financial elites.

Some Qualifications

Although the accumulation of advantages that favor business elites in their tussles with presidents is imposing, those elites do not always win.[22] During episodes of economic and political upheaval, special circumstances can give presidents and other political decision makers the upper hand in dealing with business elites. Three circumstances in particular stand out in American economic history:

1. When markets crash: market failures belie the claim that owners of capital are the drivers of prosperity, diminishing their prestige and providing an opening for political officials to call them to heel. It was of course during the Great Depression of the 1930s that significant constraints were placed on Wall Street (the Securities and Exchange Commission), higher labor costs were imposed on industry (unemployment insurance and fair labor standards), and collective bargaining rights gave unions, for a time, the muscle to challenge employers. The Great Recession that began in 2008 had a milder impact on economic elites, but the Dodd-Frank legislation, discussed later in this chapter, did put something of a period to an era when financial elites were treated as "masters of the universe."

2. When there are egregious contradictions to the market promise of free competition: periodic bursts of corporate mergers and the exercise of quasi-monopoly power over particular economic sectors violate official norms and legitimate governmental efforts to make the American capitalist system live up to its own claims. In one form or another, antitrust legislation and litigation have come to the fore at such moments—the Progressive Era, the New Deal, and the most recent Democratic administrations—with mixed success.

3. When reformers publicize harmful business practices or externalities that threaten the public welfare, mobilizing popular support behind their campaigns: economic elites can become vulnerable when they can be made to look exploitative toward their employees and callous toward the public interest. For example, pure food and drug legislation and child labor laws were Progressive remedies for business abuses, while the early 1970s featured a flurry of liberal regulatory laws to halt environmental degradation, safeguard worker health and safety, and protect consumers from dangerous products.

DEMOCRATIC PRESIDENTS AND THE BUSINESS COMMUNITY

Compared to Republican presidents, Democratic ones are ushered into office primarily through the votes of lower-income and minority voters. Their political ideology is less enamored of the magic of the free market. And they do not have personal backgrounds in the profitable haunts of the corporate or banking worlds. For all of these reasons, their relationship with the business community is bound to be more uneasy than when Republicans occupy the White House.

In what follows I concentrate on three Democratic presidents of the postwar era, John F. Kennedy, Bill Clinton, and Barack Obama, because each of them experienced similar tensions with the business community. Before turning to this trio, however, I take an abbreviated look at Franklin D. Roosevelt's relationship with business. Especially for liberals, FDR has served as the benchmark against which later Democratic presidents have been judged as backsliders for their timidity toward business. The image of FDR as tough on business is not wrong, but his story is more complicated—and closer to that of his Democratic successors—than appears in nostalgia for the New Deal.

Franklin D. Roosevelt

Before there were the "economic royalists," there were the "money changers" in the "temple" whom FDR lacerated in his first inaugural address. But when he moved swiftly to rescue a banking system on the verge of collapse, his program was cautiously designed to avoid fatal shocks to American finance. "It was," historian David Kennedy observes, "a thoroughly conservative measure." The big bankers got to stay in the temple. FDR was equally conciliatory at first toward the top leadership of American industry. Aiming to revive production and employment at the nadir of the Great Depression, the president's National Recovery Administration (NRA) offered industries large and small the chance to draft codes of self-regulation under the federal government's aegis.[23]

Desperate for recovery, the business community was responsive to Roosevelt's new direction in political economy at first. However, within a year the business backlash began. An assortment of complaints turned many corporate and financial elites against the New Deal: the new government bureaucracy was too large; labor unions were mobilizing under Section 7(a) of the NRA legislation, and the ideology of state planning was an ominous break from laissez-faire thought. Corporate and Wall Street discontent took organizational form in 1934 with the creation of the American Liberty League. The League brought together top executives from the private sector with leaders of the conservative wing of FDR's own party.[24]

On top of the business backlash, a conservative Supreme Court began to knock down the central pillars of the New Deal economic program. It was in the context of the challenge from his right, coupled with mounting discontent on his left at the slow pace of economic progress, that FDR moved in a more radical direction in the "Second New Deal," beginning in 1935. The move leftward was manifest in rhetoric. Along with the "economic royalists" address, an equally inflammatory speech at the end of the 1936 campaign threw down the gauntlet to the champions of "business and financial monopoly": "Never before in our history," Roosevelt intoned, "have these forces been so united against one candidate as they stand today. They are unanimous in their hate for me—and I welcome their hatred." Several "Second New Deal" policies took direct aim at Roosevelt's foes. His 1935 tax reform proposal, dubbed a "soak-the-rich" bill by its critics, called for higher taxes on the incomes and inheritances of the upper class. In 1938, he called upon Congress to address the threat of corporate concentration to a democratic society.[25]

Yet for all of FDR's more radical rhetoric and proposals, there was less to his challenge to the business community than it appeared. Despite his rhetoric, business elites were far from unanimous in their hostility to the president. Some titans in the banking community, along with most executives from labor-intensive industries, were indeed vehement opponents of the New Deal. But Roosevelt's free-trade policies won him friends at the top of capital-intensive firms and international investment houses, and his programs to lift the purchasing power of ordinary Americans brought support from businessmen oriented to mass consumption in such fields as large-scale retailing, entertainment, and housing. Roosevelt policies aimed to curb corporate and financial power also fell well short of the objectives they proclaimed. Congress worked over FDR's tax reform bill until it became toothless. The challenge to corporate concentration produced a three-year investigation whose massive findings were largely ignored by a nation whose concerns had shifted from depression to war. The most effective New Deal check on corporate power—the Wagner Act of 1935, ensuring collective bargaining rights for workers—was crafted in the Senate and endorsed only at the eleventh hour by the president. [26]

The war years produced a critical coda to the story of FDR and the business community: whatever big business and finance lost during the New Deal, it largely won back during World War II. As previously mentioned, even before the war the New Dealers were beginning to back away from direct intervention in the affairs of business in favor of fiscal policy. Equally important, with the onset of war in Europe in 1939, Roosevelt needed rapidly to ramp up industrial production for defense, and to staff the government agencies in charge of industrial mobilization he saw little choice but to recruit top-level economic royalists. The bitter irony was not lost on the president: as he wrote in a 1941 letter: "I am somewhat appalled by the fact that at least nine out of ten men being brought here by the Production people are not only Republicans but are mostly violent anti-Administration Republicans." Corporate "dollar-a-year" men, still drawing salaries from their companies, assumed most of the key posts on the civilian side of the defense buildup. Forming a formidable network with a rapidly expanding military freed from the normal constraints of America's isolationist and antimilitarist tradition, they laid the foundation of the postwar military-industrial complex.[27]

With corporate and financial elites in key positions directing procurement for the federal government, big business prospered mightily during World War II, while smaller businesses lost market share. As historian John Morton Blum observed, 100 big companies received 70 percent of federal contracts relating to the war effort. The same 100 firms received government subsidies or low-interest loans to expand their existing factories for wartime production. Large defense contractors even were given assurances that they would be able to purchase new factories built at government expense at bargain prices upon war's end. A furtherance of the very corporate concentration against which FDR had inveighed before the war was certainly not his intention. A guide to the progressive postwar America that he envisioned was his Economic Bill of Rights proposal, announced in his 1944 State of the Union address. Nonetheless, the political economy at the time of his death clearly featured the comeback of corporate power.[28]

John F. Kennedy

The pattern for postwar Democratic presidents in relations with the business community is evident in the Kennedy administration. From the start, President Kennedy recognized that both the structure of the American economy and the political economy of the party system necessitated business cooperation if he was to achieve his principal domestic objective: more rapid economic growth. Pledging to "get America moving again" on the economic front, Kennedy hoped that a speed-up in growth would bring down unemployment and utilize the slack potential of a sputtering economy. The goal of rapid growth also reflected Kennedy's rejection of New Deal–style class conflict amid scarcity in favor of consensus politics amid abundance. In addition, economic growth was a component of Kennedy's Cold War strategy: in the face of Soviet premier Khrushchev's boasts about the superior productivity of communism, the American president wanted to bolster the international prestige of free enterprise.[29]

To achieve accelerated growth, the corporate sector would have to raise its level of investment in plant and equipment. To coax this increase from business, Kennedy directed friendly words and policies toward it. In his first speech before a major industrial group, Kennedy said: "Our revenues and thus our success are

PRESIDENTS AND ECONOMIC ROYALISTS   59

dependent upon your profits and your success. . . . Whatever past differences may have existed, we seek more than an attitude of truce, more than a treaty—we seek the spirit of a full-fledged alliance." The president backed his promise of alliance with solid tax breaks for business investment: an investment tax credit proposed in 1961 (passed by Congress the next year) and a liberalization of depreciation allowances implemented by the Treasury Department in 1962, amounting in combination to an 11 percent tax cut for corporations. Well before Kennedy's more famous innovation in tax policy—1963's proposed cuts in personal and corporate rates—he was charting a new course in what Republicans would later call supply-side economics.[30]

Yet corporate America was not eager to shake the hand of friendship that Kennedy offered. Business complaints were numerous: the investment tax credit was not generous enough; Commerce Secretary Luther Hodges took the side of small business against big business; Kennedy surrounded himself with too many academic economists; the president did not invite industrialists and bankers to White House functions as frequently as his Republican predecessor had. Even at their best, relations between Democratic presidents and the business community are not smooth. In Kennedy's case, simmering tensions boiled over in the spring of 1962.

To ward off the threat that accelerated economic growth would spark inflation, Kennedy's Council of Economic Advisers established a set of wage-price guidelines in January 1962. The crucial test of the guidelines arrived almost immediately with contract negotiations in the steel industry. Closely involved in the negotiations, Kennedy and his aides prevailed on the steelworkers' union to accept the most modest gains for its members in decades. From the tenor of the tripartite negotiations, they were led to expect that the steel companies would reciprocate by holding the line on prices. But on April 10, Roger Blough, the CEO of U.S. Steel, visited the White House to inform the president that his corporation was raising the price of all of its products by $6 per ton. Most other steel corporations quickly followed Blough's lead.

Feeling that he had been misled by Blough and his colleagues, and made to look weak in the eyes of the unions and the public, Kennedy responded in cold fury. At a press conference the day after Blough's announcement, the president blistered Big Steel: "The American people will find it hard, as I do, to accept a situation in which a tiny handful of steel executives whose pursuit of private power and profit exceeds their sense of public responsibility can show such utter contempt for the interests of 185 million Americans." To White House aides (in a remark that soon leaked to the press), Kennedy was more pungent: "My father always told me that steel men were sons of bitches, but I never realized till now how right he was." He backed up his verbal fusillade with threats of punitive action against any steel company maintaining the price increase: loss of Defense Department contracts and a Justice Department investigation into price-fixing. Within three days, the increase in the price of steel had been rescinded.[31]

But Kennedy paid a steep price for facing down Big Steel. For the moment, his proposed alliance with corporate America was in tatters. Businessmen indignantly asserted that Kennedy's actions had been dictatorial and that his "sons of bitches" remark revealed his true antibusiness sentiments. A month and a half after the steel affair, when the stock market, in the midst of a bubble, suddenly plummeted, Wall Street was all too eager to blame the downward plunge on the president's blow against business confidence. With talk rising in business circles about corporate reluctance to invest amid a hostile political climate, economists began to warn of a potential recession.

The force of economic structure and private power now shook the Kennedy administration hard, and it spent the next year seeking along multiple paths to placate business so that it might get another shot at building the alliance it had originally proposed. An array of symbolic gestures and concrete benefits were now directed toward Kennedy's corporate critics. At the president's request, his top domestic adviser, Theodore Sorensen, drafted a strategy paper, "The Kennedy Administration and Business." The paper laid out a fourteen-point "psychological" campaign that aimed to "soften the business hostility which reached an emotional peak during the steel price-stock market sequence of events." Among the fourteen points was a proposal for "black-tie stag dinners for business leaders." But Sorensen had more in mind than simply hand-holding. To prevent further grievances among businessmen, he asked: "Can the President, or the Attorney General, or the Special Counsel, meet quietly and individually with the heads of the regulatory agencies, the anti-trust division, the wage-hour, Food-and-Drug, and other enforcement activities—to emphasize that there are times to steam ahead, to pursue, to be zealous, and there are times to be cooperative and understanding (and the latter is more appropriate now)?"[32]

Kennedy's conciliatory campaign toward the business community vexed the leadership of organized labor, which recognized that the president that it had consistently supported was nicer to his adversaries than to his union friends. But organized labor was, by Kennedy's time, largely a political captive of the Democratic Party. Because Kennedy needed business cooperation so badly, he saw no alternative other than to woo it back. The chairman of his Council of Economic Advisers, Walter Heller, facetiously described the Administration's approach as "making love to business."[33]

It was Heller who played a pivotal role in crafting the policy that finally stitched the government-business alliance together: the tax plan of 1963. A neutral technocrat and neo-Keynesian, Heller worked hard to persuade Kennedy that a large-scale cut in individual and corporate rates was the key to accelerating economic growth even if it resulted in a deficit. The economist's persistent argument was that the high rate of federal taxation represented a "drag" on economic expansion. Kennedy could grasp Heller's logic, but out of political concerns he hesitated to take action. The business community and its congressional friends in the Republican Party, and the conservative wing of the Democratic Party, were likely, he worried, to say no to any planned deficit and hand him a stinging defeat.

Kennedy eventually decided to test the waters to see if he could win business backing for a neo-Keynesian tax cut. Appearing before the Economic Club of New York in December 1962, he turned Keynes into a conservative. Reducing individual and corporate tax rates, he told the business audience, was a way to expand incentives for private investment and consumption in contrast to "a program of excessive increases in public expenditures." In Kennedy's "commercial Keynesianism," tax cuts were business-friendly while increased public spending was antithetical to the alliance between government and business. (Two months later, the president informed an audience of bankers that "we have submitted a budget which provides for a reduction in expenditures with the exception of space, defense, and interest on the debt."). Kennedy's in-house liberal critic of "commercial Keynesianism," John Kenneth Galbraith, grumbled that the Economic Club speech was "the most Republican speech since McKinley," but the president and his other economic advisers were jubilant about the favorable business reaction. Perceiving that a conservatively designed and packaged tax cut might actually help him with business, Kennedy was ready to go forward with the most important economic proposal of his presidency.[34]

Introducing his tax bill to Congress early in 1963, Kennedy portrayed it as the most important step the nation could take to accelerate economic growth and create a larger economic pie for everyone. Compared to the later tax cuts of Ronald Reagan and George W. Bush, Kennedy's was far more equitable in its distributional aims. Nonetheless, the proposed reduction in the top nominal rate for individual taxes from 91 percent to 65 percent was a warming gesture to the wealthy. So, too, was a reduction of corporate income taxes to the pre–Korean War level. Wealthy bankers and businesspeople were less happy about the tax reforms that appeared in the legislative proposal, closing or narrowing some of the loopholes in the tax code that benefited the rich. These were included in the omnibus legislation to compensate for some of the federal revenue lost by the tax cuts and to placate liberals in Kennedy's party. The tax cuts made their way through Congress, slowed by conservative resistance to planned deficits, but were ultimately enacted under Lyndon Johnson. The tax reforms, however, were jettisoned, in part because the group of corporate notables that the Kennedy White House had assembled to lobby for the tax bill, the Business Committee for Tax Reduction, was, as its name suggested, only interested in cuts and used its clout to help scuttle reform.

Judged on the basis of their contribution to economic growth rates, the Kennedy-Johnson tax cuts were successful. For the next few years, until the onset of massive spending on the war in Vietnam fueled inflation, the United States enjoyed the then longest period of peacetime economic expansion in the nation's history. At a time of prosperity, few Americans were troubled by the division of a larger economic pie. As is usually the case, however, the rewards of the new economic policy were skewed in favor of the already advantaged: corporate profits, for example, rose three times as fast as take-home pay. Even more significant were the long-term implications of Kennedy's innovation in economic policy. As economic historian Kim McQuaid observes: "Kennedy was not Reagan, not by a long shot, but his decision to buy popularity in business circles in the wake of the steel price hike imbroglio via a conservative Keynesian tax cut nevertheless set the stage for the decades of economic conservatism that were to come."[35]

To the very end of his brief presidency, Kennedy was pitching the advantages of his alliance with business. In his final appearance in front of a business group, four days before he was assassinated, the president was still swatting down business complaints by touting his probusiness achievements. Businessmen, he pointed out, "are prospering as never before during this administration. . . . The new figures on corporate profits after taxes . . . reached an all-time high, running some 43 percent higher than they were just 3 years ago." It would take several years—perhaps until President Nixon announced that he too was a Keynesian—before conservative elements in the business community appreciated the thrust of Kennedy's economic approach. But Kennedy's men expected that day to come. His secretary of the treasury, C. Douglas Dillon, summed up the story of Kennedy and business: "I don't think there had been a president in a long time who had basically done as much for business. . . . It took the business community a long time to recognize this."[36]

Bill Clinton

Of the three postwar presidents covered in this book, Bill Clinton came to the White House with the strongest probusiness background. Clinton came of political age at the height of the war in Vietnam, and in 1972 he was a campaign organizer in Texas for the populist McGovern presidential campaign. But in his multiple terms as governor of Arkansas, he had repositioned himself in the center and adopted business-friendly policies. He served as chairman of the centrist Democratic Leadership Council, a launching pad for his bid for the presidency in 1992.[37]

However, during the 1992 campaign, Clinton adopted a populist message of his own in running against a Republican incumbent in a downbeat economy. His campaign manifesto was entitled *Putting People First*. Clinton's economic agenda was geared to the middle and working classes, pledging a tax cut for the middle class and social "investments" in such areas as education and worker retraining for a globalized economy.

Two numbers rattled Clinton's economic agenda even before he took office. Ross Perot won 19 percent of the popular vote in 1992, the best third-candidate showing since Theodore Roosevelt in 1912, largely on the issue of the deficit. And the Bush administration's parting gift to Clinton was an announcement that the federal deficit was likely to be approximately $50 billion more than in its previous projection. With the political and economic context increasingly highlighting the importance of the deficit—and making new spending on populist programs a tough sell—Clinton was ready to listen to a celebrated economic sage. His new mentor on the economy would be a Republican with a libertarian background: Federal Reserve chair Alan Greenspan.

President-elect Clinton met with the Fed chair a month after the election. In their conversation, Greenspan set out to school Clinton on the structural realities of a finance-driven economy. With deficits already running high, the Fed chair told the president-elect, traditional Democratic spending programs would not revive a weak economy and expand employment. The road to economic growth and employment lay through deficit reduction instead. Only a credible deficit-reduction plan would impress the bond markets and thus hold down the long-term interest rates that they determined. Wall Street needed the right signals from Washington to spark a recovery. Clinton understood Greenspan's message, and after this first meeting the two men functioned as de facto partners in economic policy making for the next eight years. As a show of respect for Greenspan, and a dramatic gesture to Wall Street, the White House seated the Fed chair next to the first lady in the gallery at the president's first address to a joint session of Congress.[38]

In the Clinton administration's opening months, as Bob Woodward's invaluable fly-on-the-wall account, *The Agenda*, relates in detail, a debate raged between the president's campaign consultants, who held to the populist positions of 1992, and his economic team, who stood firmly for deficit reduction. Since the deficit-reduction side was insistent that Clinton's populist proposals of a middle-class tax cut and social "investments" had to be slashed or eliminated altogether, the campaign consultants countered with politics and ethics: going back on *Putting People First* would alienate the president's base and represent a sell-out of principles. But the economic heavyweights echoed Greenspan's dictums and made the case that long-term economic growth, and with it the prospects for Clinton's reelection in 1996, depended on keeping Wall Street satisfied. Despite Clinton's own ambivalence, the populist consultants—Paul Begala, James Carville, Stanley Greenberg, and Mandy Grunwald—were no match for the likes of Secretary of the Treasury Lloyd Bentsen and Director of the National Economic Council Robert Rubin, who spoke with the voice of market orthodoxy and economic power.

Clinton sided with the deficit hawks, but he was not happy about it. Inside the White House, rather than on the campaign trail, economic policy making felt like a trap and not a window of opportunity. Several of Clinton's notorious red-faced outbursts expressed his frustration at feeling caught in this trap. At one meeting on the economy, he exploded: "You mean to tell me that the success of the program and my reelection hinges on the Federal Reserve and a bunch of fucking bond traders." Later in the same meeting, when Vice President Al Gore invoked the bold spirit of New Deal legislation, Clinton retorted: "Roosevelt was trying to help people. . . . Here we help the bond market, and we hurt the people who voted us in."[39]

Although the deficit-reduction plan necessitated a capitulation on populist spending, its tax-raising side left some room for Democratic-style values. In a televised speech from the Oval Office a few weeks after his inauguration, Clinton informed the public that 70 percent of the new tax revenue he proposed to raise would come from the rich. The wealthy had been the beneficiary of lavish tax breaks under Republican rule, he said, and now it was time for a rebalancing of tax burdens.[40]

The day after Clinton's speech, the stock market plunged. The White House quickly dispatched Robert Rubin and Alice Rivlin of OMB as emissaries to Wall Street, where they got an earful. In an off-the-record meeting with CEOs from several large companies that same evening, one corporate executive compared Clinton not to the supposedly antibusiness John F. Kennedy but to the more radical George McGovern. The executives at the meeting were especially angered by the president's remarks about the wealthy; they warned that increasing taxes on the rich represented old-time Democratic class warfare that would shatter business confidence and stall economic recovery. Back in Washington, Rubin reported to Clinton that "you're being seen as anti-business. You're seen as punishing the rich." According to Woodward's account, "Clinton appreciated Rubin's argument, and in his public statements he began scaling back, and even cutting out altogether, his rhetoric about taxing the rich."[41]

As a denouement to the one-sided debate between populists and deficit hawks in the crucial early months of Clinton's presidency, consider a dialogue between Paul Begala and Robert Rubin as Clinton's economic agenda made its way through Congress. Begala insisted that though Clinton leaned in the direction of deficit reduction, he could not dispense with populist rhetoric to sell his economic program to the public. Rubin, a multimillionaire whose previous position had been as co-chairman of Goldman Sachs, replied that he hated his president's use of the word "rich" and wanted more respectful language toward the successful. When Begala was unmoved, Rubin brought out his clinching argument about Wall Street and corporate America: "Look, they're running the economy and they make the decisions about the economy. And so if you attack them, you wind up hurting the economy and hurting the president." In two blunt sentences, Rubin expressed the essence of academic structuralists' perspective on the American political economy.[42]

Clinton's 1993 deficit-reduction package barely passed Congress, with Republicans unanimous in opposition due to the tax increases. With the GOP shortly to capture congressional majorities after the 1994 midterm elections, the deficit-reduction package proved to be Clinton's major macroeconomic victory during his two terms in office. Combined with cyclical growth and a boom in technology, the positive responses of the bond market and the Federal Reserve to the Clinton plan helped to launch a period of strong economic growth. And with that growth, the stock of the deficit hawks soared within the administration. His initial ambivalence fading, Clinton was now happy to be known as a fan of free markets.[43]

Once Clinton appointed Robert Rubin to replace Lloyd Bentsen as secretary of the treasury, Rubin became the administration's economic star. It was telling that a popular label for the economic approach ascribed credit for the prosperous nineties became "Rubinomics." Ronald Reagan was less personally involved in crafting economic policy than Clinton, but his name was associated with the reigning economic doctrine of the eighties. With Wall Street even more integral to the expansion under Clinton, Rubin's economic thinking, which boiled down, in the words of journalist Michael Hirsh, to "let the markets rip," held sway in Washington for the remainder of the decade.[44]

Often thrown on the defensive after 1994 by an aggressive Republican majority in Congress, in areas outside economic policy, such as social security, abortion rights, affirmative action, and environmentalism, Clinton mostly defended traditional Democratic priorities and values. On economic questions, however, his approach was considerably closer to the Republicans. Consistent with a free-market emphasis, and guided principally by Rubin and his acolytes, the most important moves that the administration made were to support the deregulation of Wall Street even as a scattering of skeptics in official positions were posting warning signs of danger ahead. In 1998, when Brooksley Born, chair of the Commodity Futures Trading Commission, proposed a government investigation into the exploding, and unregulated, global market in derivatives, her worries about a speculative bubble were dismissed by the secretary of the treasury. Born bravely persisted, to the irritation of Rubin, but she was powerless to prevent Treasury, in alliance with the Fed, from squashing her efforts.[45]

The following year, the New Deal era Glass-Steagall Act, which forced apart investment banking and commercial banking, insuring customer deposits for the latter through the Federal Deposit Insurance Corporation, was repealed. Allowing mergers between the two types of banks, thereby permitting federally insured depositors' money to be used for trading in increasingly opaque financial instruments such as derivatives, the Gramm-Leach-Bliley Act was an initiative of the Republican Congress. Republicans had pushed this initiative unsuccessfully since the Reagan administration, but by the closing years of the Clinton presidency neither the majority of congressional Democrats nor Clinton's economic team had objections. Indeed, Rubin had called for the repeal of Glass-Steagall almost immediately upon assuming his position as secretary of the treasury.[46]

Assessing the performance of the American economy during Clinton's two presidential terms, a balanced judgment looks much like the prior discussion of the Kennedy years. On one hand, economic growth under Clinton bestowed benefits on most Americans. Unemployment fell sharply, median household income rose, inflation was contained, and minorities, Clinton's most loyal electoral backers, enjoyed some of their best economic years in decades. The deficit, which had exploded at the hands of the Reagan administration, was supplanted by surpluses by the final years of Clinton's second term. With the incubus of the deficit off economic policy making, it was now possible to talk about addressing unmet societal needs—or at least it would have been if free-market thinking had not become so bipartisan.[47]

However, as in Kennedy's case, the picture looks different when the focus shifts to the distribution of wealth and power. Workers made moderate gains under Clinton, but with a roaring stock market and rampant deregulation of the financial sector, the wealthy did far better. According to statistical measures of income inequality, the gap between the rich and everyone else grew even faster under Clinton than under his Republican predecessors.[48]

During the 2000 presidential campaign, Robert Reich, an old friend of Clinton's who served as his secretary of labor during the first term, sounded like C. Douglas Dillon describing the Kennedy years: "No administration in modern history has been as good for American business as has the Clinton-Gore team; none have been as solicitous of the concerns of business leaders, generated as much profit for business, presided over as buoyant a stock market or as huge a run-up in executive pay." The difference between the remarks from Dillon and from Reich was that the latter, who had opposed the deficit hawks and become progressively disillusioned with the administration's policies, had an ironic edge. Yet Reich, from the vantage point of 2000, could hardly have anticipated the long-term contribution of Rubinomics to the financial disaster that loomed from the start over the next Democratic administration.[49]

Barack Obama

The historic financial crisis that coldly greeted Barack Obama when he entered the White House drove home the structural realities of the American economy more powerfully than the typical cyclical downturns that Kennedy and Clinton had faced at the beginning of their terms. Obama had campaigned for the presidency for nearly two years before Election Day in 2008. For all but the final month and a half of that campaign, the expansive policy agenda upon which he ran was based on an assumption of normal economic times. He did not abandon this agenda because of the financial crisis, but its fate became intimately linked with the grimness of the worst American economy since the Great Depression. Borne into the White House largely with the support of moderate-income and minority voters in coalition with highly educated professionals, Obama in office had a very different constituency that wanted help: the Wall Street firms and banks that had risen to dominance in the financial revolution that had remade the American economy during the previous three decades.

The first order of economic business for the new administration was a rapid response to the severe downturn that had spread like a virus from the financial sector to the rest of the American economy. With unemployment soaring, consumption drying up, and credit markets frozen, Obama and congressional Democrats rushed the largest stimulus bill in American history into law in February 2009. Conservatives denounced the bill as an egregious and feckless federal overreach into the free market, but the more striking critique of the stimulus came from liberals, including two Nobel laureates in economics, Joseph Stiglitz and Paul Krugman. According to this critique, Obama's stimulus may have helped stave off a depression, but it was much too small to launch a genuine economic recovery. While the critics' economic case for a bolder stimulus was strong, their analysis was weaker on the politics: they tended to overlook the political economy of the party system. With Senate Republicans mounting a filibuster, and Democrats holding only fifty-eight Senate seats in February, the Obama administration had to pay a price for a successful cloture vote. A stimulus whose size was already suboptimal because of perceived political constraints was pared down even further late in the negotiations to meet the demands not only of three Republican moderates but also a larger number of centrist Democrats who claimed to share their deficit worries.[50]

With the stimulus in place, the focus of argument within the White House shifted to how to approach the financial giants whose reckless pursuit of outsized rewards had crashed the economy. Candidate Obama had already signed on to bailing out the banks when President George W. Bush proposed the Troubled Asset Relief Program (TARP). As president-elect, Obama chose an economic team whose composition would shape the administration's subsequent debates about Wall Street. His chief criteria for the top figures on his economic team were that they had to be experienced in handling financial crises and acceptable to a Wall Street community whose confidence was presumed to be none too strong at the moment. To the dismay of his liberal supporters, this meant the return of the Rubinites in the form of Timothy Geithner as secretary of the treasury and Lawrence Summers as director of the National Economic Council.[51]

In several books by journalists that came out during Obama's first term, Geithner was regularly portrayed as the most influential player on Obama's economic team—and as the person most responsible for steering the president toward an overly cautious stance toward the wayward Wall Street giants. Unlike many of his predecessors at the Treasury Department, Geithner had never been a top executive in the private sector. But as a protégé of Summers, himself a protégé of Rubin, during the Clinton administration, and later as president of the New York Federal Reserve, Geithner had developed a proclivity, as Noam Scheiber describes it, "to see the world through the eyes of large financial institutions." In White House debates, he insisted that the priority had to be on propping up the banks in order to unfreeze the credit upon which the American economy depends. Any sharp move toward playing to public anger and punishing financial miscreants would, he warned, threaten to bring the whole financial system down.[52]

According to Ron Suskind's *Confidence Men: Wall Street, Washington, and the Education of a President*, Geithner's most decisive intervention on behalf of Wall Street involved Citigroup, perhaps the model post–Glass-Steagall financial behemoth (and the institutional home of Robert Rubin after he left the Clinton administration). During the spring of 2009, there was growing sentiment within the administration to take bold action that would restructure the financial order and end the era of "too big to fail." With the president seemingly on board, even Summers endorsed a plan to "take down" the financially troubled Citigroup as a forceful first step toward bringing back the banking industry's traditional prudence in behavior. Adamantly opposed to the plan, Geithner fended off action until "stress tests" of the financial capacities of the major banks, his preferred alternative, were completed. Claiming that the tests showed that the worst of the financial crisis had passed, Geithner preserved Citigroup and effectively stifled the momentum for systemic change on Wall Street.[53]

As the storm over Wall Street subsided and many banks rebounded quickly with the assistance of bailout funds, financial firms persisted in their old habits. One of these habits, handing out enormous bonuses to their executives, especially angered the public and rattled the president's customary calm. Having treated Wall Street so gingerly, Obama's ire at their ingratitude was all the stronger, akin to Kennedy's fury at Roger Blough in the steel showdown. At a meeting in December 2009, Obama reportedly said to his economic team: "Wait, let me get this straight. These guys are reserving record bonuses because they're profitable, and they're profitable only because we rescued them." He expressed the same sentiment more provocatively on national television at about the same time. Appearing on the *60 Minutes* program, Obama hit hard at Wall Street's greed: "I did not run for office to be helping out a bunch of fat cat bankers on Wall Street. They're still puzzled why is it that people are mad at the banks. Well, let's see. You guys are drawing down $10, $20 million bonuses after America went through the worst economic year that it's gone through in decades, and you guys caused the problem. And we've got 10% unemployment."[54]

Years later, journalists reported, many on Wall Street and in corporate America were still incensed over the "fat cat" remarks. Obama had raised far more money from Wall Street titans in his campaign for the presidency than Kennedy or Clinton, and in office he had eschewed plans for fundamental change in their world, yet their backlash against his presidency was the most intense since New Deal days. Complaints from the business community were legion. Obama, it was alleged, not only was antibusiness, but had the instincts of Soviet-era planners. He demonized business and made the rich the villains in his narrative of the economic crisis. His hostility to the private sector established an unfavorable climate for investment and job creation, holding back the economic recovery. There were no business-men in his inner circle but too many ivory-tower academics with the president's ear. Even when he met with business elites at social functions, he was uninterested in their accomplishments and loath to schmooze with them. Hedge fund manag-ers, some of them among the richest of the rich on Wall Street, were particularly furious at the president. Obama not only refused to show them the respect they thought they were owed, but he threatened their wealth by proposing to treat the bulk of their earnings as ordinary income at the top tax rate (35 percent until 2013) rather than as capital gains (at a 15 percent rate).[55]

Although striking out rhetorically at business vented presidential frustra-tions—and played to abundant populist anger at the culprits for the economy's implosion in the Great Recession—it carried costs for Obama just as it had for Kennedy and Clinton. Mindful of the structural realities and power dynamics in the political economy, Obama muted his tone toward business most of the time after his "fat cat" blast. He pursued remedies for the pathologies of Wall Street through financial regulatory reform, but there was no Obama narrative at this point comparable to FDR's "economic royalists" speech. Some of the complaints from the business community were eventually addressed: after the disastrous mid-term elections of 2010, when the president replaced the departing Rahm Emanuel as his chief of staff with William Daley, it was Daley's experience as an executive at JP Morgan that the White House hoped would send a conciliatory signal to his Wall Street and corporate critics.[56]

Obama's most significant accomplishment in response to the financial disas-ter wrought by Wall Street was the passage in 2010 of the Wall Street Reform and Consumer Protection Act, commonly named Dodd-Frank after its congressional sponsors (Senator Christopher Dodd and Representative Barney Frank). Analysts initially rendered a mixed verdict on Obama's financial regulatory reform. For example, Lawrence Jacobs and Desmond King wrote that "the scope of change is unprecedented since the New Deal, but the final legislation was substantially watered down and falls short of the restructuring that the administration proposed and that many experts recommend to prevent future system breakdowns."[57]

Critics of Obama on the left suggested that the president could have been more tenacious in fighting for far-reaching reforms of Wall Street behavior. Yet to dwell on the administration's shortcomings is to overlook how the legislative process that the Dodd-Frank bill had to survive illustrates the thorny field for presidential management of the economy. Many of the features of this field discussed at the beginning of the chapter were present in the case of Dodd-Frank. Both economic structure (the concern that stringent controls on banks might limit the availability of credit) and economic ideology (the need to pay obeisance to free markets) promoted a moderate approach to financial regulatory reform. The political economy of the party system was manifest in the role of probusiness New Democrats, who softened the impact of regulations on Wall Street in the bill's final stages.[58] It was also manifest in the concessions required to recruit the three moderate Republican supporters who carried the bill to the requisite sixty votes against their fellow partisans' filibuster. A phalanx of lobbyists from the financial industry played a significant role in blocking or tempering some of the provisions in draft legislation that they considered most onerous to the individual firms or business-wide organizations that employed them.[59]

The most controversial provision in Dodd-Frank—and the one most overtly disliked by the financial industry—was the creation of a Consumer Financial Protection Bureau as a safeguard against the predatory financial practices that had been central to the devastation of the Great Recession. The bureau was the brainchild of Harvard Law professor Elizabeth Warren, and liberals promoted her to be its first director. But Obama instead asked her to serve as a special adviser to the president, tasked with organizing and staffing the new agency. A confirmation fight in the Senate, he said, might leave Warren—and the bureau—in limbo for too long. The calculation that the White House did not have the votes in the Senate to overcome a filibuster against a reformer to whom the GOP and its friends in finance vehemently objected was certainly correct. Republican filibusters blocked Obama's less controversial nominee to head the new bureau, Richard Cordray, from all but a recess appointment until July 2013 in an effort to emasculate consumer financial protection.[60]

Five years after the enactment of the Dodd-Frank law, the pulling and tugging between reformers and the financial industry continued unabated. Employing a horde of lobbyists to influence Congress and regulators alike, Wall Street tried to chip away at the law, especially taking aim at esoteric provisions that would attract little public notice. Its task was made easier after Republicans gained control of both houses of Congress in the 2014 elections.[61] Yet pessimistic observers who predicted that Dodd-Frank would make little difference were pleasantly surprised that the law, gradually put into place through the writing of regulations, actually turned out to have some teeth. The requirement that banks and other financial institutions hold larger amounts of capital had the effect of shifting a significant share of their operations away from riskier trading.[62] The famous Volcker Rule, prohibiting banks from "proprietary trading" that seeks profits while foisting losses off on taxpayers, was, when finally issued, tougher on Wall Street than almost anyone anticipated.[63] Whether Dodd-Frank, the Obama administration's response to the crash on Wall Street, can be counted as a major success will not be fully determined for years—and will crucially depend on which party captures the presidency in the elections of 2016.

The "shellacking" that President Obama and congressional Democrats took in the 2010 midterm elections made the field of macroeconomic management even tougher for the president. A shrunken Democratic majority in the Senate made overcoming filibusters less likely; more important, the new Republican majority in the House, infused with a large contingent of Tea Party freshmen, was intent on opposing anything with the president's name on it. Aggressive Republican House members threw Obama onto the defensive in the summer of 2011 by their refusal to vote for an increase in the debt ceiling without major Democratic concessions on spending. Accepting conservative terms of debate about the deficit, and entering into fruitless negotiations with Speaker John Boehner, Obama came across to friends and foes alike as weak, and his presidency hit its nadir in public approval.

Getting back into the game, Obama came out with a large-scale jobs bill in September 2011. Although the administration expected most of its provisions to be declared dead in the House, the new economic agenda repositioned the president as a populist battling against the defenders of the status quo. Three months later, Obama's altered economic identity crystallized through a major speech. On the 100th anniversary of Theodore Roosevelt's "New Nationalism" address in Osawatomie, Kansas, Obama spoke in the same small town. Although the symbolism evoked TR in his most progressive phase, the president's language was more evocative of FDR in the "economic royalists" speech.

Like FDR, Obama at Osawatomie pulled no punches in denouncing "the breathtaking greed of a few." Like FDR, he portrayed in vivid terms the victims of greed: the crisis brought on by the abuses of the financial industry "claimed the jobs and the homes and the basic security of millions of people—innocent, hardworking Americans who had met their responsibilities but were still left holding the bag." And like FDR, he emphasized a deeper structural malady behind the current economic crisis: a growing inequality that threatened the fundamental bases of American political and economic life. Inequality, Obama argued, "distorts our democracy. It gives an outsized voice to the few who can afford high-priced lobbyists and unlimited campaign contributions, and it runs the risk of selling out our democracy to the highest bidder." Even worse, he insisted, inequality stacked the economic deck in favor of a few more thoroughly than ever before. "This kind of gaping inequality gives lie to the promise that's at the very heart of America: that this is a place where you can make it if you try."[64]

Obama's new populist persona obviously did not win back big donors from Wall Street, but it was valuable in reassembling the coalition that had taken him to the White House in 2008. It didn't hurt to have an opponent in 2012 that had a plutocratic persona and a trickle-down economic message. But the mixed electoral results of 2012 left the field of economic policy relatively unchanged. With the Bush tax cuts scheduled to expire at the end of 2012, Obama had the whip hand in a post-electoral congressional session, finally succeeding in rolling back Bush's tax cuts for the rich, although not as far as he had previously proposed. Beyond that victory, however, the House Republicans remained Obama's nemesis in policy making. Even as the American economy began to pick up steam from cyclical factors, sequesters (mandatory limits) on domestic and defense spending that Obama had supported as part of the deficit fiasco of 2011 were a persistent drag on economic growth.

Six months into his second term as president, Obama reprised his attack on inequality in a major speech at Knox College in Galesburg, Illinois. He could legitimately claim to be more of a populist than Kennedy or Clinton, both of whom had shied away from substantial talk about inequality. Measured in terms of the rise of inequality, however, his presidency looked worse than theirs. During the years of economic hardship that coincided with the first term of the Obama presidency, median family income declined and unemployment rates were slow to come down. Yet at the upper reaches of the American economy, a soaring stock market and renewed increases in executive salaries more than cushioned the blows of a weak economy. The richest 1 percent of Americans took 22.46 percent of national income in 2012, up from 18.12 percent in 2009. As Timothy Noah observed: "Income inequality has gotten worse under President Barack Obama. But it could be worse still if President George W. Bush's tax policies remained in place—which makes it almost certain that inequality would be worse today had John McCain been elected president in 2008 or Mitt Romney in 2012."[65]

Despite rants from Wall Street executives about the "antibusiness" Obama, the financial industry was, compared to other sectors of the economy, a winner during his presidency. A *New York Times* headline from May 2015 heralded the basic story: "Wall Street Is Back, Almost as Big as Ever." Obama's policies had successfully imposed new regulatory restraints upon the riskier forms of behavior by Wall Street firms, and eye-popping pay increases for CEOs had become less common. Yet fundamental reductions in the power or profitability of the financial sector, on a scale at all comparable to what the New Deal accomplished, were not evident. In the words of *Times* reporter Neil Irwin: "Seven years after a crisis that shook Wall Street to its core, the financial sector's economic imprint has largely recovered. The number of people working in the securities business nationally has returned to 2007 levels, as has the gap between the compensation of Wall Street workers and that of everyone else. The financial sector as a whole is reporting profits that are as large a share of the overall economy as in the early 2000s and more than double their average level over the 70 years ended in 1999."[66]

CONCLUSION

When the formidable weaponry of economic elites is deployed to beat back challenges from the White House, presidents usually find themselves on the most difficult of political terrains. Presidents hope to keep the reigning powers of American industry and finance placated for the sake of macroeconomic performance that pleases the public and secures the path to reelection. Yet at least for Democrats in the White House, the policy agenda and electoral coalition they support push them at times into explosive contests with "economic royalists." Only under unusual circumstances do presidents prevail in these contests.

The brief case studies in this chapter of the relationship between Democratic presidents and the business community display considerable variation. Interactions between the two have been shaped by the distinctive personalities and viewpoints of the presidents, the changing issues at the core of White House conflicts with business, and larger structural transformations of the American political economy. Nonetheless, it is possible to discern patterns in these relationships that persist across time. With Roosevelt as a partial exception due to the extremity of the Great Depression and World War II, Kennedy, Clinton, and Obama have all experienced similar dynamics in dealing with American business. The relationship between Democratic presidents and the business community tends to follow a common sequence.

At the outset of their administrations, Democratic presidents are already attuned to, or else quickly made aware of, the structural realities of the American political economy. Franklin Roosevelt perceived that he had to save the money changers along with their banks and to seek cooperative arrangements with the leaders of industry. John F. Kennedy urged business executives to forgo outdated suspicions and regard a Democratic president as their ally. Bill Clinton was tutored by Alan Greenspan about the power of bond traders to pave the way for his economic success through low long-term interest rates. Barack Obama was pre-committed to bailing out the banks and alerted to the perils posed by frozen credit markets.

However, lacking Republican presidents' ideological and coalitional affinities with the business community, Democratic presidents are likely, sooner or later, to experience frictions and frustrations in their relations with business, with tensions ultimately erupting into a public clash. FDR was incensed at the backlash from ungrateful businessmen when he believed that he had saved the capitalist system, and he struck back with the policies of the Second New Deal and the rhetoric of "economic royalists." Kennedy was enraged by the "sons of bitches" in Big Steel that he faced down over an inflationary price hike. Clinton complained about the "fucking bond traders" who held in their selfish hands the economic and political fate of his presidency. Obama lashed out at "fat cat bankers" whose outrageous bonuses at a time of mass misery underscored their refusal to take responsibility for the economic destruction they had caused.

When Democratic presidents get tough with business for offenses it has committed, the business community pulls out its trusty weapons: allegations that the president is antibusiness and warnings that corporate or financial confidence is on the verge of collapse as a result, conveniently backed up in the cases of Kennedy and Clinton with tumbling stock prices. At the signs of a business slowdown, Democratic presidents tend to back off, turning to milder words and placating gestures. With black-tie dinners and corporate-friendly tax cuts, Kennedy resumed, in Walter Heller's phrase, "making love to business." Clinton dropped disparaging words about the rich and successfully courted new friends on Wall Street by placing Robert Rubin at the head of his economic team. Obama tried to patch up his tattered relationship with Wall Street, appointing a chief of staff who could credibly serve as an ambassador to the business community. FDR represents something of an exception to this pattern, at least until the onset of World War II, while Obama, after not making much headway in repairing his relationship with Wall Street, took a belated turn to Rooseveltian populism.

For all of their verbal bashing of Democratic presidents, industry and finance profit handsomely during their administrations. In FDR's case, good times for big business had to wait until the war, but with his Democratic successors the rewards came sooner. Kennedy and Clinton ushered in periods of vigorous economic growth, during which corporate and financial profits strongly outpaced income gains for the middle and working classes. Contrary to his concerns about inequality, Obama presided over a bifurcated economic recovery in which corporate profits and bank earnings soared even as median incomes stagnated and unemployment figures came down painfully slowly. The business community, it seems, does not need to have one of its avowed champions in the White House to thrive; it does well under Democratic and Republican presidents alike.

Unsurprisingly, the foregoing patterns bewilder and dishearten liberals. When they succeed in electing a Democrat as president, they expect a tougher hand toward the few along with a kinder hand toward the many. What they subsequently perceive, instead, is that Democratic presidents appear intimidated by the rich and powerful, ineffectual in serving the middle class, and delinquent in helping the disadvantaged.

In "Death to My Hometown," a song from *Wrecking Ball* (2012), his Great Recession CD, Bruce Springsteen, America's premier populist artist, bitterly expressed this classic liberal frustration. The song used images of military assault to describe a scene of utter devastation. But it was financial predators, not conventional armed forces, who deployed the weapons of death. The greatest outrage of all was that the profit-hungry perpetrators were never punished for their crimes against ordinary folks.[67]

Springsteen declined until the closing days of the 2012 campaign to perform at rallies with Obama, as he had four years earlier. According to an ABC News report, he explained that "he still supports Obama but expressed disappointment in his handling of the job market and home foreclosures and disapproved of the attention Obama paid to corporations rather than the middle class."[68] Had Springsteen and other liberals realized how closely this behavior followed the pattern that marked previous Democratic presidents as well, they might have been less surprised by the Obama record. Of all the political grounds upon which Democratic presidents initially might hope to advance, the political-economic field is the one upon which the most frequent outcome instead has been retreat.

3. Presidents and Coalition Politics

An important tract of the political ground upon which presidents must maneuver is coalition politics. Yet this tract has been less often charted by presidency scholars than others, such as Congress or public opinion. Presidents prefer to muddy their tracks in coalition politics because their actions do not square with the image of the chief executive as the sole representative of the national electorate and champion of the common good. Other elected officials have partial constituencies and partial perspectives, but presidents like to claim that they occupy a unique eminence from which they can see and serve the whole people.

The appealing image of the presidency as the representative of national unity has long been clouded by political realities. As early as the first decade of the American constitutional republic, presidents came to be leaders of rival political parties even as they swore fidelity to a conception of their office as transcending party.[1] Beginning with the New Deal, they began to construct personal parties centered in the executive branch itself.[2] Even as the lingering conceit of a presidency that represents the nation more fully and fairly than does the parochial Congress is accepted by many observers of the office, some recent works of scholarship have begun to batter away at this conceit. In their policy proposals and in the rhetoric they employ to promote these proposals, B. Dan Wood demonstrates, presidents are "partisan representatives" rather than representatives of the nation.[3] The benefits that flow from their policy achievements, Douglas Kriner and Andrew Reeves demonstrate, are primarily distributed to the battleground states and partisan constituencies that are critical for reelection.[4]

The fact that presidents primarily serve some groups and interests, and not others, is an awkward reminder that presidents must rhetorically distance themselves from, but nonetheless remain a charter member of, the unloved tribe of the politician. Nowhere is this more evident than in the management of coalitions. Tending coalitions is a quintessential skill for the politician. At the level of presidential politics, it ranges in quality from a virtuoso like Franklin Roosevelt to a novice like Jimmy Carter. Success at managing coalitions appears, at first glance, primarily to serve the president's personal interest in maintaining and expanding power. Lacking this success, however, larger accomplishments that determine a president's legacy will be hard to come by. Focusing on the often grubby details of coalition politics can make presidents appear tawdry or ruthless. So it is essential to remember that the "low" arts of the politician are often indispensable to "high" achievements.

In the history of political theory, the author who most vividly scoffs at claims of unity as chimerical and postulates that leaders must choose from which elements of society to seek support and from which to expect opposition remains Machiavelli. For the prince, Machiavelli writes, a fundamental choice in establishing a new state is which group to favor: the nobles or the people. As the highest leader emerging from among the political elite, it might seem natural for a prince to ally himself with other aristocrats. However, says Machiavelli, that course of action would be shortsighted. As a political leader, the prince needs to determine how the demands of the competing groups can be met and then calculate which among them is easier to satisfy with the resources at his disposal. The nobles, Machiavelli writes, arrogantly assume themselves to be the peers of the prince and insist upon their right to oppress the common people; allying himself with them will leave the prince in a perpetually exposed state. But the common people wish only not to be oppressed, and they will be grateful to a prince who frees them from the oppressiveness of the nobles. Even in Machiavelli's autocratic political regime, the logic of coalition politics points to a democratic strategy.[5]

In the study of American politics, coalitions are primarily associated with political parties. A few presidents, such as Andrew Jackson, Franklin Roosevelt, or Ronald Reagan, may play a formidable role in stitching together partisan coalitions, but these coalitions outlive their creators and are presumed to endure for a generation or so. Scholars who study party politics tend to focus on durable partisan coalitions. For instance, The Party Decides, an influential work on political parties and presidential nominations, defines parties as "long coalitions" made up of "intense policy demanders."[6]

The durability of party coalitions is an important premise for understanding ongoing party competition, but it is an inadequate basis for understanding presidents and coalition politics. In The Party Decides, it is longstanding party elites who are decisive in determining presidential nominations. In this chapter, it is presidents in office whose actions can reconfigure the makeup of party elites.

For presidents, the ground of coalitional politics is unstable. To the White House, the field of coalitions appears to be dynamic, contingent, and often perilous. Even the friendliest groups sometimes ask for more than presidents can deliver. The most volatile supporters, social movements, retain the ability to challenge, provoke, and embarrass the White House. The opposing party is regularly trying to steal away less reliable supporters. And demographic changes among largely unorganized blocs of voters shift the ground itself. Coalition politics is a major preoccupation for presidents—and a critical test of their capacities as political leaders.

This chapter seeks to chart the tract of coalition politics within which presidents have to maneuver. Compared to the two grounds for presidential actions covered in the preceding chapters, the ground of coalition politics is the most overtly political of the three. Spectacle traffics in appearances, while political economy determines the balance of money and power in policy confrontations. But the management of coalitions concerns the most basic question for a leader: who supports and who opposes me?

The chapter touches only tangentially on presidents' relations with political parties, a related subject that has been prominently treated in a historical fashion by the likes of James MacGregor Burns, Sidney Milkis, and Daniel Galvin.[7] One of my objectives here is to distinguish different forms of coalitions and different compositional elements of coalitions. Another is to examine the varying advantages and disadvantages for coalition politics accruing to presidents who come into office under dissimilar circumstances. Rather than employing substantial case studies, as in the previous two chapters, here I illustrate my analysis with shorter examples drawn mostly from the history of the modern presidency.

MANAGING COALITIONS

In the modern history of the presidency, there has been a notable shift in the principal vehicle for managing coalitions. Prior to the emergence of a large White House staff, conventionally marked in its origins by the Executive Reorganization Act of 1939, presidents perforce relied on party leaders to manage their coalitions. It was traditional to place the president's chief political aide and coalition manager in the cabinet position of postmaster general. Thus, if we look to how Franklin Roosevelt assembled the New Deal coalition before 1939, a central figure is Postmaster General James Farley.

There are no Jim Farleys anymore. (Indeed, there is no longer a postmaster general.) Today, the White House has several institutional units engaged in coalition management. White House media and scheduling units send specialized messages to interest groups and book the president for what is by now a large number of appearances before such groups. An Office of Public Liaison, first formally established under President Ford and continued by successors of both parties, contains staffers who perform liaison functions with a proliferation of special interests. A political director, an invention of the Reagan administration, oversees White House operations in key electoral contests. Two and a half decades ago, Lester Seligman and Cary Covington characterized this organizational apparatus as the "presidential party."[8] This "presidential party" has grown even more elaborate in the years since.

The most important White House unit for the management of coalitions is the Office of Public Liaison, which was renamed the Office of Public Engagement (an even more democratic-sounding euphemism) by President Obama. Prior to the Nixon administration, White House liaison with interest groups had been ad hoc and unsystematic, but the Nixon White House, concerned about its minority-party status in the era of the New Deal coalition, was determined to manage coalitions in a more businesslike fashion. Charles Colson, special counsel to the president—and later notorious for his hardball political tactics—headed the effort. Colson had twin objectives: to draw organized interests into the White House orbit and leverage their resources in support of the president's agenda and to woo specific voting blocs (e.g., women and senior citizens) with more sustained outreach.[9]

Situated in an even weaker political position than Nixon, Gerald Ford institutionalized Colson's portfolio by establishing the Office of Public Liaison. Ford's liaison mapped the array of organized groups and scheduled regular meetings with their representatives. Couched in the language of greater transparency and openness in the wake of the Watergate scandal, the Office of Public Liaison was even more useful to Ford in building up his base for the anticipated primary challenge from Ronald Reagan in 1976.[10]

The importance and role of the public liaison unit has waxed and waned with the varying electoral and policy concerns of succeeding administrations. Although Republican and Democratic administrations alike designate liaison staffers to serve as ambassadors to some of the same major groups in American society (such as African Americans and veterans), liaison assignments also vary by party. Thus, the Reagan White House was the first to provide liaison to evangelical Christians.[11]

Reagan was also the first president to establish an Office of Political Affairs in the White House. Although the purview of this office has primarily been elections rather than the ongoing management of coalitions, the office has been tasked with sensitizing the White House inner circle to cross-currents in the political environment, including the potential effects of policy proposals on friendly and unfriendly interest groups as well as on larger voting blocs.[12] President Obama came under pressure after his election to abolish the office, which critics alleged was using taxpayer funds solely to promote partisan objectives. The office was shut down early in 2011, much to the dismay of Democratic operatives who complained of the lack of political assistance and coordination from the White House. Facing a grim electoral environment in 2014, Obama recreated a White House unit named the Office of Political Strategy and Outreach.[13]

A description of the specialized White House units devoted to politics does not do justice to the place of coalition management in the contemporary presidency. Recent presidents have placed close at hand "senior advisers" whose portfolios range freely over politics and policy. Dick Morris's brief, stormy tenure in the Clinton White House in 1995–1996 was the most notorious. Karl Rove's role in the George W. Bush administration and David Axelrod's in the Obama administration have been nearly as prominent and, in Rove's case, controversial. The president's chief of staff is also involved in managing coalition politics, though few chiefs of staff have had the political pedigree of Rahm Emanuel in the early Obama White House.

Almost every aspect of the presidency touches upon the management of coalitions. Legislative politics has the most obvious connection to managing coalitions and will be discussed shortly. Administrative politics is another important realm for managing coalitions. A recent body of presidential scholarship from the rational-choice perspective, associated primarily with Terry Moe and his former students, has advanced the argument that presidents use executive orders (along with other tools) to politicize the bureaucracy because it is one of the few instruments for their purposes over which they have much unilateral control.[14] Without denying the force of this argument, it might be supplemented with the observation that executive orders issued by the president are often designed to please coalition partners. For example, President Reagan banned federal funding for international agencies that engaged in abortion counseling, President Clinton rescinded the ban, the second President Bush restored it, and President Obama rescinded it for the second time.

Appointment politics is central to the managing of coalitions. Executive branch appointees are often chosen with an eye to gratifying elements of the president's coalition and are expected to make decisions that please not only the White House but also the interest groups from which they came. In this vein, there is a stark difference between Republican and Democratic presidents in appointments to such agencies as the Department of the Interior, the Environmental Protection Agency, and the Occupational Safety and Health Administration (part of the Department of Labor). Republican presidents typically appoint individuals to these agencies who come from the corporate world and conservative law firms, whereas Democratic presidents are more likely to recruit from the ranks of academics, environmentalists, and unions. Even some presidential nominations to the Supreme Court can be interpreted through the lens of coalition management. President Reagan's first nominee to the Supreme Court, Sandra Day O'Connor, shored up his shaky standing with female voters. President Obama's first nominee, Sonia Sotomayor, solidified his standing among both Hispanics and female voters.

In addition to legislation, executive orders, and appointments, the presidential management of coalitions includes symbolism. The presidential spectacle, the subject of chapter 1, can be aimed not only at the general public, but at narrower slices of it as well. Through their public appearances, their words, and their deeds, presidents provide current and prospective elements of their coalitions with grat-ifying gestures. When a Republican president is warmly welcomed by a veterans' group, or a Democratic president is enthusiastically greeted at a NAACP conven-tion, the affiliation of the group with the president's coalition is demonstrably re-affirmed. Indeed, the symbolic value of such an event extends beyond the group's membership to the larger number that considers the group a positive reference point. When a president honors a revered member of a group with featured seat-ing in the gallery at the State of the Union address or with a presidential medal at a White House ceremony, the bonds of allegiance between presidents and their political friends are similarly signified. In a metaphorical sense, it is by observing upon whom presidents smile—and upon whom they occasionally frown—that one can discern the contours of their coalitions.

THE DYNAMICS OF COALITION POLITICS

Two kinds of coalitions are central to presidential politics: legislative and electoral. These two generally—indeed increasingly—overlap, but the differences between them remain important to examine.

Legislative Coalitions

Writing before the recent intensification of partisan polarization, political scien-tists emphasized how coalition formation fundamentally differed between par-liamentary and presidential systems of governance. In a parliamentary system, coalitions had to be established before a government could be formed in the wake of an election, and the majority coalition in the legislature thereafter consistently supported executive leadership or else the government collapsed. But in a presi-dential system featuring the separation of powers, coalitions had to be assembled in the legislature after the elections and on an ad hoc basis.[15]

For American presidents, the preponderance of legislative support for their priority proposals has come from their own partisan coalitions, but save for highly favorable and usually fleeting circumstances they have also needed some measure of support from opposition party members. President Johnson could not have steered the 1964 Civil Rights Act past fierce resistance from southern Democrats without support from Republican leaders. President Reagan could not have passed his budget and tax cut, the heart of "Reaganomics," without the votes of "Boll Weevil" Democrats from the South. As recently as 2001, President George W. Bush needed to win over prominent liberal Democrats in the House and Senate in order to enact his "No Child Left Behind" program of federal standards in education.

Such cross-party coalitions in Congress have largely vanished since Bush's first term. President Obama's signature policy victory during his first two years in office, the Affordable Care Act, did not receive a single Republican vote for final passage in either the House or the Senate. The health-care reform bill surmounted a filibuster in the Senate only because every single Democrat (and two independents caucusing with Democrats) repeatedly voted for cloture. For that moment at least, the difference between presidential and parliamentary systems almost disappeared. Meanwhile, the demise of cross-party coalitions had a devastating effect on other parts of Obama's agenda in the absence of total party unity. In 2010, his cap-and-trade bill to combat global warming could not make it past a threatened Senate filibuster due to the defection of a small number of Democrats from energy-producing states.

The potential for cross-party coalitions in Congress requires some degree of overlap in ideology and interest between at least some Republicans and Democrats. In today's polarized political climate, the least conservative congressional Republicans are located to the right of the most conservative congressional Democrats.[16] Moreover, possible positioning by members of Congress toward the center of the ideological spectrum runs the risk of inspiring primary challenges backed by a polarized base, especially for Republicans. Just how polarized the base of the two parties has become is evident in presidential approval scores. According to data from Gallup, in their respective sixth years in office, the second President Bush and President Obama each received only 9 percent approval ratings from identifiers with the opposing party.[17] The signal that such approval scores send to members of Congress is that their electoral incentives lie strictly in opposition to a president from the other party.

Although partisan polarization has sharply curtailed cross-partisan coalitions in support of the president's agenda, it has not entirely ruled them out. One issue area that typically features scrambled party coalitions is international trade. For reasons that include both the tasks of economic management and the orthodoxies of economic doctrine, presidents of both parties tend to be free traders, whereas many members of Congress, especially Democrats, defend threatened producers and workers. Winning a legislative battle on trade thus may require the construction of a coalition of groups whose interests favor free trade and that has influence on members of Congress from both parties. President Clinton's successful struggle to pass the North American Free Trade Agreement (NAFTA) is a good illustration of the phenomenon. Clinton's policy coalition for NAFTA drew in corporate elites, gaining him Republican votes in Congress, while the opposing policy coalition, centering on organized labor, was spearheaded in Congress by some of the leaders from Clinton's own party. A very similar story unfolded in President Obama's difficult campaign to win "fast-track" authority in negotiations for the Trans-Pacific Partnership.

In other cases, presidents might seek to incorporate interest groups that normally spurn them—and side with the rival party—into their policy coalitions in order to neutralize the potential danger they pose to legislation. President Obama's landmark victory in health-care reform serves as an important example. Alert to how damaging were the allied interest groups that opposed President Clinton's failed bid for health-care reform in 1993–1994, the Obama White House preemptively cut deals with some of those same interests so as to keep them from joining the opposing coalition. In the most notorious of these transactions, the trade association representing the giant pharmaceutical companies agreed to provide roughly $80 billion in drug discounts and $150 million in supportive advertising for health-care reform in exchange for a White House promise not to pursue liberal measures to negotiate lower prices for Medicare recipients or to allow the re-importation of prescription drugs from Canada. This bargain (and others like it) outraged many of Obama's supporters when the details became public, and it was one of the reasons why progressive groups, such as MoveOn, came for a brief time to oppose passage of the health-care legislation. Yet Obama's ultimate success, compared to Clinton's eventual failure, suggests that his coalitional tactics were shrewd.

Electoral Coalitions

The dynamics of electoral coalitions are fundamental to presidential politics. Daniel Galvin has posited that presidents from majority parties approach these dynamics differently than presidents from minority parties. Presidents from majority parties seek to "exploit" their coalition, aiming to "deliver on shared ideological purposes within the party and reward stalwart supporters." By contrast, presidents from minority parties seek to "expand" their coalition, aiming to "attract new groups, cut into the opposition party's electoral coalition, and expand the party's appeal to new and emerging demographics." Galvin's distinction is illuminating, and I will make use of it, but it requires a couple of qualifications. In some periods of American history there has not been a clear-cut partisan majority and minority; that was the case between 1876 and 1896, and that also seems to be the case since the elections of 1994. Moreover, even when there is evident disparity in party strength, some of the same dynamics of coalition politics operate within both parties.[18]

The dynamics between presidents and their electoral coalitions can become complicated to untangle, so to sort them out I focus on three dimensions: coalition maintenance, difficult partners, and poaching from the opposing party.

COALITION MAINTENANCE

All presidents, regardless of the competitive status of their parties, regularly engage in coalition maintenance. As previously mentioned, presidents deploy an array of benefits and services—legislative proposals, administrative actions, executive and judicial appointments, and symbolic gestures large and small—to satisfy the leaders and rank-and-file of allied groups. Presidential actions are invariably couched in terms of the general welfare, yet with few exceptions their role in coalition maintenance can be discerned by the careful observer.

Coalition maintenance provides a link between campaigning and governing. Many of the campaign promises that presidential candidates make are directed to specific coalition members. Promises off-handedly delivered in the heat of a campaign can get a new president in hot water. Bill Clinton was driven off-message at the outset of his first term because of a campaign pledge he had made to gays and lesbians to end the ban on their service in the armed forces. Promises to key coalition supporters that presidents cannot turn into successful legislation may have to be fulfilled in other ways. For example, George W. Bush, stymied on Capitol Hill, implemented "faith-based initiatives" by invoking his authority over the executive branch.[19]

The interest groups and voting blocs that constitute a partisan coalition may be more or less easy to satisfy. On one end of the spectrum lie "captured" groups; on the other end are constraining groups.

Paul Frymer developed the concept of a "captured" group to explain the fate of African Americans as an electoral constituency first of the post–Civil War Republican Party and then of the Democratic Party since the mid-1960s. Fearing that support for black interests would drive away too many white voters, party politicians in both eras marginalized the concerns of their faithful minority followers. They could safely assume the continuing loyalty of black voters because those voters had no viable alternative in electoral politics; the opposing party did not want to be identified with them or to include them in its coalition. Frymer observed that even when black voters provided the margin of electoral victory, the party to which they gave their suffrage offered them smaller rewards than those bestowed on other groups in its coalition.[20] (According to recent scholarship, a qualification is in order to Frymer's findings: quantitative measures of material well-being indicate that African Americans do significantly better under Democratic presidents than under Republican ones.)[21]

Can organized labor as a mainstay of the Democratic coalition and evangelical conservatives as a mainstay of the Republican coalition also be regarded as captured groups? Daniel Schlozman instead depicts them as "anchoring groups," influential players in their respective parties that contribute "access to votes, and the money, time, and networks that help in winning votes" in exchange for policy rewards and other compensations.[22] Rather than marginalized members of their parties' coalitions, anchoring groups are veto players; for example, aspiring Republican presidential candidates must be pro-life if they are not to run afoul of the powerful evangelical vote in primaries and caucuses.[23]

Schlozman's treatment of organized labor and evangelical conservatives is illuminating. Yet from the standpoint of the presidency, especially after these two groups have been ensconced in their parties' coalitions for a long time, they still usefully can be regarded as captured by two of Frymer's criteria: only one party wants a group's support, and that group consequently does not receive benefits for its loyalty commensurate to the magnitude of its electoral contributions.[24] The location of organized labor in the Democratic Party since the New Deal is not only a matter of ideological affinity, but a result as well of the hostility of business interests at the core of the traditional Republican coalition. The heyday of organized labor in the Democratic Party did not last much beyond the New Deal and Fair Deal years. By the time of the Kennedy administration, labor lobbyists complained that the White House directed more benefits to placate an antagonistic business community than it did to reward a friendly labor movement.[25] Later, organized labor suffered bitter defeats on international trade agreements at the hands of their party's presidents: Clinton and the North American Free Trade Agreement in 1993 and Obama's fast-track authority for the Trans-Pacific Partnership in 2015.

On labor's priority legislation, Democratic presidents from Kennedy through Obama have not expended much of their political capital.[26] Progressively weakening in numbers and influence, organized labor threw its full support behind Barack Obama in 2008 in the belief that a Democratic president and Congress might pass "card-check" legislation to improve unions' odds of winning certification and recouping lost strength. But when "card-check" received only a modest push from the White House and died in Congress during the same session that witnessed the passage of health-care reform and financial regulatory reform, organized labor once again had to swallow the defeat and soldier on as loyal Democrats.[27]

Evangelical conservatives, like organized labor, have become a captured group. Democrats largely leave evangelicals to the Republicans because appeals to conservative Christians would alienate women voters concerned with reproductive rights and secular voters worried about the separation of church and state.

Although the born-again Jimmy Carter ran strongly among evangelical Christians in 1976, since 1980, when Ronald Reagan welcomed them into the Republican coalition, they have become the party's largest single voting bloc. Evangelicals accelerated the shift of the white South into the Republican column, and they have continued to provide the party with an expanded base among Americans of moderate income. Yet Reagan himself subordinated the agenda of his evangelical supporters—to halt abortions and restore prayer in the schools—to the interests of his business supporters, giving priority to his economic program over his conservative cultural platform. George W. Bush was perhaps the Republican president most supportive of Christian conservatives with his "faith-based initiatives" and judicial appointments. Yet the second Bush, like his father and Reagan, was a president primarily responsive to the business wing of the Republican Party. The benefits that evangelical conservatives have received from Republican presidents pale beside the massive tax cuts and extensive deregulation that have been showered on the business community.[28]

Presidents can exploit captured groups, gaining in support far more than they distribute in benefits, but the flow of influence is the opposite in the case of constraining groups. The most dramatic instance, of course, is the role of southern segregationists in the Democratic Party between the 1930s and the 1960s, the decades during which their clout in both Congress and the Electoral College was a recurring headache for Democratic presidents. As Roosevelt's New Deal created the central pillars of the American welfare state, southern members of Congress saw to it that agricultural and domestic workers, the majority of the African American labor force in the South, were excluded from the protections of the Social Security Act and Fair Labor Standards Act.[29] Southern congressmen allied with Republicans against organized labor in passing the Taft-Hartley Act over President Truman's veto in 1947.[30] Filibusters by southern senators repeatedly killed even the mildest civil rights legislation until 1957, and they blocked any major advances in the civil rights field until 1964.

For a recent instance of constraint from within a president's own coalition, George W. Bush's frustrations with immigration reform in his second term are illustrative. For Bush and his chief political adviser, Karl Rove, immigration reform promised important political benefits. Immigration reform was desired by the business community as a means to enhance the supply of both high-tech and low-wage workers from abroad. It was desired by party strategists, concerned with the fast-growing electoral strength of Hispanics in several battleground states. Yet Bush could not steer immigration legislation through a Republican Congress in 2005–2006 or win with a bipartisan coalition in the Democratic Congress of 2007–2008. The principal barrier to his plans was nativists from his own party. As Daniel Tichenor points out, survey data "showed that conservative white Republicans were the most hostile to the Bush administration's plans to provide a path to legal status for undocumented immigrants, and that they overwhelmingly favored mass deportations, denial of public benefits for immigrants, and a constitutional amendment depriving birthright citizenship to the children of undocumented immigrants."[31]

DIFFICULT PARTNERS

Of all the constitutive elements of a president's coalition, social movements can be the most difficult partners. Unlike interest groups, which typically favor insider tactics such as lobbying, or voting blocs, which are activated only in elections, social movements put distinctive pressures on presidents from the outside, often in explosive fashion. Even when their goals are congruent with presidents' positions, they draw a contrast between the moral urgency of their causes and the cautious political timetable of the White House. In demanding that presidents move unequivocally to their side, social movements are heedless of how they may drive away other coalition partners or "swing" voters. If presidents resist social-movement pressures for full-throated commitment, movement activists may question the very authenticity of a president's character. And they may mount dramatic protests that prove embarrassing to their ostensible ally in the White House.[32]

It is through protest politics that the tension between presidents and their social-movement allies is most vividly manifested. Social-movement activists can launch direct protests against the president or White House, or they can stage demonstrations elsewhere that, intentionally or not, put the administration on the spot. Perhaps the iconic case of direct protests was the campaign mounted by Alice Paul and the National Woman's Party in 1917 on behalf of a constitutional amendment to enfranchise women. Confronting President Wilson with the contradiction between his war for democracy abroad and his refusal to back democratic rights for women at home, Paul and her supporters began daily picketing of the White House. Attacked by irate onlookers, and arrested by police, likely with the collusion of the administration, jailed militants further embarrassed Wilson with hunger strikes. The wave of bad publicity for the White House on the issue of suffrage broke only in January 1918, when the president officially came out in support of the constitutional amendment.[33]

Although social movements have caused personal and political grief to presidents positioned on the same side of issues, they have also provided the compelling ideals and grass-roots energy that have proved indispensable for signal presidential accomplishments. Social movements have challenged structures of privilege and hierarchy that presidents, as calculating politicians, are loath to confront, producing disruptions to the status quo that can be turned into openings for changes that previously seemed unthinkable. It is the often awkward collaboration between movements and presidents, Sidney Milkis, Daniel Tichenor, and Laura Blessing observe, that allows both "to break through the imposing obstacles to change that define the American political system."[34] Their principal case in point is the alliance of President Johnson with the civil rights movement in 1964–1965. In those two years, the symbiosis between movement demonstrations and presidential activism generated two landmark civil rights laws that reshaped American politics and remain LBJ's most honored achievement.

Johnson was already poised to collaborate with the civil rights movement when he became president, but initial presidential reluctance to ally with movements is more common. One case in point, the relationship between John F. Kennedy and the civil rights movement, will be taken up in the next chapter. A more contemporary case involves Barack Obama and LGBT rights.

Beginning with the McGovern presidential campaign of 1972, gays and lesbians were incorporated into the Democratic coalition.[35] Their votes were important in a few states, notably California and New York; their role as campaign donors became even more significant. Yet overt identification with the LGBT cause was risky for Democratic presidents or presidential candidates so long as it involved extending the logic and laws of equal rights to the most stigmatized minority in America. Barack Obama took office in 2009 at a time when LGBT issues were highly controversial, and regardless of his past statements or private convictions, he was reluctant to take a strong public stand. As the LGBT movement pushed hard for change, first to end the "Don't Ask, Don't Tell" policy on military service, and then to legalize same-sex marriage, the president whom they had enthusiastically backed in 2008 was a disappointment. Fearful of offending swing-state voters, as well as socially conservative blacks and Hispanics (who had voted against same-sex marriage in a California referendum—Proposition 8—at the same time they had voted for him), Obama argued that the issue of military service for LGBTs needed further review by the Pentagon and suggested that his views on same-sex marriage were "evolving."[36]

Leaders of moderate LGBT organizations had access to high-level Obama aides, and gay and lesbian staffers within the Obama administration worked hard to move the president and his cautious political strategists toward support for marriage equality.[37] Yet similar to the African American civil rights movement under Kennedy and Johnson, LGBT activists needed to keep outside pressure on Obama through litigation and protest politics. Successful lawsuits in the lower federal courts to overturn Proposition 8 in California and to void the key section of the 1996 Defense of Marriage Act as unconstitutional forced the Obama Justice Department to choose a side on cases involving LGBT rights. Meanwhile, LGBT protestors repeatedly confronted the first president to be a direct beneficiary of past civil rights victories. Obama was heckled by demonstrators at a California fundraiser in April 2010 for the slow pace in repealing "Don't Ask, Don't Tell."[38] In November 2010, as Congress considered repeal, thirteen LGBT activists, recreating iconic images of Alice Paul's militants, handcuffed themselves to the fence in front of the White House.[39] Once the ban on open homosexuality in the military was repealed, the focus of the protestors shifted to the issue of marriage equality.

With a tough reelection fight looming in 2012, Obama remained evasive about his stance on same-sex marriage. But activists continued to call into question the courage and authenticity of the man who had authored *The Audacity of Hope*. Their charges resonated not only in the LGBT community but also in Obama's base among young voters who, polls showed, overwhelmingly supported marriage equality. If the threat to important parts of his electoral coalition began to pull Obama off the fence, so too did increasingly encouraging news from polls. A poll commissioned by Freedom to Marry showed majority support for same-sex marriage in 2011, and by election year conventional polling organizations produced comparable numbers.[40] Prodded by comments from Vice President Biden in the spring of 2012, Obama finally told an ABC interviewer that "same-sex couples should be able to get married." A headline the following day in *LA Weekly* humorously captured the closing of this chapter in Obama's relationship with the LGBT movement: "Obama Totally Screws up Gay Activists' Plans to Protest His L.A. Visit Tomorrow."[41] In his second inaugural address in January 2013, Obama, like Kennedy and Johnson before him, stood firmly on the side of equal rights, linking the emblematic site of the LGBT struggle, Stonewall, to the emblematic sites (Seneca Falls and Selma) of now hallowed American struggles for women's rights and black civil rights.[42]

Poaching

Presidents who attend closely to coalition politics are looking to reshuffle the deck in favor of themselves and their party, whether that involves diminishing the other party's prior voting edge among important constituencies or shifting a few of those constituencies into their own electoral column. As previously noted, the incentives for poaching groups from the opposition coalition are greater when presidents perceive their party to have been stuck over the recent past in a minority status, such as the Democrats during the long era of Republican hegemony up to 1932 or the Republicans during the era of the New Deal coalition. Presidents seeking to expand their coalition through poaching will look to elements in the coalition of the rival party that are displaying signs of discontent or that might be successfully won over with favorable policies and flattering gestures. But successful poaching requires effort and art; the group the president is trying to woo away from the opposition may be made wary by the historical unfriendliness of the president's party, while the opposing party can adopt counter-measures to repair fraying loyalties.

In the face of both forms of resistance, the durable shift of a group from one party's coalition to the other's coalition may necessitate more than one stage, with the gains made by the original poacher in the White House only solidified during a later administration. To trace the transformations of partisan coalitions that have been sparked by presidential efforts thus requires the identification of a dynamic that may unfold rapidly or alternatively proceed in fits and starts over a substantial span of years. The following brief examples involve three pairs of presidents: Franklin Roosevelt and Lyndon Johnson for African Americans, Richard Nixon and Ronald Reagan for working-class whites, and, in a peculiar contemporary twist, George W. Bush and Barack Obama for senior citizens.

One of the most historically consequential instances of coalition poaching was Franklin D. Roosevelt's relationship with African Americans. Blacks had voted Republican since the Civil War on the basis of historical memories and political patronage. Democrats had been the champions of the South's racial order in the antebellum era, and they had continued to oppose black advances for decades after the war. The "progressive" Democratic precursor to FDR, Woodrow Wilson, had reinstituted segregation in federal agencies. But African Americans were "poor relations" in the Republican coalition, with little tangible to show for their loyalty to "the party of Lincoln."

Franklin Roosevelt was constrained in his courtship of blacks because of the power of the white South in his party. Nonetheless, the economic relief that the New Deal offered to impoverished African Americans during the Depression, the appointment of blacks to lower-level federal offices (FDR's "Black Cabinet"), and the visible sympathy of Eleanor Roosevelt and a few top New Dealers to the cause of equal rights were enough to shift the allegiance of the black majority to FDR by the time of the 1936 election. Once the Democrats captured the greater share of the black vote that year, they have never lost it since.[43]

However, because the Democratic Party remained mortgaged to its southern base after the New Deal, the loyalty of African Americans to the party of FDR was far from secured. So long as Democratic presidential candidates, especially Adlai Stevenson in the 1950s and John Kennedy in 1960, sought to placate the white South, Republican candidates could still claim a sizable share of the black vote. Dwight Eisenhower picked up nearly 40 percent of the black vote in 1956. Richard Nixon's share dropped to a third in 1960, but he might have come closer to Eisenhower's figure had Kennedy not engaged in a well-publicized intervention to free Martin Luther King Jr. from a Georgia jail in the campaign's closing days.[44] It was only with the 1964 presidential election, after Lyndon Johnson brilliantly maneuvered a landmark civil rights law through Congress, and after his Republican opponent, Barry Goldwater, voted against it, that African Americans became the most loyal component of the Democratic coalition. Like Kennedy, Johnson recognized the political price to be paid for destroying segregation; the white South swiftly became lost to Democratic presidential candidates unless they hailed from the region. But a black voting bloc that regularly exceeded 85 percent support for

Democrats was valuable compensation, especially in northern battleground states that now became the key to Democrats winning the White House.

Richard Nixon divided southern electoral votes with George Wallace in 1968, while Hubert Humphrey could carry only Texas. Once in office, the president's "southern strategy" sought to make permanent the shift of the white South from the Democrats to the Republicans. But Nixon was perhaps the most strategic and relentless poacher in recent presidential history, and he was after other game as well in a bid to construct a "new majority" for himself and his party. He had what can be termed a "northern strategy," aiming squarely to lure to his side northern ethnics, Catholics, and, above all, a white working class that had been the linchpin of the New Deal coalition.[45]

As a probusiness Republican, Nixon knew that he could not compete with Democrats for the support of the white working class through the provision of material benefits. Yet the political, racial, and cultural upheaval that had shaken the Democratic Party to its roots during the 1960s opened an alternative approach to white workers. Nixon's appeal fused patriotism, cultural traditionalism, religion, and race into a heady brew for disgruntled white workers. It was pitched to both labor leaders and the rank-and-file. The president undertook an on-again-off-again courtship of George Meany, AFL-CIO president and a fierce Vietnam hawk, feting Meany at a Labor Day dinner in the White House in 1970, alienating him in the implementation of wage-price controls in 1971–1972, then wooing him back during the 1972 campaign with golf and cigars as Nixon cemented their mutual dislike of Democratic candidate George McGovern. Even more potent was his embrace of the most conservative sectors of labor as his kinsmen in resentments. When New York City construction workers beat up antiwar protestors in May 1970, nothing was heard from the Nixon White House about the law and order that the president ordinarily claimed to uphold. On the contrary, Nixon invited top officials from New York's building-trades unions to the White House, where they presented him with a construction worker's "hard hat" to symbolize his unity with patriotic workers. Subsequently, the president appointed the New York City union leader most closely identified with hard hats, Peter Brennan, as his secretary of labor. In the short run, Nixon's poaching of the white working class from the Democrats paid off: In 1972, George McGovern suffered the largest defection of white workers from a Democratic presidential candidate since the formation of the New Deal coalition, with Nixon capturing 54 percent of the union vote, 25 percent better than he had done four years earlier.[46]

Nixon's "New Majority" went up in smoke with the Watergate scandal. Once the war in Vietnam ended, George Meany and the labor leadership returned to the Democratic fold. White workers were hardly thrilled with Gerald Ford and were pleased with Jimmy Carter's centrist message; in the 1976 election, Carter's percentages among both union and nonunion workers matched those of John Kennedy in 1960.[47] So it would take the presidency of Ronald Reagan to solidify Republican strength among white working-class voters. Reagan followed Nixon's lead in playing to white resentments around matters of patriotism, cultural traditionalism, religion, and race. He moved beyond Nixon's poaching strategy in two respects. First, he aimed to weaken organized labor, a pillar of the Democratic coalition, rather than courting it as Nixon had, sending a message when he crushed the Professional Air Traffic Controllers Organization in 1981 that union leaders had a determined foe in the White House. Second, by attacking "welfare queens" while cutting income taxes, Reagan signaled to white workers that less money would be given to low-income blacks while more would remain in their own paychecks.[48]

The current period of party politics is very different than during the era from Roosevelt to Reagan: Since the elections of 1994, control of Congress and the presidency has been volatile even as the two parties have progressively polarized. Neither side can claim a durable majority. Competition for constituencies whose loyalties are unsettled, however, is no less intense than in the past. Presidential poaching in this new context is evident in the case of George W. Bush and senior citizens.

As the generations of senior citizens with memories of and gratitude to Franklin Roosevelt for Social Security and Lyndon Johnson for Medicare began to die off, Republicans became more competitive with an electoral bloc containing the most reliable voters and growing in size with the aging of the American population. In 2000, candidates George W. Bush and Al Gore put forward rival plans for prescription drugs under Medicare, with Gore's plan promising more generous benefits.[49] Seniors still had a Democratic lean that year: Gallup Poll data showed Democrats with a nine-point advantage in partisan identification.[50] Exit polls showed Gore beating Bush among voters sixty-five and over by 50 percent to 47 percent.[51]

Taking office after a contested election verdict, President Bush and his top strategist, Karl Rove, looked to seniors as a potential component of a stronger Republican coalition. Bush would be on the defensive among senior voters when he sought reelection if he failed to deliver on his promise of prescription benefits. But if he could be the first Republican president to expand a program that heretofore carried a Democratic brand, the potential benefits seemed enormous. As Jonathan Oberlander observes, legislative enactment of prescription drug benefits under Medicare would, Rove calculated, increase Bush's share of the senior vote in 2004 and begin to realign seniors as part of a new Republican majority. Bringing in private insurers to Medicare for the first time as a conservative twist on what had been a fully public health-care system, the approach of the Bush White House to prescription-drug benefits was also pitched to the business side of the Republican coalition and aimed to pacify conservatives alarmed that their party was enlarging entitlements. The latter group almost sank Bush's program: Republican leaders needed to cut deals, twist arms, and violate normal voting rules before the bill squeaked through the House in 2003.[52]

Democratic charges of giveaways to big business and early implementation problems in the new Part D of Medicare limited anticipated gains among seniors for Bush in 2004, and Rove's realignment scenario imploded in his president's second term amid a cascade of disasters. Yet by 2012, seniors had moved toward the Republican Party much as Rove had hoped. President Obama still had one card to play with seniors: his defense of traditional Medicare against the unpopular proposal of congressional Republicans to transform it into a "voucher" system.[53] Nonetheless, Gallup Poll data for 2012 showed Republicans with a four-point advantage in partisan identification, a thirteen-point swing in their favor since 2000.[54] Exit polls showed Romney beating Obama among voters sixty-five and over by 56 percent to 44 percent, a fifteen-point swing in the Republican direction since 2000.[55]

Ironically, the Obama presidency appears to have inadvertently solidified the switch of seniors to the Republicans that Bush had initiated. Part of that switch owes indirectly to Bush's prescription-drug program for seniors: having outdone the Democrats and expanded Medicare in 2003, Republicans could for the first time assume the role of its defenders and charge Obama's Affordable Care Act with taking away benefits from seniors to subsidize health care for the uninsured. Another part, one might speculate, is traceable to the protracted culture war that Republican presidents have waged since Nixon. Demographically, seniors are the whitest age cohort in the U.S. population. Culturally, they were socialized before the upheavals of the 1960s and thereafter. Obama represents the coming of a multiracial and multicultural America. It is not surprising, therefore, that the same values and gestures that enhance his appeal to younger voters and voters of color have put off white seniors that feel no affinity for him.

OPPORTUNITIES AND CONSTRAINTS IN THE TENDING OF COALITIONS

The distinction between majority-party presidents and minority-party presidents does not capture the full range of historical variability in the relationships between presidents and their partisan coalitions. In the effort to map more systematically this ground for presidential action, a good place to look for guidance is the work of Stephen Skowronek on "political time." Although Skowronek's major book on the presidency, *The Politics Presidents Make*, is typically used for other purposes, I deploy his categories here as a historical guide to the tending of coalitions, drawing on examples from his book and adding some of my own.[56]

Coming into office in opposition to a discredited and failing political regime, Skowronek writes, a "president of reconstruction" is in the most favorable position to assemble a new coalition. Presidents of this type—Jefferson, Jackson, Lincoln, FDR, and Reagan—reshape the landscape of American politics in a lasting fashion, buoyed by the new majority coalition that assembles behind their person and policies. Their signature policies and their new coalitional forces are intertwined, as with the cases of Lincoln, emancipation, and African American support, or FDR, the Wagner Act, and labor support.

Presidents of reconstruction enjoy leeway in coalitional politics that will not be available to their successors in the regimes they establish. They are uniquely able both to embody and to transcend contradictions among their supporters. The regime founded by FDR united the white South and blacks; the regime founded by Reagan united corporate elites and low-income white workers. The acceptance by regime supporters of such contradictions in the reconstructive president they admire might, one can speculate, have a number of sources. Among these sources might be personal appeal, shared opposition to disliked elements of the old regime, bridging issues that divert contradictory interests from the subjects about which they most sharply disagree, and distributional payoffs that permit each interest to feel that it is a net winner. For example, FDR's coalition was at its strongest when white southerners and blacks both focused on measures of economic relief, and most jeopardized by issues of civil rights that highlighted their antagonism.

However, the leeway enjoyed by presidents of reconstruction should not be exaggerated. The need to retain the political support of the conservative white South constrained FDR at a number of junctures. Since the white South was vastly more powerful than African Americans in the 1930s, Roosevelt would not touch antilynching legislation, even though his private sympathies were behind it. In constructing the American welfare state, Roosevelt wanted its core programs to be universal in coverage; in compromises to win the votes of southern congressmen, however, African Americans were mostly excluded from them.[57] The white South was not the only element of the New Deal coalition that could block FDR from pursuing his preferences. Politically weakened and in declining health as he sought his party's nomination for a fourth presidential term in 1944, Roosevelt had to yield to Democratic urban bosses and accept their candidate for the vice presidency, Harry Truman.[58]

For "presidents of articulation," who come to office as affiliates of a partisan regime established by a president of reconstruction, the central task is to manage and maintain the coalition they have been bequeathed. Over time, this inheritance becomes increasingly hard to sustain. Presidents of articulation lack the elevated stature of the regime founder; often they suffer from invidious comparisons with him. More important, increasing strains within the inherited coalition demand the president's attention. Interests within the coalition now look past shared objectives to zero-sum differences. Past policies that have defined the regime become tattered and ineffectual, further loosening the ties that bind the coalition together. Healing fractures in the regime's coalition demands political skill; successfully containing regime tensions may take just as much art as constructing the regime in the first place, even though it will never receive the same measure of praise.

As Skowronek writes, a few presidents of articulation, coming to office at a time in which the regime appears especially robust, aim for more than coalition maintenance. These leaders—Skowronek counts Monroe, Polk, Theodore Roosevelt, Lyndon Johnson, and George W. Bush in this class—seek to deliver on the unfulfilled promises of the regime and to expand its coalition even further. Unlike the regime founder, however, their bold efforts backfire. Operating on the treacherous terrain of factionalism, their ambitious overreaching widens rather than narrows the divisions within the coalition. Seeking new policies that will bind together increasingly antagonistic forces within their party, they succeed instead only in turning each of these forces against the White House. Eschewing the cautious course of regime management in an aggressive bid to revitalize the regime (and achieve greatness), presidents of this type leave to a partisan successor a schism nearly beyond repair.

The failures of the bolder presidents of articulation make for a dramatic and often tragic tale. Even in the case of more cautious leaders in this category, however, the strains of coalition management are sometimes too much to withstand. FDR could hold the white South in his New Deal coalition, albeit with significant compromises and frustrations. But Harry Truman could not: as the civil rights movement gained new energy during World War II and its aftermath, its liberal sympathizers successfully incorporated a plank in the 1948 Democratic platform that prompted a southern walkout and a third-party challenge to Truman from the Dixiecrats. Ronald Reagan could raise taxes as well as reduce them, and he was able to placate religious conservatives with court appointments while subordinating their legislative agenda to that of his business constituency. But George H. W. Bush could do neither: feeling compelled to sign off on tax increases as the contradictions of "Reaganomics" came home to roost, and hard-pressed to overcome the distrust of the Christian right in light of his moderate past, his political coalition was fatally disrupted as both supply-side hardliners and the prophets of culture war within the Republican party denounced him in turn.

A third type of president in Skowronek's historical-institutional approach is the unfortunate "president of disjunction." Entering the White House in a regime's final period, this type of president is candid about his party's state of disrepair. His initial objective is to rehabilitate the regime's coalition and modernize its aging agenda to cope with the new problems of the day. Yet the regime proves beyond saving, and the president of disjunction only accelerates its crumbling with his hapless patchwork. Distancing himself from the inherited coalition to demonstrate his reform credentials, this type of president alienates the party's core elements; at the same time, the distance established is too small to impress opposition elements, emboldened as they have become by the sense that they have the opportunity to topple the regime and supplant it with their own. Ironically then, the abject failure of the president of disjunction to repair his party's coalition clears the ground for the next moment of successful coalition-building in the presidential reconstruction that follows in its wake.

A vivid illustration of the politics of disjunction is the presidency of Jimmy Carter. Divided and demoralized at the end of the Johnson administration, Democrats were given fresh life by Watergate and economic stagnation. In the massive field of contenders who sought the party's nomination in 1976, Carter was the one candidate who represented a new and more moderate version of the party's traditional liberalism. No admirer of the welfare state built by FDR and his successors, Carter pioneered the skepticism toward big government that would later become the calling card of Reagan through such nostrums as "zero-based budgeting." But as he searched for a middle ground between a faltering Democratic liberalism and a confident Republican conservatism, Carter found himself with fewer and fewer friends. It would be the conservative Ronald Reagan who defeated—and in a sense humiliated—him in the 1980 election. But before that, Carter had been politically crippled in the Democratic primaries by a challenge from Senator Edward Kennedy, who assembled the remnants of the liberal New Deal coalition in a campaign that may well have denied Carter renomination save for the unpredictable contingency of the Iranian hostage crisis.[59]

There is a fourth type in Skowronek's work: a "president of preemption," a candidate from the opposition party elected to the presidency when the regime has suffered a short-term setback yet is still vital in its coalition and governing philosophy. This political situation invites a president to probe for new coalitional possibilities, as we have seen in the case of Richard Nixon. The trick here is to develop what Bill Clinton, like Nixon an example of the preemptive type, described as a "third way," sufficiently familiar to the coalition elements of the opposition party to retain their support yet sufficiently novel in its borrowings from the regime party to win over its more discontented factions. A president of preemption is the type most capable of surprises, announcing unexpected twists in policy that can alarm old friends and charm old foes, as when Nixon went to China and Clinton signed off on the Republican brand of welfare reform.

Unlike the president of reconstruction, however, the president of preemption is unable to pull off the shuffling of coalitional elements at which he has aimed. Suspicious of his authenticity, maybe even wise to his game, most members of the regime's coalition resist his blandishments and stay where they have long been located. Clinton and the New Democrats sought to dramatize their independence from feminists and racial minorities, hoping thereby to woo back to the party the blue-collar elements known since the 1980s as Reagan Democrats. Yet once the third-way president got into deep water with the Lewinsky scandal, it was women and African Americans who rallied to his defense and liberals in the party's congressional wing who saved his job. Clinton's Democratic heirs—Gore, Kerry, and Obama—did not inherit from him a revived base in the white working class; on the contrary, their electoral coalitions would primarily consist of the same elements of the Democratic Party from which Clinton had tried to distance himself.

CONCLUSION

As the ceremonial heads of state and high priests of America's civil religion, presidents are expected to recite paeans to national unity and proclaim their commitment to represent the whole people. As practical politicians in a pluralistic polity, they need to assemble governing coalitions that divide the nation and serve some citizens and groups better than others. If this divisive role often smacks of self-interested behavior on the part of presidents, usually it reflects sincere belief as well that the interests they prioritize are more deserving or more vital to the nation's welfare than the interests represented by the opposing party.

Managing coalitions can take presidents onto treacherous ground. Some of the allies in their coalitions are relatively docile (captured). But most are demanding, and some (especially social movements) can be exceptionally difficult to handle. A few coalition members constrain presidents' agendas for governance, extracting a high price in policy in exchange for the president's reward in votes. And always there is the opposing party, poaching whatever stray supporters they can take away from the existing coalition. Opportunities in coalition politics are historically contingent, depending on the regime sequence that Skowronek calls "political time."

The Republican Party, Abraham Lincoln observed in the "House Divided" speech of 1858, was a coalition "of strange, discordant, and even hostile elements."[60] Something similar might be said of most major party coalitions in American history. During the Civil War, the "discordant" Republican coalition caused Lincoln considerable grief, yet it collaborated with him in carrying out a transformative policy of emancipation. Coalition politics draws presidents onto the political ground of stratagems, maneuvers, and bargains that tarnish traditional claims of national leadership and statesmanship. Yet unless presidents proceed shrewdly and skillfully across this ground, the achievements that will accrue from their leadership and define their legacy will be limited.

4. Tough Terrain: Making Domestic Policy

Machiavelli's essential advice to princes on how to keep their (male) subjects satisfied was simple: don't touch their property or their women.[1] For contemporary presidents, satisfying the citizenry is anything but simple. In particular, domestic policies—especially those in areas like health care, education, and civil rights that directly impact the daily lives of citizens—carry high stakes. To succeed in making domestic policy, presidents have to maneuver on tough terrain.

Reverting to the Machiavellian metaphor with which this book began, the ground of domestic policy is that terrain upon which presidents lead their coalitions into battle with the hope of winning some of the most valuable of all political prizes. This chapter begins by observing that the terrain has grown tougher in recent years, as the forces arrayed against the White House increase in scope and seek to drive away potential followers of the president with fearful pronouncements. Nonetheless, presidents still score some notable victories on the ground of domestic policy. Upon closer inspection, these victories take distinctive forms. In the most impressive display of executive agency, presidents design the strategy and lead their forces across tough terrain to domestic policy triumphs. In a second form of battle, presidents are cautious strategists whose victories owe more to their bold allies than to their own plans. Finally, some domestic policy achievements are more for show than about substance, as presidents opportunistically outflank their rivals to steal their political thunder.

OBSTACLES

In contemporary presidential politics, the ground for initiating new domestic policies is tougher to traverse than for new macroeconomic or foreign policies. Presidents today are able, albeit with some exceptions, to put into place their basic economic or foreign policies, whether or not those policies ultimately prove effective. But the major domestic initiatives undertaken by the White House are frequently thwarted at the outset. Once a president introduces a controversial domestic proposal, passionate and well-organized forces are sure to rise in opposition. Whether or not these forces defeat the proposal, its sponsor may pay a high price. Bill Clinton suffered his most consequential defeat with health-care reform, a political disaster that profoundly affected the remainder of his tenure in the White House. George W. Bush found it easier to send troops into Iraq and to cut taxes than to alter Social Security or to reform immigration policy. Although he secured a historic victory with the Affordable Care Act, Barack Obama learned how costly domestic reform could be for his public approval ratings and his party's standing in Congress.

Even a cursory examination of the obstacles confronting presidents once they venture onto the political ground for domestic policy change should drive home the difficulties they typically encounter and the risks they typically run. Congress is the most obvious obstacle, especially in an age of partisan polarization. Overcoming all of the veto points along the passageway to legislative enactments has always been hard but has been made much harder with the routine use of Senate filibusters. The budget reconciliation process potentially offers an easier path for some macroeconomic measures, but it is not available for changes in law on domestic matters. Presidents also can expect diminished numbers of their partisans after their first two years in office because of the longstanding pattern of midterm election losses.

Interest-group opposition is another factor that is more formidable for domestic initiatives than for macroeconomic or foreign policy initiatives. Because new domestic policies upend the status quo, threatening entrenched and organized beneficiaries of existing arrangements, those beneficiaries will mobilize to thwart change. If they are well-heeled, massive sums will be spent to lobby, to offer campaign contributions, and perhaps to send alarming messages to affected publics in order to defeat the president.

Cost is a third consideration. It is hardly an accident that so many of the landmark domestic achievements we associate with presidents came during the era from Franklin Roosevelt to Lyndon Johnson, when federal deficits were modest. Once large federal deficits came to loom over domestic policy making, presidents faced pressures to scale back their domestic initiatives or come up with convoluted financing mechanisms.

Beyond Congress, interest groups, and deficit worries, there are two more subtle obstacles presidents encounter on the political ground of domestic policy. The first is internal to the White House: the difficulty of balancing conflicting considerations of "good policy" and "good politics." Self-described "wonks" from the policy shops in the White House seek to develop proposals that they hope will prove effective in solving problems. They view their foes as the "hacks" on the White House staff that press for domestic proposals that will play well with important political constituencies.[2] To be sure, tensions between policy and politics are not unknown in economic and national security decision making, but these tensions are more frequent and fundamental in the sphere of domestic policy.

The second subtle obstacle concerns the public and stems from the phenomenon that behavioral psychologists label "loss aversion": the common propensity of individuals to fear losses more than to hope for gains.[3] Prone to "loss aversion," many members of the public are anxious that a domestic reform might jeopardize their existing well-being. When presidents put forth complex domestic initiatives in the name of reform, opponents can have considerable success warning of prospective hazards, real or imaginary. The sizable drop in initial public support for Clinton's health-care reform, Bush's social-security reform, and Obama's health-care overhaul is a potent reminder of how often "loss aversion" provides an advantage for the opposition to presidential leadership in domestic policy.

"Loss aversion" has implications for understanding the historical dynamics in domestic policy making. Simply put, the more the majority of citizens already have, the more they worry about what they may lose. Consider the contrast between FDR's Social Security Act of 1935 and Barack Obama's Affordable Care Act of 2010. Roosevelt could offer old-age insurance to a population few of whose members already enjoyed this form of security. When Obama proposed a new system to aid those without health insurance, 80 percent or more of Americans were already insured—and would be bombarded with messages from partisan opponents about how much they stood to lose from "Obamacare."

To this point I have been delineating the obstacles to domestic policy reform through legislation. But, say some prominent scholars of the presidency, there is an alternative to making domestic policy via the legislative route: unilateral action. Executive orders have been the tool through which recent presidents have pursued bold changes in such domestic areas as affirmative action (Kennedy, Johnson, and Nixon), abortion (Reagan), and climate change (Obama). By their powers over the apparatus of administration, they have inserted their own policy choices in the implementation of laws, regardless of whether Congress ever intended to make such choices. Unilateral action offers presidents, William Howell writes in *Power without Persuasion*, an opportunity to bypass Congress and make domestic policy all on their own: "When considering how to enact their legislative agendas, presidents can either engage the legislative process, and all of the uncertainties that come along with it, or, by issuing some kind of directive, they can just act on their own. Both processes yield policies that carry the weight of law."[4]

That executive directives can accomplish important presidential objectives is certainly true. The scholarship on unilateral action tells us why that can happen—why, for example, a majority in Congress is seldom able to undo executive orders with which it disagrees. Yet if this scholarship powerfully reveals the reach of unilateral action, it is too often vague about its limits. For several reasons, unilateral action does not function as the equivalent of legislation.

First, unilateral actions need to be justified through existing constitutional or statutory law; they cannot make new law. If presidents could transform the nation's laws on taxes, health care, education, civil rights, or immigration through executive orders, they would not bother with following the arduous route of legislation. That they do follow this route for their top domestic priorities—and often fail to reach their goal—suggests one of the most important limits to executive orders.

Second, the scope of executive orders is constrained by the appropriations power of Congress. Should a majority in Congress dislike an executive order, it may not be able to take collective action to reverse the order—but neither will it be willing to fund its implementation. Presidents know that they can't get much money for controversial unilateral actions in domestic affairs, so even when their executive orders have significant impact they entail modest expenditures. By contrast, major domestic initiatives adopted through the legislative route often require substantial sums.

Third, executive orders lead a precarious existence. A president who wishes to reverse the legislative accomplishments of a predecessor from the opposite political party must surmount the same array of congressional veto points that had to be cleared in the first place. But to undo an executive order requires only a "stroke of a pen." Executive orders—or at least most controversial ones—only survive so long as the White House remains in the possession of the same party.[5]

Despite the obstacles to success, presidents regularly seek major changes to the nation's laws in domestic affairs—and sometimes they win major victories. The incentives for gamely venturing onto this tough terrain are powerful. The incentives may be personal: most presidents do care deeply about at least some reforms to domestic policy. The incentives may be political: presidents need to deliver on the promises they made to get elected if they want to increase the odds that they will be reelected. Finally, the incentives extend to historical reputation: for many presidents, it is by their domestic policy triumphs that they are most warmly remembered (especially true for LBJ with civil rights and the Great Society).

Consequently, the remainder of this chapter focuses not on presidential frustrations in domestic policy but on presidential successes. Presidents sometimes maneuver across the tough political terrain of domestic policy and achieve the results for which they are later hailed. Yet their journey may not look like what they originally planned, and the results are not always what they truly wanted. There is more politics to making successful domestic policy, I aim to demonstrate, than meets the eye.

DOMESTIC POLICIES ON POLITICAL GROUND

In the American political system, new domestic policies with high visibility are usually associated with the presidency. Especially for the relatively small number of major bills that the president supports and Congress enacts, presidents normally garner the lion's share of the credit. At the end of a legislative session, or in the campaign for reelection, the White House will certainly boast of these policy accomplishments. And in the longer run, as historians write textbook surveys or studies of particular administrations, these major laws will be listed under the president's name.

To what extent does this textbook image of presidential leadership in the making of landmark domestic policy accurately capture reality? How often are major domestic policies the products of presidential ambitions and talents? How often instead do they reflect the pressures and constraints that presidents encounter as they attempt to traverse political ground? By examining the creation of landmark domestic policies through a historical lens, I attempt to answer these questions. I offer six short case studies involving presidents and landmark legislation. The cases are:

Franklin D. Roosevelt and the Social Security Act
George W. Bush and No Child Left Behind
Franklin D. Roosevelt and the National Labor Relations (Wagner) Act
John F. Kennedy and the Civil Rights Act of 1964
Richard Nixon and environmental legislation
Bill Clinton's crime bill.

These six cases were selected out of an initial surmise that they potentially represented three distinct types of presidential leadership in domestic policy:

1. *Leadership as entrepreneurial initiation*, in which presidents pursue their own preferences and dominate the process of policy development.
2. *Leadership as policy responsiveness*, in which presidents respond to the demands of others and provide essential services in policy development that they did not intend or initiate.
3. *Leadership as policy credit claiming*, in which presidents advance policies that run counter to their own preferences in order to steal the thunder from opponents with a more genuine claim.

Domestic Leadership as Entrepreneurial Initiation

FRANKLIN D. ROOSEVELT AND THE SOCIAL SECURITY ACT

The Social Security Act of 1935 is indisputably one of the chief landmarks of Franklin D. Roosevelt's New Deal. More than any other single piece of legislation, it is the cornerstone of America's modern welfare state. The substantial literature that has grown up around the Social Security Act suggests that it is a paradigmatic example of domestic policy leadership as entrepreneurial initiation.

The two pillars of the Social Security Act are old-age insurance and unemployment insurance. Both ideas had been staples on the policy agenda of progressives for several decades before the New Deal. And both were endorsed by Franklin Roosevelt before he became president. At a governors conference in 1930 he took the lead in advocating unemployment insurance. The Democratic platform of 1932 called for the establishment of both unemployment insurance and old-age insurance.[6] As Roosevelt's secretary of labor, Frances Perkins, his point person for the Social Security Act, related in her memoir, "Before his Inauguration in 1933, Roosevelt had agreed that we should explore at once methods for setting up unemployment and old-age insurance in the United States."[7]

Under pressure to pass measures for immediate economic recovery, and recognizing that the establishment of unemployment and old-age insurance was a dramatic departure from past federal policy, subject to challenge on constitutional as well as economic grounds, Roosevelt and Perkins did not move precipitously on a social-security agenda. Instead, they carefully laid the groundwork for innovative legislation. The president encouraged Senator Robert Wagner and Representative David Lewis to introduce an unemployment insurance measure in 1933 designed to educate public opinion on the subject. Perkins repeatedly raised the topic at cabinet meetings and developed support among FDR's inner circle. She "made over a hundred speeches in different parts of the country that year [1933], always stressing social insurance."[8]

By the spring of 1934, Roosevelt was ready to make his move. The policy-making flurry of the "first one hundred days" was past, and pressure for old-age pensions was building with the popularity of the Townsend Plan, a radical proposal to supply every citizen over the age of sixty with $200 per month provided the money was spent in the next thirty days. On June 8, 1934, the president sent a special message to Congress on social insurance, and three weeks later he created a Committee on Economic Security through an executive order. The committee included the principal cabinet officers involved with the economy along with relief administrator Harry Hopkins. It hired an executive director and numerous policy specialists tasked with research and the development of policy options. Policy planning for social insurance thus proceeded mainly within the executive branch.[9]

As the committee and its staff fleshed out the details of the new social insurance system, Roosevelt made the crucial strategic decisions. The most important was to combine old-age insurance and unemployment insurance with old-age assistance (support for those currently aged through general revenues) in an omnibus bill. By 1934, the idea of old-age assistance had become popular, and the president saw that its popularity could be leveraged to enact unemployment insurance and old-age insurance as well. As Edwin Witte, executive director of the Committee on Economic Security, wrote:

As the situation developed, I doubt whether any part of the social security program other than the old-age assistance title would have been enacted into law but for the fact that the president throughout insisted that the entire program must be kept together. Had the measure been presented in separate bills, it is quite possible that the old-age assistance title might have become law much earlier. I doubt whether anything else would have gone through at all.[10]

Once the "economic security" bill (the name was changed later to "social security") was introduced in Congress early in 1935, Roosevelt pushed for prompt enactment. Committees in both the House and Senate quickly went to work on the legislation. According to Witte's account, the majority of the House Ways and Means Committee was personally unsympathetic to the bill, but the strong support of a popular president with a large partisan majority carried great weight in committee deliberations. The Senate Finance Committee, stacked with conservative southern Democrats, was even more unfavorable terrain, but skilled leadership from the committee chair, Patrick Harrison, moved the bill through successfully. Once the legislation had cleared these legislative hurdles, its passage was overwhelming, with favorable votes of 371–33 in the House and 77–6 in the Senate.[11]

Most of the resistance to Roosevelt's social insurance came from conservatives, with business interests assailing the new taxes involved and southerners decrying violations of federalism. Legislative rivals to the administration proposal emerged from the left. Thousands of letters poured into legislators' offices on behalf of the Townsend Plan, but it was so wildly costly that it stood no chance of serious consideration. Ernest Lundeen, a Farmer-Labor congressman from Minnesota, sponsored a bill that would have created a national system of unemployment compensation derived from general revenues, omitting both the employer contributions and state-based administration in the Roosevelt bill. Left-wing support for the measure may have hurt its prospects, with opponents tagging it as a communist proposal.[12]

Although Roosevelt initiated the development of social security legislation and successfully shepherded his program through Congress and into law, critical compromises made during the policy process delimited its reach and circumscribed the president's original aspirations. The most consequential compromise concerned the extent of coverage. The president wanted a universal system of social insurance. As Perkins relates, "At cabinet meetings and when he talked privately with a group of us, he would say, 'You want to make it simple—very simple. So simple that everybody will understand it. And what's more, there is no reason why everybody in the United States should not be covered. I see no reason why every child, from the day he is born, should not be covered.'"[13]

But others saw reasons to restrict coverage. Secretary of the Treasury Henry Morgenthau, deviating from the rest of Roosevelt's cabinet committee, told Congress that it was not administratively feasible to collect payroll taxes from agricultural, domestic, or sporadic workers, and that these occupational categories therefore should be excluded from the social insurance system. Since the majority of these workers were African Americans in the South, whose inclusion in the new system would have threatened exploitative practices in that region's racial labor market, southern Democrats in Congress had their own reasons for limiting coverage (and for ensuring that administration of unemployment insurance would be through local discretion rather than national rules). What emerged from the Social Security Act of 1935, therefore, was not Roosevelt's universal system, but a dual system that privileged white workers over black workers.[14]

Despite the fact that he had fallen short of obtaining the universal coverage he desired, Roosevelt was very proud of his accomplishment in the Social Security Act. Unlike a number of other New Deal measures, he felt that this had been *his* idea from the start.[15] During World War II, when he read about the Beveridge Plan in Great Britain for "cradle to the grave" social insurance, he complained to Perkins, "Why does Beveridge get his name on this? . . . You know that I have been talking about cradle to the grave insurance ever since we first thought of it. It is my idea. It is not the Beveridge Plan. It is the Roosevelt Plan."[16]

GEORGE W. BUSH AND NO CHILD LEFT BEHIND

George W. Bush prided himself on his decisiveness, and nowhere else in the field of domestic affairs was he as decisive as in education policy. His proposal for what he titled No Child Left Behind (NCLB), a large-scale reform of the federal role in K–12 education, was the inaugural domestic initiative of his administration. Compared to the sharply partisan character of later Bush administration proposals, it was remarkably bipartisan in nature. Most important, NCLB has had a greater impact on American life than any other Bush measure in domestic policy. Although controversy dogged NCLB from the moment the legislation passed Congress at the end of Bush's first year in office, he has continued to regard it as "my signature domestic policy initiative."[17]

Preceding the introduction of NCLB were two decades of extensive efforts outside and inside government to transform federal education policy. The Elementary and Secondary Education Act (ESEA) of 1965, one of the hallmarks of Lyndon Johnson's Great Society, dramatically expanded the role of the federal government in an area traditionally controlled by local and state institutions, but its objective was confined to improving opportunity for disadvantaged students. Education policy specialists have labeled it as an "equity regime." In the early 1980s, this equity regime came under fire from an unusual coalition of reformers. Political scientist Jesse Rhodes has demonstrated that the chief components of this coalition were "business entrepreneurs," convinced that American schools were not imparting the knowledge and skills that their workforce needed in an increasingly competitive global economy, and "civil rights entrepreneurs," distressed that the equity regime of ESEA had failed to lessen the achievement gap between minority and white students. Despite divergent objectives, the two groups concurred on the need for an "excellence regime" in education policy. At the heart of the new vision was a shift of focus from resources to results; the core argument was that more money had not fixed American education, but that the establishment of standards, testing, and accountability (hereafter STA) would.[18]

Once this "excellence in education" agenda garnered increasing support, presidents of both parties began to respond. The Reagan administration highlighted the mediocre performance of American public schools in *A Nation at Risk*, a commission report that drew enormous attention. George H. W. Bush convened the nation's governors to promote education reform at the "Charlottesville Summit."[19] But Bill Clinton was the first president successfully to enact part of the reform coalition's STA agenda into law with his "Goals 2000" and "Improving America's Schools Act." Clinton's success was limited, however: in the face of traditional suspicions of federal intrusion into local control of schools, the legislation he sponsored lacked teeth. To make matters much worse, almost immediately after his two education bills were passed, the Republicans took over control of Congress and proceeded to reverse direction.[20]

Republican revolutionaries in Congress were opposed to any effort by the federal government to guide the states into the path of STA. Conservative opposition to a federal presence in education went deeper: the Department of Education, established under Jimmy Carter, was targeted for demolition. Pressed to come up with a positive agenda on education for the presidential election in 1996, Patrick McGuinn writes, Republicans talked about "morality and vouchers rather than school improvement per se."[21] Students needed to be taught abstinence and patriotism, and allowed to pray in class; low-income parents should be offered an alternative to failing public schools through private-school vouchers.

Apart from circumscribing the implementation of Clinton's STA program, conservative Republicans had little to show for their counterthrust in education policy. Clinton won a budget battle over federal spending on education, and with his image as the defender of public schools contrasted to Republican candidate Robert Dole's morality and vouchers platform during the 1996 presidential campaign, he trounced his opponent by a 2–1 margin on the education issue in exit polling.[22] When establishment Republicans began to challenge the hardline conservative stance on education in the wake of electoral defeat, they did not have to look far for a standard bearer. The governor of Texas, George W. Bush, was a committed and enthusiastic advocate of education reform through STA. Building on the work of the previous administration, Bush made a stringent STA system into his signature gubernatorial policy.[23] He worked closely with Texas business elites on education policy but also found a receptive audience among black and Hispanic educators in the state. Indeed, Bush always preferred to portray his version of STA as a civil-rights policy, blaming the failures of the "equity regime" on "the soft bigotry of low expectations."[24]

During the 2000 presidential campaign, Bush made education reform his top domestic issue and the emblem of a "compassionate conservatism" that distinguished him from unpopular congressional Republicans. He took great care not to be saddled with the baggage of conservative hostility to federal education policy, successfully lobbying the Republican platform committee to avoid any mention of abolishing the Department of Education. The NCLB campaign proposal allowed Bush to reach beyond the Republican electoral coalition of the 1990s. As Frederick Hess writes, "Bush used education reform to reassure moderates that the GOP could govern 'compassionately,' woo liberal constituencies like Latinos and African Americans, and fracture the Democratic coalition by weakening the teachers' unions."[25] Exit polls indicated that Bush's identification with education reform was effective: unlike almost all Republican predecessors in recent decades, Bush was seen as the equal of his Democratic rival, Al Gore, in the field of education policy (no small matter in one of the closest elections in American history).[26]

Two days after his inauguration, Bush presented his NCLB blueprint to Congress. Many of the features of his plan were modeled after the STA system in Texas, except that now he was proposing to have the federal government become the driver of educational reform by tying federal aid to the states to their adoption of STA. Stringent requirements were the centerpiece of the blueprint: every state would have to test students annually on reading and math in grades 3–8, and states would be rewarded or punished financially depending on student performance scores. For both pragmatic reasons (Republican majorities in the House and Senate were narrow) and symbolic reasons (he had promised to be a "uniter" during the campaign), the new president determined at the outset that he would seek a bipartisan and centrist bill. In a political move that was indispensable to this strategy—but that he would not or could not repeat for subsequent domestic proposals—Bush skillfully courted the most important Democratic leaders in the field of education, Ted Kennedy in the Senate and George Miller in the House.[27]

Like FDR with the Social Security Act, Bush had to accept crucial compromises to steer NCLB past congressional opposition from both left and right. To hold the support of key Democrats, he dropped an educational proposal beloved of conservatives, vouchers that could be used for private schools. In the same vein, he agreed to raise the level of federal spending on education well beyond what he had initially requested. However, these compromises did not seem to faze Bush. Andrew Rudalevige observes that the president's "core accountability priority was annual testing. What was in the tests, and how they were used, was less critical. Vouchers were less critical still."[28] The bipartisan, centrist coalition that Bush had assembled surmounted challenges from disgruntled conservatives and liberals. Attempts by conservative Republicans in the House to restore "school choice" vouchers to NCLB were soundly defeated. The heart of Bush's plan, annual testing, was threatened by an unusual coalition of liberals (who believed that the testing regime would prove harmful to minority students) and conservatives (who feared a slippery slope toward the imposition of a national curriculum), but the bipartisan coalition beat back this challenge as well in both the House and the Senate.[29]

Reconciling more than 2,000 differences between the chambers' respective versions of NCLB, a conference committee report easily passed the House (381–41) and Senate (87–10) in December 2001. Most of the negative votes came from conservative Republicans. Yet the majority of conservatives, not wanting to embarrass their party's new president on his signature domestic initiative, swallowed their doubts and voted for an education reform whose expansion of federal authority ran directly counter to their ideology.[30] When the president signed the bill into law in January 2002, he received mostly favorable press. Public opinion was positive as well, but there was an ominous harbinger for the future of NCLB in polls at that time: a majority of Americans indicated that they did not know much about how this complex and controversial legislation would impact the nation's schools.[31]

FDR's Social Security Act became increasingly popular over time, but Bush's NCLB was not so fortunate. As the states began to implement the newly mandated STA regime in education, familiarity with the new system grew—and a growing number of Americans did not like what they were learning. A decade after Bush signed his signature domestic initiative into law, a Gallup Poll found that 16 percent of Americans thought NCLB had improved public education, 29 percent thought it had a negative effect, and the largest number, 38 percent, thought it had not made a significant difference. Among respondents who claimed to be "very familiar" with the law, negative views topped positive views by 48 percent to 28 percent.[32]

Elites of many stripes became as unhappy with NCLB as was the mass public. State and local officials complained that the law imposed unrealistic standards and was fiscally and administratively burdensome. Never well-disposed to Bush's brainchild, conservatives increasingly regarded it as a mark of his apostasy in championing "big government conservatism." Liberals decried how NCLB fostered "teaching to the test," demoralizing students and teachers alike. Yet while Barack Obama entered office in 2009 with an agenda of reversing most of what Bush had put into place, in education policy he largely followed in his predecessor's footsteps. The new president signaled his support for the idea of an "excellence regime" in education policy by choosing Arne Duncan, an advocate of STA while head of Chicago's school system, as secretary of education.[33] Obama's own signature policy in education, Race to the Top, revised but essentially continued the STA system that was Bush's entrepreneurial achievement in domestic policy.[34] No Child Left Behind remained the cornerstone of federal education policy until 2015, when Congress restored greater state and local authority through the Every Student Succeeds Act.

Domestic Leadership as Policy Responsiveness

FRANKLIN D. ROOSEVELT AND THE NATIONAL LABOR RELATIONS ACT

The National Labor Relations Act of 1935 (Wagner Act) nearly equals the Social Security Act of the same year as a landmark of the New Deal. This law revolutionized labor relations in the United States, establishing the right of unions to engage in collective bargaining and thereby modifying power relations in the American political economy. Considering the strength of management and the weakness of labor in American history when compared to other advanced capitalist nations, the Wagner Act (as I will hereafter refer to it) was, James MacGregor Burns wrote, "the most radical legislation passed during the New Deal."[35]

Who or what deserves the credit for the genesis and passage of the Wagner Act? A lively debate within the field of American political development (APD) puts forward several contenders. According to Michael Goldfield, an exogenous explanation for the Wagner Act works best: the legislation was a response to the fierce strikes and growing radicalism of insurgent unions, and it sought "to constrain, limit, and control the increasingly militant labor movement."[36] In a rejoinder to Goldfield, Theda Skocpol and Kenneth Finegold suggest an endogenous explanation: taking advantage of Democratic gains in the 1934 elections, and moving past the failed labor regime of the National Industrial Recovery Act of 1933, a political entrepreneur, Senator Robert Wagner of New York, was the pivotal actor in drafting and pushing a new system of labor rights through Congress.[37] David Plotke offers a broader network analysis in his work on the construction of the New Deal order: passage of the Wagner Act "was due primarily to the efforts of progressive liberals inside and outside the government, allied with a mass labor movement."[38]

What is notable about this debate within APD is that no scholar ascribes a formative role to President Roosevelt.

At the outset of the Great Depression, labor unions in the United States were
in a weak position. Labor organization was given its first boost by the New Deal
through Section 7(a) of the National Industrial Recovery Act of 1933. In this omnibus bill that offered each player in the industrial economy some advantage, labor won a vague guarantee of collective bargaining rights. The bill was a defensive
reaction by the Roosevelt administration to more radical legislation introduced
by Senator Hugo Black of Alabama that would have mandated a thirty-hour work
week in order to spread employment opportunities. In the bargaining between
administration officials and interest-group representatives, the inclusion of 7(a)
was primarily the handiwork of Jett Lauck, an adviser to mineworkers leader
John L. Lewis.[39]

Lewis rushed to take advantage of 7(a). The United Mineworkers plastered the
coalfields with posters claiming that "PRESIDENT ROOSEVELT WANTS YOU TO JOIN
THE UNION." Other union leaders too seized upon the promise of a new labor regime to speed up their organizing activities. Union membership began to soar, and
with it came a surge in strikes. By 1934, the labor upheaval was nationwide, with
violence-tinged general strikes in San Francisco and Minneapolis.[40]

In retrospect, it is evident that this mobilization of organized labor created a
powerful new political formation that could be vital to the emerging New Deal
coalition. Available evidence, however, suggests that this was not so apparent to
President Roosevelt at the time. Roosevelt wanted to be a benefactor to workers
and to raise their standard of living, but he was hardly attracted to the prospect of
muscular unions and class conflict. As Burns wrote, "the political implications of
a vastly expanded labor movement, solidly grounded in the millions of workers in
the great mass-production industries, seemed to escape him."[41]

Business interests reacted to 7(a) mostly with the dodge of company unions,
ostensible labor representatives under management control. After many decades
of enjoying the upper hand in labor relations, they were understandably alarmed
by the rise of worker insurgency; some retorted with violent repression. Trying to
weave his way through the conflicting class interests, Roosevelt moved cautiously
in labor relations after the establishment of 7(a). The labor board established in
the 1933 legislation lacked enforcement power, as did a successor that Roosevelt
created the following year. Administration policy made space for the company
unions that labor leaders despised.[42]

In this highly unsettled state of labor relations, Senator Robert Wagner of
New York and his allies inside and outside the government began working on a
new system outside the faltering National Industrial Recovery Act and its Section

7(a). Wagner's proposed legislation established a strong enforcement mechanism through a National Labor Relations Board. It encouraged "the practice and procedure of collective bargaining, . . . protecting the exercise by workers of full freedom of association, self-organization, and designation of representatives of their own choosing, for the purpose of the terms and conditions of their employment or other mutual aid or protection." Wagner first introduced this legislation in 1934. It did not receive backing from the president—and it failed to pass.[43]

Although Wagner was more sympathetic than the president to independent unionism, the legislation he drafted actually served a multiplicity of objectives. Along with his desire to level the playing field in management-employee relations, Plotke wrote, Wagner aimed to boost the purchasing power of workers as a tool of demand management in averting future depressions. Further, he sought to end the unfolding chaos at the workplace and create an orderly system of handling labor disputes.[44] These latter two goals were congruent with the president's concerns, but it was Wagner who possessed the more comprehensive vision.

Historic Democratic gains in the 1934 elections opened a window for Wagner in the 1935 congressional session. His bill was introduced in February, still lacking any expression of support from Roosevelt. Yet Wagner guided it skillfully over the hurdles, and it easily passed the Senate by a vote of 63–12 on May 16. Eight days later, with the House about to take up the bill, the president belatedly announced his support. Once he came down on the side of Wagner's bill, however, Roosevelt put his own muscle behind it. The new labor bill was, he proclaimed, high on the list of his administration's "must" legislation. He firmly associated himself with the new regime in American labor law—but only at almost the last possible moment.[45]

The political and economic effects of the Wagner Act were more immediate than those of the Social Security Act. As David Kennedy writes, "the Wagner Act opened a world of possibility to American labor. . . . The act helped initiate a historic organizing drive that rearranged the balance of power between American capital and labor. Labor's awakening also secured a broad working-class constituent base that would help to make the Democrats the majority party for a long time to come."[46] Intending to be a benefactor to American workers, Roosevelt (and the Democratic regime he founded) proved to be the political beneficiary of the rise of organized labor. He neither envisioned nor shaped the policy that brought all of this about, but he was responsive to it in the end.

JOHN F. KENNEDY AND THE CIVIL RIGHTS ACT
The Civil Rights Act of 1964, introduced the year before by President John F. Kennedy and guided to passage after his assassination by President Lyndon B. Johnson, was the most important advance in equal rights for African Americans since the constitutional amendments of the Civil War and Reconstruction. Kennedy's

sponsorship of this law became, in the eyes of sympathetic historians, his greatest domestic achievement.[47] It also cemented his glowing reputation among blacks; for decades afterwards, as civil-rights leader John Lewis relates, the homes of many poor blacks contained portraits of three saintly figures: Jesus Christ, Martin Luther King Jr., and John F. Kennedy.[48]

Yet it was a winding political road that brought Kennedy to the introduction of a landmark civil-rights bill. As a wealthy New Englander whose primary interests while in Congress had been in foreign affairs, Kennedy had little personal background or political passion for the issue of civil rights. As an aspiring presidential candidate, he had a powerful incentive to sustain friendly relations with Democratic leaders in the South who were staunch segregationists. However, about the same time that Kennedy formally announced for the presidency in early 1960, the civil-rights movement moved into a dramatic new phase of "direct action" with lunch-counter sit-ins across the South. Faced with competition from Republican Richard Nixon for the black vote, which was critical in a number of urbanized northern states rich in electoral votes, Kennedy promised strong civil-rights actions if he was elected president.[49]

Once in office, however, Kennedy announced that civil-rights legislation was not part of the agenda of his New Frontier. The narrowness of his electoral victory was advanced as an argument for treading carefully in the explosive field of race relations. Even more important was the strategic power of the white South in Congress: with southern Democrats holding many of the key committee chairmanships thanks to the seniority system, Kennedy and his aides believed that any push for a civil-rights bill might jeopardize his entire legislative program. To the unhappy leadership of the civil-rights groups, who felt that black votes had put Kennedy over the top in 1960, the administration responded that progress could still be made through litigation and executive action. In neither area was the president heavily involved: the first was delegated to Attorney General Robert F. Kennedy and the second primarily to Vice President Lyndon Johnson.[50]

As the leader of a paradoxical partisan coalition that combined equality-minded blacks with segregationist whites, Kennedy hoped to move quietly and incrementally so as to keep both groups in his camp. By 1961, however, the civil-rights movement was determined to speed up the pace of its struggle. Starting with the Freedom Rides in the spring of that year, movement activists staged a series of dramatic public confrontations in the deep South that derailed the administration's plans to control the civil-rights issue. Keeping up the pressure on the Kennedy Administration, the activists compelled the federal government to intervene in the South to cope with racist violence. Concerned not to alienate white southerners any more than was necessary, Kennedy justified these interventions in law-and-order terms, refusing, despite pleas from liberal supporters, to address the moral evil of the Jim Crow system. And he still was silent on the subject of civil-rights legislation.[51]

Impatience with Kennedy among black activists and their white supporters was mounting by the winter of 1962–1963. Martin Luther King Jr. took to print to lament that the Kennedy Administration was content with token progress toward racial justice.[52] Civil-rights supporters in Congress began to draft legislation of their own. Ominously for Kennedy's reelection prospects in 1964, Republican Governor Nelson Rockefeller of New York moved out ahead of the president on the issue. Rockefeller blasted Kennedy for "abdicat[ing] virtually all leadership toward achieving necessary civil rights legislation."[53]

In response, Kennedy proposed civil-rights legislation on the last day of February 1963. For the first time, he began to couch the civil-rights issue in moral terms. Yet if he was finally willing to ratchet up the presidential rhetoric, he was not eager to do the same with policy. The proposed legislation was cautious and narrow in application. A sympathetic Arthur Schlesinger Jr. described it as "piecemeal improvements in existing voting legislation, technical assistance to school districts voluntarily seeking to desegregate, an extension to the life of the Civil Rights Commission."[54] Kennedy's weak bill of February was hardly what the civil-rights movement had been urging on him from the start of his presidency. Its lack of enthusiasm for the legislation was matched by the president's, since he did little to promote the bill after its initial announcement.[55]

Once again, Kennedy's cautious civil-rights strategy was disrupted by the movement. Martin Luther King Jr. and his Southern Christian Leadership Conference launched a mass-action campaign in April 1963 in Birmingham, Alabama, designed to force not only the local white elite but also the Kennedy White House to end a palpable state of injustice. Dramatic photos from Birmingham of nonviolent civil-rights demonstrators attacked by police dogs and blasted by fire hoses shocked the nation and altered the political climate. As civil-rights demonstrations rapidly spread to other southern cities and towns, and as violence broke out in Birmingham and elsewhere, the Kennedy administration was confronted with the civil-rights crisis it had long tried to forestall.[56]

No longer able to placate both antagonists, Kennedy sided with black freedom at the risk of losing the solid South for the Democratic Party. On June 11, 1963, he came out with the bold legislation that civil-rights supporters had been urging on him all along. Kennedy's language rose to the occasion: racial justice was "a moral issue, . . . as old as the Scriptures and . . . as clear as the Constitution."[57] So, too, did the proposed bill meet the moment; its chief provisions moved forcefully in such areas as public accommodations, school desegregation, and equal employment opportunity.

The story of the landmark Civil Rights Act of 1964 does not properly end with

Kennedy's proposal, however. Other actors played critical roles even after Kennedy became the sponsor of the legislation. Spurning the president's admonition that a "march on Washington" might spark a backlash from Congress, civil-rights leaders went ahead with their plans for what proved to be the largest demonstration to that date in American history, an event whose moral grandeur further expanded public support for the Civil Rights Act. Rejecting the administration's warning that further strengthening provisions of the bill might play into the hands of segregationists and sink the legislation altogether, congressional liberals rewrote parts of Kennedy's package to make it even tougher. Overcoming remaining obstacles to the legislation after Kennedy's death, President Johnson skillfully drew Republican Senate leader Everett Dirksen into a bipartisan coalition large enough to defeat a last-ditch southern filibuster.[58]

President Kennedy had not planned to be a champion of landmark civil-rights legislation. Indeed, it was only his inability to control the dynamic of events that brought him to this stance. Yet if he was hardly the initiator of civil-rights progress in this story, he was the responsive policy leader. His ultimate commitment was stronger than that of presidents in the credit-claiming cases I am about to consider.

Leadership as Credit Claiming

RICHARD NIXON AND ENVIRONMENTAL LEGISLATION

The landmarks of modern environmental legislation not only were passed by a Democratic Congress during the presidency of Richard Nixon but bear the Republican's distinctive policy imprint. In one year alone, 1970, Nixon signed into law the National Environmental Policy Act, the Water Quality Improvement Act, the Resource Recovery Act, and Clean Air Act amendments, while establishing the Environmental Protection Agency through executive action.[59] Historians have taken note of an accomplishment that seems surprising for such a conservative president. In the conclusion of Melvin Small's study of the Nixon presidency, he writes that Nixon "signed legislation that made him the most environmentally conscious president since Theodore Roosevelt."[60]

Nixon not only acted as a champion of environmental protection in this period but sounded like one as well. On New Year's Day of 1970, he told the public: "The nineteen-seventies absolutely must be the years when America pays its debt to the past by reclaiming the purity of its air, its waters, and our living environment. It is literally now or never."[61] A year later, he announced that "I have proposed to Congress a sweeping and comprehensive program . . . to end the plunder of America's natural heritage."[62]

Was Nixon actually committed to protecting the environment? Or was he concerned with claiming credit in this field for political reasons alone? Certainly he had no record at all in environmental protection prior to his presidency, and he never indicated that the environmental field would be among his administration's priorities.[63] Nor was there anything in his 1968 presidential campaign that previewed the environmental actions to come. Nevertheless, Nixon entered the White House just as public interest in environmental problems was beginning to explode and as an environmental movement was rapidly growing. Poll data suggested the magnitude of risk and opportunity in this area. In the spring of 1969, only 1 percent ranked the environment as a major domestic problem; two years later, the number had swelled to 25 percent.[64]

The political threat to Nixon from the environmental issue came primarily from the Democratic majority in Congress. Despite the Democrats' loss of the White House in 1968, the party's congressional contingent was still fired by the policy activism of the Kennedy-Johnson era. Most worrisome to Nixon was the fact that the leading environmental champions in the Senate, Edmund Muskie of Maine and Henry "Scoop" Jackson of Washington, were in the top tier of likely challengers to Nixon in the 1972 presidential election.[65]

An ideological conservative in the White House might have resisted the Democrats' congressional offensive on the environment. But Nixon was far more a politician than he was an ideologue (and was more interested in foreign affairs than in domestic policy anyway). Moreover, one of his top White House aides, John Ehrlichman, was interested in the environmental issue. In this explosive political climate, Ehrlichman and the pro-environment aides he had hired pressed Nixon to turn his attention to a subject that he had previously ignored. Their argument to the president was, as J. Brooks Flippen, author of *Nixon and the Environment*, observes, that the "administration should embrace the new environmentalism, take the offensive, or risk being run over on an issue that increasingly appeared politically potent."[66]

Nixon's shift to environmental supporter followed this advice. From the second half of 1969 through roughly the first half of 1971, he compiled the environmental record that historians have hailed. Sometimes, as when he signed the National Environmental Policy Act, he claimed credit for legislation that his administration had initially resisted and in whose passage it had played no role.[67] At other times, as with the creation of the Environmental Protection Agency, the president was genuinely proactive.[68] Whatever his actual role, Nixon's decisions in this period were consistently favorable to environmental protection.

Yet in the political terms that most mattered to him, Nixon had little to show for this strong environmental record. Although revisionist historians would later bestow credit on him, at the time the press, his old foe, did not, granting the environmental laurels to Muskie or Jackson instead. It was galling to Nixon that

Muskie—who had pulled ahead in a hypothetical 1972 match-up against the president in polls taken after the 1970 midterm elections—was named "Conservationist of the Year" by a major environmental organization. Nixon had blunted the risk that he would be viewed by voters as an obstacle to environmental progress. But the environmental issue continued to favor the Democrats no matter what the president seemed to do.[69]

By 1971, Nixon was reassessing his stance on environmental policy. His supporters in the business community, unhappy over the costs they were incurring from the new environmental laws, were lobbying him to stem the tide of further environmental actions. The president was increasingly receptive to their arguments, especially because he was inaugurating a broad policy shift toward the right. Frustrated by his paltry political gains from trying to compete with the Democrats on their traditional policy turf, Nixon now perceived more advantage in opposing liberalism than in co-opting it. As Flippen writes, he began to de-emphasize "welfare reform, civil rights, and the environment" and to prioritize "lower taxes, deregulation, economic efficiency, and, most importantly, an embrace of industry."[70]

Abundant evidence from his White House tapes and from the memoirs of his aides suggests that Nixon was more comfortable in opposing environmental protection than in championing it. His motivation from the start was evident in his words to Ehrlichman: "Just keep me out of trouble on environmental issues."[71] Even in his brief stint as an environmentalist, he was hopeful that "interest in this will recede."[72] Nixon was particularly hostile to the environmental movement: its activists, he told Ehrlichman, were "clowns" and their issue was "crap."[73] The president was relieved once he concluded that the momentum for environmental change had subsided. During the 1972 campaign, he told his aides in a White House meeting that "people don't give a shit about the environment."[74]

In private, though not usually in public, Nixon strongly defended corporate interests against the environmentalists' challenge. In a meeting with executives from Ford Motor Company, he said, "Whether it's the environment or pollution or Naderism or consumerism, we are extremely pro-business."[75] To Nixon, economic growth was the priority and environmental protection had to take a backseat. "In a flat choice between smoke and jobs," he told business supporters, "we're for jobs."[76]

During his final years in office (1972–1974), Nixon went public with his new antienvironmental stance. In the fall of 1972, he vetoed the Federal Water Pollution Control Act on the grounds that it appropriated an excessive amount for purifying the waters and contributed to inflationary pressures. Even congressional Republicans did not stand with the president in this case: the veto was overridden by votes of 247–23 in the House and 52–12 in the Senate. Nixon proceeded to impound half of the funds that the bill had authorized.[77]

As his political demise drew near in 1974, Nixon became ever less constrained in repudiating the environmental positions that his administration had taken earlier. In a cabinet meeting in spring 1974, the president ordered: "Promote energy developments. . . . Get off the environmental kick."[78] On his last full day in office in August, he vetoed the annual appropriation bill for the Environmental Protection Agency that he had created four years earlier.[79]

Landmark legislation on the environment was enacted during the presidency of Richard Nixon. Yet contrary to the argument of those historians who ascribe environmental advances to him, this case study suggests how we should understand his environmental actions: as policy credit claiming.

BILL CLINTON AND THE CRIME BILL

Before Bill Clinton was elected president in 1992, the crime issue belonged to the Republican Party. Richard Nixon had pioneered the use of crime as a wedge issue against Democrats in his 1968 campaign, and his innovation became a standard tactic in the Republican electoral playbook for the next two decades. No Republican candidate made such effective use of the crime issue as George H. W. Bush in 1988, as he pummeled Democrat Michael Dukakis for his opposition to capital punishment and alleged softness toward violent inmates. With crime rates—and public alarm—on the rise, the issue posed a serious threat to Democratic hopes in 1992 of recapturing the White House after a dozen years of Republican control.

Bill Clinton came gradually to the "tough on crime" stance that was designed to blunt the Republican advantage on the crime issue in the 1992 campaign. As the attorney general of Arkansas, and then as its first-term governor, Clinton was a moderate on the crime issue. But after losing his office in 1980 to a Republican who charged that he was "soft on crime," Clinton returned for multiple two-year gubernatorial terms with a toughened stance, becoming more comfortable, in particular, with imposition of the death penalty. During the 1992 New Hampshire primary, Clinton famously flew home to sign a warrant for the execution of Rickey Ray Rector, a mentally impaired inmate.[80]

Clinton's crime agenda in 1992 owed less, however, to his Arkansas experience than to his association with the centrist Democratic Leadership Council (DLC), established after the 1984 election to combat the Democratic Party's liberal direction—and its loss of four of the five previous presidential contests. Clinton became chairman of the organization in 1990, and he was viewed as its dream candidate for the White House. As DLC chair, he inherited a set of policy proposals that he put to use in his campaign for the White House, among them federal funding for more police officers on the street, tough "boot camps" for youthful first-time offenders, and longer mandatory sentences when guns were used during the commission of crimes.[81]

As president, Clinton's approach to the crime issue was characteristically centrist in its attempt to combine a traditional Democratic priority, prevention of crime, with the signature Republican stance, punishment of crime. The most important steps toward prevention were in the field of gun control: the Brady Handgun Violence Prevention Act (1993), mandating background checks for handgun purchasers, and an originally freestanding ban on nineteen semiautomatic weapons that was eventually folded into the omnibus Violent Crime Control and Law Enforcement Act (1994), the largest anticrime bill in American history. Also incorporated in the latter bill, at the urging of House Democrats, were funds to combat the social pathologies that liberals saw as the roots of crime; among these prevention efforts was a program of "midnight basketball" leagues for inner-city young males. As its name indicated, however, the Violent Crime Control and Law Enforcement Act was heavily loaded with Republican-sounding "tough on crime" provisions. A centerpiece of the act was a provision for the hiring of 100,000 more police officers. Nearly $10 billion was offered to state governments to finance the building of more prisons. Title VI of the act established sixty new death-penalty provisions under federal laws. A "three strikes and you're out" provision mandated a life sentence for three violent federal felonies. A punitive tone was even set for those already incarcerated through the elimination of federal grants for inmate education.

During congressional negotiations over the 1994 crime bill, a controversial provision championed by the Black Caucus in the House was scrapped. The Supreme Court had ruled in *McClesky v. Kemp* (1987) that statistical evidence of systematic racial disparities in a state's imposition of capital punishment was not sufficient to overturn death sentences without a demonstration of deliberate bias. Responding to this decision, Senator Edward Kennedy and Representative John Conyers introduced the Racial Justice Act (RJA) in 1988, which provided that the type of evidence the Court had slighted in the *McClesky* case could be dispositive.[82] The House version of the Clinton Crime Bill included the RJA provision, but the president, who had never been enthusiastic about the measure, agreed with Senate Republicans that it should be eliminated from the omnibus bill.[83] Clinton had a practical reason to drop the RJA language: Republicans were threatening a filibuster over it. But he had a political motive as well: a bill carrying his stamp that would restrict imposition of the death penalty because of statistical evidence of racial discrimination would undercut his "tough on crime" image.

In the short run, Clinton's bid to take the crime issue away from the Republican Party backfired. Ignoring the punishment provisions in Clinton's crime bill, Republicans effectively focused on the funding for preventive measures, especially midnight basketball, to tag the law as yet another instance of wasteful federal spending targeted to reward low-income and minority voters.[84] Meanwhile, actor Charlton Heston, president of the National Rifle Association, stirred up its membership for the midterm elections, scathingly denouncing the president for the assault-weapons ban in a series of television commercials.[85] Clinton and his party soon suffered a historic defeat in the 1994 elections, losing both chambers of Congress to the Republicans, the House for the first time in forty years. There were several contributors to the Democrats' debacle, with the failed health-care reform proposal topping the list. Among these contributors was a crime bill that was supposed to inoculate Clinton from Republican attacks yet only added to his party's electoral ills.

Only after Clinton's political fortunes turned around through his showdown with House Speaker Newt Gingrich was the president able successfully to claim credit for his crime bill. During the run-up to the 1996 elections, he regularly touted his crime-fighting accomplishments: his first three campaign ads, broadcast more than a year before Election Day, highlighted his support for an expanded death penalty. Public opinion at last was suitably impressed: polls showed Clinton with a double-digit lead over Republican Robert Dole on the crime issue (the first time since 1968 that the Democratic presidential candidate had the advantage on crime).[86] During the 1996 campaign, *New York Times* reporters David Johnston and Tim Weiner wrote: "After nearly three decades of Republican dominance of the issue, President Clinton has scrapped his party's traditional approach to crime and criminal justice, embracing a series of punitive measures that have given him conservative credentials and threatened the Republicans' lock on law and order . . . Mr. Clinton has caused consternation in Republican ranks and in Bob Dole's campaign for the presidency."[87] On the campaign trail, Dole complained plaintively—and accurately—that Clinton had stolen his issue.

How happy was President Clinton to be identified in the long run as a champion of punishment as central to combating crime in America? Safely past re-election, during his second term he spoke much less about punishing than about preventing crime.[88] Ten years after passage of the crime bill, when he published his autobiography, Clinton's recollections of the crime issue focused almost entirely on the subject of gun control. Thus he proudly observed of the Brady Bill that by the end of his presidency it "had kept more than 600,000 felons, fugitives, and stalkers from buying handguns . . . [and] had saved countless lives."[89] By contrast, the punitive measures in the 1994 crime bill, such as funds to construct more state prisons, received only passing mention.

Twenty years after the passage of the crime bill, some of its punitive measures had become an embarrassment to Clinton. With the nation's prisons overflowing with inmates who are disproportionately black and Hispanic, even as crime rates have been falling for two decades, critics have looked back on the 1994 crime bill as an unfortunate contributor to the inequities of the current criminal justice system.[90] In an October 2014 speech observing the twentieth anniversary of the Violent Crime Control and Law Enforcement Act, Clinton himself lamented: "We basically took a shotgun to a problem that needed a .22—a very significant percentage of serious crimes in this country are committed by a very small number [of people]. . . . We took a shotgun to it and just sent everybody to jail for too long."[91]

CONCLUSION: DISTINGUISHING TYPES OF PRESIDENTIAL POLICY LEADERSHIP

The six cases presented above were initially sorted on the basis of previous familiarity with them into three types of presidential leadership in domestic policy: entrepreneurial initiation, policy responsiveness, and policy credit claiming. Research into the details of the six cases led to the recognition of patterns that help to distinguish more clearly the different types. Of course, additional cases need to be investigated before the existence of these patterns can be made more than tentative. In this conclusion, I describe the indicators that serve to mark off one type of presidential policy leadership from another.

Entrepreneurial Initiation

The cases of Franklin D. Roosevelt and Social Security and of George W. Bush and No Child Left Behind reveal the following patterns that seem indicative of presidential leadership as entrepreneurial initiation:

1. Presidents have signaled their personal preferences and firm commitments to policy innovation before winning office. These commitments may take the form of policy innovation in previous political roles and promises during the campaign for the presidency. As governor of New York and as the Democratic candidate in 1932, Roosevelt had come out for the basic elements of a social security system. Education reform was a signature issue for George W. Bush in the Texas governorship and a centerpiece of his presidential run in 2000.

2. Presidential policy entrepreneurship should not be confused with intellectual entrepreneurship. Presidents ordinarily are not the intellectual creators of their policy innovations, but they are the decisive players in promoting their adoption. Roosevelt drew on a long progressive tradition in the area of social insurance, and he delegated the key tasks of policy formation to Secretary of Labor Frances Perkins. Bush built on two decades of efforts by an unusual coalition of business groups and civil-rights groups to promote an "excellence in education" agenda of standards, testing, and accountability.

3. Presidents remain largely in control of the process of policy development. The administration sets the agenda and lays the groundwork for policy innovation, with policy-planning task forces, legislative testimony, and the like. Congressional committees largely follow their lead. Alternative proposals to theirs are soundly defeated. Roosevelt's strength within his party helped bring along skeptics on the congressional committees, and his supporters defeated the more radical Townsend and Lundeen proposals. Bush put together a bipartisan coalition in the center that overcame opposition from both the right and the left in Congress.

4. Even when entrepreneurial initiation is successful, generating landmark legislation that accomplishes the president's original objectives, there will be compromises that delimit the range of the achievement. Put differently, presidents almost never get everything they want. Roosevelt and his advisers wanted the new system of social insurance to be universal in coverage, yet administrative caution from the Treasury Department and the power of southern Democrats in Congress wrote exclusions into the law that markedly discriminated against African Americans. To hold the support of key congressional Democrats, Bush sacrificed vouchers for private schools and agreed to far more spending on education than he had originally proposed.

Policy Responsiveness

The cases of Franklin D. Roosevelt and the National Labor Relations Act and of John F. Kennedy and the Civil Rights Act reveal the following patterns that seem indicative of presidential leadership as policy responsiveness:

1. In presidential leadership as policy responsiveness, strong external demand for major legislation from elements of the president's coalition drives the process of policy development. The genesis of landmark legislation cannot be ascribed to the president's personal preferences or prior commitments. Labor militancy—and the sympathetic response of congressional liberals—had more to do with the development of the National Labor Relations Act than Roosevelt's own objectives or actions. The militancy of the civil-rights movement pulled Kennedy away from the cautious posture that he had assumed for the first two and a quarter years of his administration.

2. The president is on record as supporting the cause in question, but the issue is not a priority for the administration and the legislation it initially proposes is on the weak side. Indeed, the external forces pressing for stronger action are likely to deride the president's legislative or administrative plans as thoroughly inadequate to the problems at hand. Senator Wagner and

his union allies were unhappy with the feckless enforcement efforts of the Roosevelt administration in labor relations up to 1935. The civil-rights movement unsuccessfully pressured the Kennedy White House to introduce civil-rights legislation for two years and then was disappointed when Kennedy's proposal of February 1963 was so tepid.

3. When the president finally comes down on the side of innovative legislation, the motive appears to be less to satisfy a personal preference than to end a political threat. The administration's objective is not only to tackle a major domestic problem but to put an end to disorder that threatens both social peace and the administration's own peace. For Roosevelt, endorsement of Senator Wagner's bill was a response to both the surge of militant strikes and the growing hostility of business interests. For Kennedy, the racial crisis initiated by King's Birmingham campaign in the spring of 1963 necessitated that he finally abandon the straddle on the civil-rights issue that had characterized his actions heretofore.

4. The landmark legislation with which the president is associated in the end carries serious political risks as well as potential political gains—a prime reason why the president has been reluctant to push very far in the first place. Unlike legislation that makes universal claims, as with the social security system, legislation that sides with one social group over another runs the risk of establishing controversial presidential identifications. Roosevelt was not eager to upset the middle class, or even large corporations, by identifying himself with militant unionism. Kennedy knew that a full-fledged commitment on civil rights would cost him heavily in the white South.

Policy Credit Claiming

The cases of Richard Nixon and environmental legislation and of Bill Clinton and the crime bill reveal the following patterns that seem indicative of presidential leadership as policy credit claiming:

1. In the case of credit claiming, the president does not have a strong prior record of support for policy development on the issue in question. The issue chosen for credit claiming may be peripheral to the president's agenda, perhaps reflecting personal ambivalence or even distaste. Nixon was a probusiness Republican with no record of support for environmental protection. Clinton came slowly and seemingly reluctantly to a "tough on crime" posture.

2. Presidential support for landmark legislation in this type of leadership is a response to a challenge from political rivals. Most often, the challenge will

come from the opposition party, whether in electoral politics or in Congress, and the president's goal will be to steal their thunder. Nixon's surprising record on environmental protection in 1970–1971 was a response to the emergence of the environmental movement and the entrepreneurial actions of Senate Democrats who were prospective challengers in 1972. The punitive dimensions of Clinton's crime bill were a response to decades of Republicans beating up Democrats as "soft on crime."

3. Electoral considerations appear to play by far the largest part in policy leadership as credit claiming. Presidents in this case set aside their own policy preferences in order to fend off electoral threats or aim for electoral advantages. Nixon attempted to overshadow Senators Muskie and Jackson and to co-opt the popularity of environmental protection legislation; although he did not reap the credit for which he had hoped from his pro-environmental stance in 1970–1971, at least the environmental issue could not be used against him in the 1972 election. Clinton's outflanking of the Republicans on punishment did not pay off immediately, but by the 1996 elections it placed him in a far stronger position than any of his Democratic predecessors since Nixon first tarred their party on the crime issue.

4. Presidential actions subsequent to the passage of the landmark legislation in question indicate that the president's heart was never really in it. Later statements or policies show a lack of interest in or enthusiasm for the president's electorally motivated achievement. Nixon's vetoes and impoundments, and his scathing private comments on environmentalism, tell us more about his view of environmental protection than his signature on new laws. By his second term, Clinton was eager to switch the subject from punishing to preventing crime, and in his postpresidential years he has further distanced himself from policies that built more prisons and sentenced more minorities to fill them up.

Of course there are examples of presidents and major domestic legislation that don't fit squarely into a single category. A case in point is Barack Obama and the Affordable Care Act. Before running for president, Obama was not closely associated with health-care reform. The three leading competitors for the 2008 Democratic presidential nomination—Obama, Hillary Rodham Clinton, and John Edwards—all got in line with this longstanding Democratic goal, with Clinton having the strongest credentials. However, once in the White House, Obama was determined to make good on his campaign pledge on health care. His politically astute chief of staff, Rahm Emanuel, urged him to hold off on this pledge amid an economic crisis. But Obama, aware that if he missed a brief opening for health-care reform it might not occur again for yet another generation, insisted on an immediate push for what would become his signature domestic accomplishment.[92]

The three types of presidential leadership in domestic policy depend on both personal preferences and political circumstances. Entrepreneurial initiation proceeds on a political ground open to personal choice and policy innovation, with the opening more expansive during what Skowronek calls a "reconstructive" presidency and more time-bound at the outset of any president's first term. Policy responsiveness reflects coalition politics, as assertive forces on the president's side of the political spectrum reject admonitions to go slow and push him or her onto unstable political ground. Policy credit claiming is called into play when the White House fears that the opposition will monopolize a popular issue and position the president on the losing side.

Each of the three types of domestic policy leadership involves the interplay between agency and structure, personal choices and political imperatives. Only the first—leadership as entrepreneurial initiation—is consistent with the textbook image of presidential accomplishments in domestic policy. The other two look very different than standard listings of presidential achievements once the dynamics of major domestic legislation are examined in detail. Presidents have to traverse hard political ground in the making of domestic policy. A scorecard of wins and losses obscures the real story of what happens to them along the way.

5. Foreign Policy Making on Partisan Ground

The Cold War adage that "politics stops at the water's edge" rings falsely today. Partisan polarization affects foreign policy nearly as much as it does domestic policy. Democrats and Republicans now disagree on nearly every global issue, with international trade a cross-cutting exception. Yet while awareness of the sweep of partisan polarization has been growing among analysts of American politics, its impact on presidential leadership in foreign policy has not received much attention.[1]

To Machiavelli, extreme partisanship was the bane of republican governments, especially in foreign affairs. His Florence was something of a national security state in miniature, with rival Italian city-states and larger nation-states (France and Spain) posing a constant threat to the city's independence. Before he was exiled, Machiavelli himself was a diplomat and military strategist. Writing *The History of Florence* in his later years, he repeatedly returned to the theme of pernicious partisanship: "It is true that some divisions harm republics and some divisions benefit them. Those do harm that are accompanied with factions and partisans. . . . The enmities in Florence were always those of factions and therefore always dangerous."[2]

Machiavelli has been regarded as a forerunner of the "realist" approach to international relations, but his comments about partisanship have not been much heeded. The factors that are conventionally assumed by scholars to influence presidential leadership in U.S. foreign policy can be divided into two categories: strategic and domestic. On the strategic side, the list might begin with individual agency: the personalities, degree of interest in foreign policy, cognitive abilities, and decision-making styles of presidents. Next might follow strategic doctrines: the guidelines that presidents formulate (or fail to formulate) to orient foreign policy toward the central conflicts of their times. Institutional forces complicate the picture, as State, Pentagon, and CIA pursue their familiar missions and promote continuity in the face of presidential initiatives for change. Classic international relations "realists" downplay all of these and highlight instead the imperatives of national interest and national security.

Domestic factors usually take second place to strategic factors in analyses of presidential leadership in foreign policy. Politically pivotal ethnic groups pressure presidents to support their favorite nations or oppose their feared adversaries. Powerful economic organizations demand state backing for their global interests.

Public opinion lurks in the background, approving in crises ("rally-round-the flag" effects), restrictive in residual fears (the "Vietnam syndrome" constraining Reagan in Central America, a "Somalia syndrome" constraining Clinton in the Balkans, an "Iraq/Afghanistan syndrome" constraining Obama in the Middle East).

By contrast to the preceding chapters, where presidents had to navigate across a diversity of political terrains, foreign policy making has conventionally been regarded as less political in nature. Foreign nations, whether adversaries or allies, often gave presidents grief, but precisely because of that fact, they could tamp down opposition at home through the invocation of national security. National unity over foreign policy was of course a casualty of the war in Vietnam, but the shape of disunity today is very different than what Lyndon Johnson or Richard Nixon encountered. Today, American foreign policy is highly politicized; on this ground, presidential leadership is now dogged by vehement partisanship.

In its current form, partisan polarization over foreign policy emerged in the 1980s and has intensified ever since. One of the most notable features of this polarization is that it encompasses both global strategy and domestic politics. In their understandings of the proper role of the United States in world politics and the most effective tools of American influence, Democratic presidents and Republican presidents begin their terms guided by rival partisan doctrines. As they attempt to exercise leadership in the realm of foreign policy, they face a domestic landscape marked by sharp partisan divisions, evident both in Congress and in public opinion. Presidential leadership in foreign policy now has to operate on partisan political ground.

One significant facet of foreign policy polarization is growing resistance from the opposing party to presidential initiatives. I briefly examine this phenomenon with a focus on congressional responses to major presidential initiatives in international affairs. But my principal concern in this chapter is to look at how partisan doctrines have become intrinsic to presidential leadership itself. My argument is that recent presidents, beginning with Ronald Reagan, have entered office committed to versions of what I call *pure party doctrines*. These pure party doctrines frame the initial foreign policy orientations and objectives of Republican and Democratic presidents in polarized fashion. Over the course of their administrations, however, the other strategic and domestic factors mentioned above tend to wear down purity, leading presidents toward actions that their party's pure doctrines would never have sanctioned. For presidents, the diminishing of partisan purity is an ambivalent affair: abandoning some of their parties' cherished objectives, at the same time they gain in leeway to chart a more flexible and nuanced course in international affairs.

The chapter's starting point is the early Cold War period, marked by an overlapping partisan consensus in foreign policy. The following section elaborates the origins and tenets of "pure party doctrines" in the presidential candidacies of the parties' biggest losers: Barry Goldwater and George McGovern. Next, I trace the historical processes through which their insurgent doctrines turned into partisan orthodoxies, first on the Republican side and then on the Democratic side. Remaining sections of the chapter home in on presidential leadership in foreign policy on partisan ground, initially in presidential campaigns, beginning with 1980, and then in each administration from Reagan to Obama.

In bringing to the fore the impact of partisan polarization on presidential leadership in foreign policy, I am not asserting that every Democrat or Republican marches in lockstep with their parties' respective global orthodoxies. These orthodox doctrines have the support of the majority in each party's ranks, whether one is considering elected officials or the electoral base. Still, there are important dissenters from orthodoxy in both parties. For the Democrats, dissent primarily comes from the centrists associated with the "Third Way" philosophy. More prominent dissent is found today in the libertarian wing of the Republican Party, led first by Ron Paul and now by his son Rand. In particular, centrist Democrats are more favorably disposed toward the uses of the military, and libertarian Republicans are less disposed toward the use of force overseas, than the majority of their fellow partisans.

OVERLAPPING PARTISAN CONSENSUS IN THE EARLY COLD WAR ERA

Over the long sweep of American history, several periods have been marked by partisan polarization in foreign policy. During the 1790s, Federalists and Democratic-Republicans battled one another over the Jay Treaty with Great Britain and the "quasi-war" with France. In the 1840s, Whigs put up strong resistance to a Democratic president's war with Mexico. In the election campaign of 1900, Republican champions of empire bested the anti-imperialist Democrat, William Jennings Bryan. But by the 1930s, partisan divisions over foreign policy were no longer stark. In the period before Pearl Harbor, interventionists and isolationists were to be found in both parties.

Global leadership as a routine enterprise for American presidents began after World War II. With the near-immediate onset of the Cold War, an overlapping consensus developed in the making of U.S. foreign policy. The Cold War consensus was neither tight nor harmonious: from the outset, Republicans were most often on the offensive and Democrats on the defensive. Militant anti-Communism was a natural ideological fit for antistatist Republicans, but it also served as a useful political club, compensating for the party's competitive disadvantage with respect to the economic growth successes and broad social provisions of the post–New Deal Democrats. Public opinion data show that by the time of the Korean War a majority preferred Republican leadership in foreign affairs.[3]

Yet Democrats were, for the most part, far from reluctant to pursue their own brand of anti-Communist militancy. Burned by the breakdown of wartime cooperation with the Soviet Union, bitter winners of internecine warfare in progressive circles after the war, Democrats were no slouches in the anti-Communist crusade. It was not only conservative Democrats such as Senator Patrick McCarran of Nevada who sounded and acted much like McCarthyite Republicans; even Hubert Humphrey, then the darling of liberal Democrats, sponsored the Communist Control Act of 1954, criminalizing membership in the Communist Party.

A handy indicator for the overlapping consensus of the early Cold War period is the pairing of Dwight Eisenhower and John F. Kennedy, especially if we consider Kennedy as a presidential aspirant who made a mark as a critic of the Republican president. By current standards, Kennedy was to the right of Eisenhower on many international issues. In the terms of today's party doctrines, the positions Eisenhower took would scarcely be imaginable for a current Republican president, while the positions Kennedy took would make him a pariah in the contemporary Democratic Party. (When Senator Joseph Lieberman of Connecticut called himself a JFK Democrat, it explained a great deal about his own pariah status among Democrats.)

We customarily think of President Kennedy's eloquent speech at American University in June 1963 as the first presidential call for Americans to break away from the apocalyptic mentality of the Cold War. A decade earlier, however, President Eisenhower had seized the occasion of Stalin's death to urge Americans to reckon with the terrible costs of the arms race with the Soviet Union. In his "Chance for Peace" address in April 1953, Eisenhower laid down a marker for what would be his most profound objective in foreign policy: the reduction of Cold War tensions:

What can the world—or any nation in it—hope for if no turning is found on this dread road? . . . The worst is atomic war. The best would be this: a life of perpetual fear and tension; a burden of arms draining the wealth and labor of all peoples. . . . Every gun that is made, every warship launched, every rocket fired signifies . . . a *theft* from those who hunger and are not fed, those who are cold and are not clothed. . . . This is not a way of life at all. . . . It is humanity hanging from a cross of iron.[4]

(Two decades later, under fire in the 1972 presidential campaign for advocating large-scale reductions in the defense budget, George McGovern cited Eisenhower as his mentor on arms spending.)[5]

To be sure, Eisenhower was also a determined and sometimes ruthless Cold Warrior in his own terms. But these were not the terms of later Republican doctrine. As a fiscal conservative, he was more resistant to a soaring defense budget than any of his Cold War successors. Yet his objections to the militarization of American foreign policy—and for that matter of the American polity itself—ran deeper, as evidenced in his famous warning about the "military-industrial complex." The war hero in the White House was not one to genuflect to his generals as would some later Republican presidents.

Neither was Eisenhower as inclined to demonize foreign leaders or refuse to negotiate with them. He may have despised Communism, but he invited Nikita Khrushchev to tour the United States. His meetings with the Soviet leader generated talk of a "Spirit of Geneva" and later a "Spirit of Camp David"—productive of little in the way of substantive progress in defusing the Cold War yet arguably valuable nonetheless in countering the grim psychology of intractable, Manichean confrontation. Eisenhower could talk tough and threaten military action in secret communications with other governments, but his public rhetoric was not as deliberately alarmist as that of his Democratic successor, much less Republicans of the Reagan era.

One final point about Eisenhower is pertinent to the pairing with Kennedy and contrast with later Republican presidents: his cautiousness and awareness of risks in overseas interventions. Only in retrospect, after the American disaster in Vietnam was unfolding, were these qualities truly appreciated, especially in what became the famous case of his refusal to intervene militarily in Indochina in 1954. Unfortunately, while Eisenhower was alert to short-term risks, his preferred Cold War strategy underestimated longer-term risks. His prudence in 1954 was mitigated by his subsequent backing of Ngo Dinh Diem, creating the conditions for the quagmire he had avoided. And his preference for covert action through the CIA had pernicious consequences in Iran, Guatemala, and Cuba, the last of these for John F. Kennedy.

During his quest for the presidency, the youthful Kennedy pledged to prosecute the Cold War more vigorously than the elderly Eisenhower. He ridiculed the "Spirit of Camp David" as exuding naïve idealism that seduced Americans into complacency. Without directly naming the popular president, Kennedy indicted the Eisenhower administration for a weakness in foreign policy that decades later would be a standard Republican charge against Democratic presidents and presidential candidates: "Attitudes, platitudes, and beatitudes have taken the place of a critical and vigilant intelligence. . . . We have allowed a soft sentimentalism to form the atmosphere we breathe."[6]

Eisenhower's concern for the costs and consequences of the arms race was not shared, at least initially, by Kennedy. A central theme of Kennedy's presidential campaign was the "missile gap" between the Soviet Union and the United States that the allegedly passive Eisenhower had failed to forestall. Upon winning the presidency, Kennedy learned that there was no missile gap and that superiority in ballistic missiles actually belonged to the United States. Nevertheless, in the increasingly tense global environment that would mark his first year in office, he asked Congress on three separate occasions to add to the defense budget. His top aide and speechwriter, Theodore Sorensen, wrote that Kennedy launched the most rapid and sizable arms buildup in America's peacetime history.[7]

Kennedy's can-do approach to foreign policy made him less cautious than Eisenhower in intervening abroad. His prepresidential rhetoric was breathtaking in its definition of the American role in the world: "Our frontiers today are on every continent . . . for our future and that of the rest of the people of the world are inseparably bound together, economically, militarily, politically."[8] The same theme was more famously expressed in his inaugural address when he proclaimed that "we shall pay any price, bear any burden, meet any hardship, support any friend, oppose any foe to assure the survival and success of liberty."[9] To his credit, Kennedy developed a greater sense of caution during his presidency, especially in the endgame to the Cuban missile crisis. Militant rhetoric for public consumption was now more frequently belied by behind-the-scenes prudence. Nonetheless, his was an administration that was not well grounded, cognitively or emotionally, in the risks of global interventionism or the limits of American power.

In the era of Ronald Reagan, Republican leaders have often cited Theodore Roosevelt as their beau ideal in adopting a muscular foreign policy. Yet no president has sounded so much like the preacher of the "strenuous life" as John F. Kennedy. Stung by his own fecklessness at the Bay of Pigs in 1961, Kennedy told Americans that he—and they—must become tougher: "The message of Cuba, of Laos, of the rising din of Communist voices in Asia and Latin America—these messages are all the same. The complacent, the self-indulgent, the soft societies are about to be swept away with the debris of history. Only the strong, only the industrious, only the determined, only the courageous, only the visionary who determine the real nature of our struggle can possibly survive."[10]

PURE PARTY DOCTRINES

The overlapping consensus of the early Cold War years began to fade even before the war in Vietnam on the Republican side and with the backlash against the war on the Democratic side. Eisenhower's foreign policy served as the foil for a new Republican doctrine, just as the Kennedy-Johnson foreign policy subsequently served as the foil for a new Democratic doctrine. Staking out polar positions, the new doctrines were articulated in their pure forms by presidential candidates Barry Goldwater and George McGovern. Landslide losers, in large part because of the purity of their positions, Goldwater and McGovern nonetheless articulated perspectives on U.S. foreign policy that would before too many years become orthodoxies that sharply divided Republicans and Democrats. Originally formulated within the Cold War context, these pure party doctrines have outlived the demise of the global struggle against Communism and continue today to polarize most foreign policy debates.

As presidential candidates, Goldwater and McGovern of course wrote and spoke at different historical moments, so their specific concerns cannot always be directly compared. Running through the particulars of their arguments, however, are polarized positions on fundamental issues in U.S. foreign policy. Their stances on at least five of these issues represent the core of rival party doctrines:

1. Basic view of the United States in world politics
2. Defense spending
3. Armed interventionism
4. Diplomacy and negotiations
5. The political and symbolic role of the United Nations

In *The Conscience of a Conservative* and in a series of speeches from the late 1950s through his 1964 presidential campaign, Barry Goldwater set down what would become the pure party doctrine of conservative Republicanism. Goldwater's view of the world was Manichean, with spotless American virtue pitted against relentless Communist evil. His Manicheanism was not new; the same moral conceit runs as a consistent thread through the entire history of U.S. foreign policy.[11] Yet in Goldwater's version, a traditional worldview that highlighted the contrast between American virtues and foreign vices hardened into a fierce dogma, resistant to doubt and inclined to conflate dissent with treason.

Rejecting Eisenhower's quest for détente with the Soviet Union, Goldwater emphasized that the Communists were an enemy whose main goal was to defeat the United States, so any talk of "coexistence" was sheer folly. In this light, the objective of American foreign policy must be "victory" rather than peace. Goldwater's military mentor was not the former general in the White House but the commander whom President Truman had fired: "If we have learned anything from the tragic lesson of Korea, if we can draw any guidance from the life of one of history's great military figures, Douglas MacArthur, it might well be this—that in war there is no substitute for victory."[12]

Goldwater drew a sharp line between the foreign policies of the two parties. Most Democratic leaders, he acknowledged, were not traitors, but they were foreign-policy Hamlets, paralyzed by their uncertainty over the nature of global conflict: "Indecision immobilizes us, lack of overriding purpose confuses us, and reaction—rather than action—restricts us." By contrast, Republicans, or at least those in Goldwater's wing of the party, were ready to heed his call to serve as "freedom's missionaries," righteous, muscular Christians in service to the global good. For Goldwater, the only real limit to the global power of the United States was in American will power—willing victory was the key to achieving it.[13]

American military superiority was one of the hallmarks of Goldwater's global vision. During the period (the late 1950s and the Kennedy years) when Democrats were pushing hard to increase defense spending, Goldwater did not break with the Eisenhower approach to the defense budget.[14] He became a champion of greater defense spending than Democrats were advocating during his presidential campaign. From the start, however, Goldwater was a vocal opponent of arms-control negotiations. "Easing the arms race," he argued, "will not ease tensions. It will encourage the Communists to adopt increasingly reckless tactics." Nuclear weapons were America's saving grace: "In the light of the West's weakness in conventional weapons, it might make sense for the Communists to seek disarmament in the nuclear field; if all nuclear weapons suddenly ceased to exist, much of the world would immediately be laid open to conquest by the masses of Russian and Chinese manpower." Consistent with this caustic view of arms control, he was one of nineteen senators to vote against Kennedy's test-ban treaty in 1963 as a Soviet "ambush."[15]

To Goldwater, American military superiority was not established merely to deter and contain the Communist enemy. On the contrary, U.S. global strategy needed to shed the reactive posture that Eisenhower shared with the Democrats and go on the offensive. Not only should peoples held captive by Communist tyranny be encouraged to revolt, but the United States, Goldwater urged in a swipe at Eisenhower for his caution toward the Hungarian revolution of 1956, must be "prepared to undertake military operations against vulnerable Communist regimes." To the challenge that such a military strategy magnified the risk of war, Goldwater replied, "Of course, but any policy, short of surrender, does that."[16]

Central to Goldwater's strategy for global victory was the downplaying of risks in general, whether they were military, technological, or even moral. Scoffing at the fear that any escalation to the use of nuclear weapons might lead to a catastrophe, Goldwater argued: "Our military experts have long recognized that for limited warfare purposes we must have a weapons superiority to offset the Communists' manpower superiority. This means we must develop and perfect a variety of small, clean nuclear weapons." Rejecting mounting scientific evidence, he insisted that concerns about radioactive fallout from atmospheric nuclear testing were the product of "Communist-induced hysteria."[17]

The flip side of Goldwater's advocacy of an aggressive deployment of American armed force was his critical stance toward diplomacy, especially negotiations with the enemy. To Goldwater, negotiating with Communists was foreign policy naïveté. Goldwater wanted nothing to do with any "spirits" of summit meetings: "I maintain there *is* harm in talking under present conditions." He listed a number of reasons why negotiations were harmful to American interests: the Communists were using talks as a tool of political warfare, invariably extracted concessions from American diplomats eager to reduce tensions, and perfidiously violated whatever agreements they signed as soon as it became advantageous to do so. Instead of enhancing American diplomatic contacts with the Soviets, Goldwater wanted to reduce them: counting the refusal to recognize "Red China" as a smart strategy, he wanted it extended to the Soviet Union by "withdrawal of recognition." Even the seemingly benign program for cultural exchanges between the two superpowers was a Soviet Trojan horse, since "the exchange program, in Soviet eyes, is simply another operation in Communist political warfare."[18]

The foremost symbol of foolish liberal multilateralism for Goldwater was the United Nations. Stopping short of calling for the United States to withdraw from the UN, Goldwater nonetheless asked Americans to judge the international organization by whether it advanced the American goal of victory over Communism. Of course it failed this test, not least, in Goldwater's eyes, because the UN, "we must remember, is in part a Communist organization." International Communism possessed a veto on the Security Council, controlled a large bloc of votes in the General Assembly, and thoroughly infiltrated the international organization's professional staff with its agents. Most galling for Goldwater, American taxpayers were stuck with obeying Marx's injunction of "each according to his ability" and had to foot roughly one-third of the bill for this hostile global forum.[19]

Inspired by the mass movement against the war in Vietnam (and even before that by the internationalism of Franklin Roosevelt and Henry Wallace), it was George McGovern, both before and during his campaign for the presidency, who most fully articulated what would become the pure party doctrine of the Democrats in international affairs. Holding on to the idea of American virtue, as inscribed in the nation's founding documents, McGovern nonetheless rejected the Manichean tradition in U.S. foreign policy. American strategy during the Cold War, he insisted, had never been rooted in an accurate assessment of world politics. During a period of greater than two decades, he told a reporter during his 1972 campaign, U.S. foreign policy had "been based on an obsession with an international Communist conspiracy that existed more in our minds than in reality." Steeped in frightening illusions about the identity of our adversaries, the nation was driven to allying itself with antidemocratic regimes that made a mockery of American pretensions of virtue: "The facts are that much of the so-called free world is not free, but a collection of self-seeking military dictators financed by hard-pressed American workers."[20] Many of the problems that the United States faced in world affairs were, from McGovern's perspective, of its own making.

Denouncing the militarization of American foreign policy, McGovern was a crusader against inflated defense spending from the moment he entered the Senate in 1963. The foreign policy establishment, Democratic and Republican, had, he alleged in 1972, "constructed a vast military colossus based on the paychecks of the American worker. That military monster, now capable of blowing up the entire world a hundred times over, is devouring two out of three of our tax dollars. It inflates our economy, picks our pockets, and starves other areas of our national life." Blasting away at the defense budget as a sacred cow, protected from serious scrutiny by the military-industrial complex, McGovern, in the most controversial of his presidential campaign proposals, called for a reduction in defense spending of approximately 35 percent.[21]

The chief lesson that the war in Vietnam taught McGovern—and a whole generation of Democrats to boot—was the riskiness of global interventionism. Blindly pursuing victory by force of superior arms, Americans blundered into situations they did not understand and fought bloody wars that they could not win. Foreign policy wisdom, in McGovern's viewpoint, needed to begin with recognition of the limits of American power to reshape the world in accordance with the design of foreign policy elites. Neither American military power nor American will power could overcome the resistance of other peoples who fought to control their own destinies.

The risk that most deeply troubled McGovern was not that American global interventionism was often feckless. He was haunted by the human carnage of interventionism. A decorated veteran from World War II, he despised the armchair warriors of Washington who sent young men into unnecessary wars. In 1970, McGovern shocked and offended his fellow senators in a floor speech: "This chamber reeks of blood. Every senator here is partly responsible for that human wreckage at Walter Reed and Bethesda and all across our land—young men without legs, or arms, or genitals, or faces, or hopes." If the American elite were callous about the violence done to ordinary American soldiers, Americans of all kinds were taught by the Manichean rhetoric of the Cold War to overlook the violence done to other peoples. Even as Americans shed tears for their troops who died in Vietnam, they seemed "indifferent to death among the Vietnamese." In the name of virtue, U.S. foreign policy cultivated a national chauvinism that regarded Americans alone as "children of God."[22]

As an opponent of Cold War America's huge defense budget and habitual armed interventionism, McGovern was naturally an advocate of diplomacy as the proper centerpiece of U.S. foreign policy. Almost from the moment that President

Johnson escalated the war in Vietnam early in 1965, McGovern, along with a handful of fellow "doves," urged him to engage in negotiations with the Vietnamese Communists. For this breach with a president of his own party, McGovern became persona non grata in the White House, even after Johnson eventually yielded and began peace talks in Paris. During his 1972 campaign, McGovern's critiques of the defense budget and global interventionism were derided as isolationism by Republicans. But McGovern contended that his view of world politics instead reflected a "new internationalism," looking to a quest for peace, democracy, and economic development as hallmarks of U.S. foreign policy in a post–Cold War world. Cutting loose dictators and apartheid regimes, freeing itself from "reflexive interventionism," the United States could demonstrate the strengths of democratic diplomacy, thereby reconciling prudent statecraft and moral activism.[23]

Whereas to Goldwater the United Nations was a monument to liberals' illusions, to McGovern it was a repository of unrealized liberal aspirations. Briefly a member of the United World Federalists organization after his combat experience in Europe, McGovern followed two of his political heroes, Woodrow Wilson and Franklin Roosevelt, in touting the pursuit of peace through collective security. With the myth of a Communist monolith shattered by the Sino-Soviet split, with Nixon chatting with the Chinese and cutting deals with the Russians by the time of the 1972 presidential election, McGovern envisioned a world where the United Nations, once liberated from Cold War conflict, could serve its original purpose and honor the hopes of its original architects.

PURE PARTY DOCTRINES BECOME ORTHODOXIES

Barry Goldwater and George McGovern led insurgent wings of their respective parties, and so their pure party doctrines faced stiff resistance for a time from the parties' establishments. The foreign policy of the next Republican administration, led by Richard Nixon and then Gerald Ford, with a central role played by Henry Kissinger, was hardly an expression of Goldwater's pure doctrine. On the Democratic side, the next administration, Jimmy Carter's, at first adopted some of McGovern's perspectives but eventually abandoned them. It was in the backlash against Nixon and Kissinger on the Republican right, and later in the backlash against Carter on the Democratic left, that pure party doctrines became orthodoxies and true foreign policy polarization emerged. I date the triumph of the new orthodoxy on the Republican side to the period from 1975 to 1980, while the new orthodoxy on the Democratic side crystallized in the period from 1979 to 1984.

In its realpolitik, bargaining with the Soviet Union, opening to China, and decreasing reliance on armed force, Nixon-Kissinger foreign policy increasingly became anathema to the followers of Goldwater's pure party doctrine. Yet it was the inheritor of the Nixon-Kissinger strategy, Gerald Ford, who became the target of the renewed conservative uprising in foreign policy. The uprising gathered steam in 1975, fueled by two largely symbolic events. First, President Ford, on the advice of Kissinger, refused to meet with famed Soviet dissident Alexander Solzhenitsyn. Cold War hawks on the right were furious at this "snub" of one of their heroes. Second, Ford attended the Helsinki conference, which produced an accord accepting postwar borders, ratifying the inclusion of the Baltic nations in the Soviet Union. For conservatives, this was another Yalta, a sellout of "captive nations" to Communism.[24]

Kissinger's hawkish adversaries were now in a perfect position to diminish his influence over U.S. foreign policy because they included Donald Rumsfeld, White House chief of staff, and his deputy, Dick Cheney. The hawks won a major victory in October 1975, when Kissinger lost his post as national security adviser, even as he retained his other position as secretary of state. In the same Ford administration shake-up, Rumsfeld became secretary of defense, where he was still effectively positioned to undermine Kissinger, while Cheney replaced him as White House chief of staff.[25]

The following year was even more momentous for the success of the new orthodoxy in foreign policy. As Ronald Reagan, chief legatee of the Goldwater mantle since 1964, challenged President Ford for the Republican nomination, Ford put distance between himself and Kissinger, even ceasing to use the word "détente." Although Reagan's primary challenge fell just short, the 1976 Republican convention ratified his rather than Ford's view of world politics. A Republican platform plank, entitled "Morality in Foreign Policy," infuriated Ford and especially Kissinger, whom it clearly rebuked, but Ford did not dare to push for a floor fight over the plank lest it jeopardize his nomination. The plank read in part: "We recognize and commend that great beacon of human courage and morality, Alexander Solzhenitsyn, for his compelling message that we must face the world with no illusions about the nature of tyranny. Ours will be a foreign policy that keeps this ever in mind. Ours will be a foreign policy which recognizes that in international negotiations we must make no undue concessions."[26]

Aside from the Reaganite party platform, two other events in 1976 furthered the triumph of the new Republican orthodoxy. At the urging of Cold War hawks, Ford's CIA director, George H. W. Bush, assembled a group, known as Team B, to evaluate (and predictably challenge) existing intelligence estimates of Soviet military strategy and strength. Team B was headed by historian Richard Pipes, well known for his anti-Soviet views, and included a number of leading figures from the anti-détente camp, among them Paul Wolfowitz and Paul Nitze. Its ominous report, leaked to the press shortly after the 1976 election, popularized the idea that the United States faced "a window of vulnerability" until it could match Soviet nuclear capacities and block a sinister new bid for Communist global domination. Not only did the report promote a new round of the arms race with the Soviets, but it handed a potent theme for the next election to Ronald Reagan.[27]

The other crucial event of 1976 was the formation of the bipartisan Committee on the Present Danger (CPD). The CPD brought together Democratic Cold Warriors hostile to McGovern's liberal internationalism with Republican Cold Warriors hostile to Kissinger's realpolitik. The organization furthered the growth of foreign policy polarization in both parties. Estranged from their party under Jimmy Carter, Democratic members of CPD would gravitate toward Reagan over the next four years (a number of them later joining his administration), thereby diminishing internal opposition to the party's shift to the left in foreign policy. Their recruitment to the new orthodoxy on the right added substantial weight to its ascendance in Republican circles.[28]

The new Republican orthodoxy was strongly in evidence in attacks on Carter's foreign policy between 1977 and 1980. Positioning himself for the 1980 election, Reagan led the charge against Senate ratification of a treaty that set a timetable for handing over control of the Panama Canal to the Panamanians. Negotiations for the treaty had begun under President Johnson and continued during the Nixon-Ford era, so here was a ripe target for conservative anger at the weakness of the bipartisan foreign policy establishment. Reagan's rhetoric on the canal played up American patriotism as against pandering to Third World anti-imperialists: "We bought it. We built it. We paid for it. It's ours and we're going to keep it."[29]

A second target representing a fading Cold War consensus was the SALT II treaty, for which negotiations had begun under President Ford and were completed under President Carter. The CPD spearheaded lobbying against Senate ratification of the treaty, arguing that this relic of Kissinger's strategy of détente only further blinded Americans to Soviet global ambitions and opened wider "the window of vulnerability." As events in the Middle East further shook the foundations of Carter's foreign policy, he gave up on Senate ratification of SALT II by the end of 1979.[30]

At the same juncture, Carter belatedly reprised the militant Cold War stance of a JFK. But his last-minute narrative of renewed Cold War struggle paled before the authentic version so vividly presented by the candidacy of Ronald Reagan. Reagan's election in 1980 clinched the dominance of the pure party doctrine originally articulated for Republicans by Goldwater.

It took several more years for the pure party doctrine originally articulated by McGovern to become orthodoxy among Democrats. Initially, President Carter, despite his centrist approach to domestic policy, largely emulated McGovern's liberal internationalism in his foreign policy. He made human rights a centerpiece of his approach in global affairs, proposed cuts in the defense budget, and proclaimed that "we are now free of that inordinate fear of communism which once led us to embrace any dictator who joined us in that fear." Yet faced with troubling Soviet moves, especially in Afghanistan, and under mounting pressure from the right, Carter became a born-again anti-Communist in his final year in office: he issued the Carter Doctrine to warn the Soviets against threatening Persian Gulf oil supplies, pushed for a larger defense budget, imposed an embargo on grain sales to the Soviet Union, announced an American boycott of the 1980 Olympic Games in Moscow, and even revived registration for the draft. Shifting to the right, Carter broached a fundamental challenge to the Democrats' post-1972 drift to the left in foreign policy.[31]

That challenge was accepted by the president's liberal rival for the 1980 presidential nomination, Senator Edward Kennedy. Kennedy's rift with Carter originally centered on health-care policy, but it widened once Carter raised his Cold War banner. The frontrunner in polls before he announced his candidacy in the fall of 1979, Kennedy watched Carter surge ahead of him as the majority of Americans rallied around the president in the Iranian hostage and Afghan affairs. In a speech at Georgetown University late in January 1980, Kennedy struck back, puncturing the patriotic silencing of foreign policy debate with a critique of Carter that resembled McGovern's attacks on the war in Vietnam. The hostility to Americans evinced by the hostage situation in Tehran, Kennedy argued, had been nurtured by decades of American support for the repressive regime of Iran's shah. The USSR's invasion of Afghanistan reflected the Soviets' difficulties in their own part of the world rather than a strategic challenge to U.S. interests. Kennedy urged Americans in this speech not to relapse into a reflexive Cold War mindset or succumb to the scare tactics of the military-industrial complex.[32]

Carter captured the 1980 Democratic presidential nomination despite a late surge by Kennedy, but his Cold War revival had no future in his party. Once Reagan was ensconced in the White House, his initial articulation of the pure party doctrine of Republicans united Democrats in an opposition reflecting Kennedy's global viewpoint. Alarmed by Reagan's massive defense buildup and loose talk among some of his underlings about winning a nuclear exchange, Democrats championed a bilateral nuclear freeze. Equally alarmed by Reagan's interventions in Central America, Democrats raised the specter of another Vietnam and cut off funds for Reagan's crusade to topple the Sandinista regime in Nicaragua. The thrust for superpower rivalry and "rollback" of Third-World Communist proxies on the right was now countered by peace initiatives and anti-interventionism on the left, as the two pure party doctrines squared off fully for the first time.[33]

Just as the "Morality in Foreign Policy" plank of 1976 was the signpost of a new conservative orthodoxy in the Republican Party, so was the foreign policy platform that Democrats adopted at their 1984 convention a signpost of its polar opposite. Dramatizing the perils of a second Reagan term, the Democratic platform warned of the escalation of the arms race, the manufacturing of new missiles that would subvert the balance of deterrence, and the spread of nuclear weapons into space. Meanwhile, Reagan would likely mistake regional conflicts for Cold War battlegrounds, dispatching young Americans "to fight and die needlessly." By contrast, the Democratic approach to foreign policy was a "strategy for peace," including "regular annual summits with the Soviet leaders," "immediate steps to stop the nuclear arms race," and a "selective, judicious use of American military power" in place of "the Reagan Administration's cavalier approach to the use of military force around the world." While the military-industrial complex sponsored war games to plan for armed conflict, a "Democratic Administration will initiate and establish a Peace Academy. In the interest of balancing this nation's investment in the study of making war, the Peace Academy will study the disciplines and train experts in the arts of waging peace."[34]

PARTISAN OPPOSITION TO PRESIDENTIAL LEADERSHIP IN FOREIGN POLICY

One of the conventional maxims about the presidency is that presidents have a freer hand in making foreign policy than they do in making economic or social policy. With the progress of polarization, however, presidents face more substantial partisan opposition to their foreign policies than during the period from the 1940s to the 1980s. Today, partisan media broadcast strident attacks on presidential actions in global affairs. In "balanced" new stories on presidential leadership in the world, the requisite quotes from opposition politicians are typically harsher than those a few decades ago. Partisan criticisms of presidential leadership in foreign policy impact a president's approval rating. Partisan opposition in Congress to presidential leadership in foreign policy has also been on the rise since the beginning of the Reagan administration.

During the era of the Cold War consensus, major presidential actions in foreign policy, including those involving the use of force, generally received support from the majority of the opposition party. Consider congressional resolutions authorizing presidents to use their discretion in deploying the armed forces to global hot spots. In 1957, President Eisenhower's Middle East resolution easily passed in a Democratic Congress, with margins of support ranging from approximately 6–1 in the House to 4–1 in the Senate. In 1964, President Johnson's Gulf of Tonkin Resolution was met with only two negative votes in the Senate, both from Democrats, while passing the House unanimously.

The Cold War consensus cracked over the war in Vietnam, as Presidents Johnson and Nixon faced mounting resistance from Congress. But congressional opposition to these presidents was not partisan in character. Under Johnson, opposition to the president's policy was more widespread among Democrats in Congress. When Congress unsuccessfully attempted to assert its authority to rein in presidential war making in Southeast Asia, its major resolutions on the war—such as the McGovern-Hatfield amendment and the Cooper-Church amendment—had bipartisan sponsorship. The same was the case for the War Powers Resolution of 1973, passed over President Nixon's veto.

Congressional votes on presidential proposals in foreign affairs have told a different story in the era of partisan polarization. Opposing President Reagan's nuclear buildup during his first term, the Democratic majority in the House passed a nuclear-freeze resolution. When President George H. W. Bush sought congressional support for military action in the first Gulf War, 45 of 55 Democrats in the Senate voted no. (Most of the ten yes votes came from southern Democrats.) A resolution authorizing President Clinton to conduct an air war against Yugoslavia to end the slaughter in Kosovo failed by a tie vote in the House, as 187 out of 217 Republicans voted in the negative. In the immediate wake of the terrorist attack on American soil in 2001, President George W. Bush easily won overwhelming bipartisan backing for the Authorization for Use of Military Force. But when he orchestrated a vote to authorize his planned attack on the regime of Saddam Hussein a month before the 2002 elections, putting congressional Democrats on the spot in the post–9/11 political environment, three-fifths of House Democrats and two-fifths of Senate Democrats still said no. When President Obama asked the Senate to ratify the New START arms-control treaty with Russia after the 2010 elections, every Democrat supported him while two-thirds of Republicans opposed him.[35]

Partisan opposition in Congress has rarely blocked presidents from either party in carrying out their chief foreign policies: Reagan continued his nuclear buildup, the first and second Bush presidencies featured wars in the Gulf, Clinton bombed the Serbs, and Obama won over just enough Republicans to ratify New START. Nonetheless, presidents pay a price in foreign policy with the rise of partisan polarization. They lead a divided rather than a united nation in global affairs, are subject to vociferous challenges from the start of almost every major global operation they undertake, and are readily and repeatedly castigated by the partisan opposition for anything that goes amiss along the way. The Republican hue and cry over the Benghazi tragedy years after that event can stand as a marker of the partisan ground that presidents now tread when conducting foreign policy.

PURE PARTY DOCTRINES AND PRESIDENTIAL CAMPAIGNS

Since the era of partisan polarization emerged in the 1980s, pure party doctrines in foreign policy have come to play an ambiguous role in presidential campaigns. During nomination contests centered on primaries and caucuses that draw disproportionately from a party's base, candidates need to take positions relatively close to the pure doctrine. During the general election season, they need to temper their purity in the hope of attracting independent voters. Shifting stances is made tricky, however, by contemporary video and audio technology, which produce an extensive catalogue of recorded statements from the earlier campaign season that can be used, either by opponents or by media, to depict changes of position as opportunistic or insincere.

The role of foreign policy doctrines in nomination contests since 1980 has been modest under two conditions. First, international issues simply may not have high salience, as was the case in the three presidential elections between the demise of the Soviet Union and the September 11 attacks. Second, there may not be visible differences between the policy stances of the competitors. However, if only one competitor stands out for the purity of his or her foreign policy positions, that candidate may gain significant political momentum. The surprising emergence of Howard Dean to lead all other Democratic hopefuls in the polls prior to the Iowa caucuses early in 2004 largely reflected the fact that only Dean was tapping into the passionate anger of the Democratic base about the war in Iraq.

Perhaps the most effective strategic use of a pure party doctrine in foreign policy for a nomination contest was by Barack Obama in 2008. Even as the media christened Hillary Clinton as the overwhelming favorite for the Democratic nomination before the Iowa caucuses, Obama and his advisers grasped her chief weakness: she had abandoned the party's pure doctrine and alienated its anti-interventionist constituency with her support for President Bush's invasion of Iraq. Moreover, Clinton compounded her problem by refusing to apologize for originally backing the war. By contrast, Obama in effect emulated McGovern's campaign slogan about Vietnam—"Right from the Start"—to highlight his original and consistent opposition to Bush's Iraq fiasco. Another of Obama's foreign policy positions, although criticized by the press and blasted by Clinton, also capitalized on the Democrats' pure doctrine: his statement that he was willing to meet, without preconditions, with a string of American adversaries (e.g., Cuba, Venezuela, and Iran) with whom the Bush administration had refused to talk. Mocked by Clinton as inexperienced and naïve in global affairs, Obama nonetheless appealed with this statement to a Democratic base that believed strongly in diplomacy and saw at least a modicum of validity to the complaints by these adversaries about their treatment by the United States.[36]

Because pure party doctrines are located at the poles of American ideology, winners of the two parties' nomination contests usually need to moderate their foreign policy postures in the search for votes in the center. Reversals are out of the question, but general election candidates tend to deemphasize or qualify some of their purer positions once they face the other party. Moreover, their strategists look to symbolic gestures or campaign ads to defend their candidates on the issues on which they appear most vulnerable to opposition attacks.

In an era of polarized partisan doctrines, the parties have opposite problems in appealing to voters in the middle: Republican candidates must demonstrate that they are not too hawkish while Democratic candidates must demonstrate that they are not too dovish. But the magnitude of their respective problems has not been symmetrical. In light of the long-standing preference in public-opinion polls for Republicans over Democrats in foreign policy, Republican presidential candidates typically have an easier time convincing the voters that they are not dangerous than Democratic presidential candidates attempting to impress upon voters that they are not weak.

The first president of the era of polarization, Ronald Reagan, faced the problem of purism effectively in 1980. Reagan clearly had the advantage over President Carter on the top issue, the sick economy, as well as on the personality dimension of likeability. But polls showed that Reagan's Cold War militancy worried many voters, who concluded that Carter was more likely to keep the nation out of war. During the fall campaign, Reagan muted his militant talk and argued that it was Carter's vacillating foreign policy that was the real threat to encourage Soviet aggressiveness and endanger the peace. As Carter pressed the charge that a Reagan presidency would be dangerous, Nancy Reagan cut a campaign ad to turn the tables on the president. The candidate's wife pronounced herself deeply offended by Carter's attacks, which distorted her husband's character: "He is not a warmonger." It was the Democrats, Nancy Reagan asserted, who were demagogues on foreign policy in 1980, playing "on fear."[37]

George W. Bush faced a comparable problem in 2000. Bush was the candidate of a party with an aggressive doctrine in international affairs, yet the public climate of the time was averse to global entanglements. By that year, Bill Clinton's brand of foreign policy, which among other features eschewed the use of American ground forces, was popular. Bush countered concerns that he would send American forces into global hot spots by borrowing a phrase typically identified with the other party's foreign policy doctrine: humility. During one of his debates with Al Gore, Bush argued that while other nations would resent an "arrogant" United States, "if we're a humble nation, but strong, they'll welcome us."[38]

Because Bush eventually squandered the Republicans' customary advantage with the public in foreign affairs, Barack Obama felt less pressure to moderate his foreign policy posture in 2008. Earlier Democratic candidates, however, were not so fortunate. Attempting to demonstrate that they were not foreign policy weaklings, Michael Dukakis and John Kerry inadvertently exacerbated their own vulnerabilities. To blunt Republican attacks on Dukakis as soft on national security, his media advisers dressed him in a flak suit, armed him with a machine gun, and had him drive around a field in a tank while the score from *Patton* blared in the background. The scene was so ludicrous that it provided fodder for a Republican campaign ad and not a Democratic one.[39]

A similar symbolic maneuver backfired on John Kerry in 2004. The 2004 Democratic convention was designed to present him as a war hero who would make a more experienced and credible commander in chief than Bush for a global war on terror. The opening words of his acceptance speech were: "I'm John Kerry, and I'm reporting for duty." As Kerry finished the line, he saluted. This transparent bid to overcome the traditional aspersions about Democratic weakness in military matters was soon subjected to a scurrilous attack by the Swift Boat Veterans for Truth. Yet there was a legitimate criticism leveled by Republicans at the same time toward Kerry's attempted identification with the military. What Democrats actually admired about Kerry's wartime performance, Republicans pointed out, was not his conduct in Vietnam but his behavior upon returning home as a leader of the Vietnam Veterans against the War. Armed with film footage of Kerry recounting atrocities committed by U.S. troops in Vietnam, Republicans nailed him even more firmly to the dovish doctrine of the Democrats.[40]

PURE PARTY DOCTRINES AND PRESIDENTIAL LEADERSHIP IN GLOBAL AFFAIRS

For the five presidencies since the onset of partisan polarization in foreign policy, a dynamic pattern has been evident regardless of whether the chief executive is a Republican or a Democrat. Despite the modifications in rhetoric that become necessary during the general election contest, presidents starting with Reagan have begun their administrations adhering fairly closely to the terms of their party's pure doctrine. However, over time party doctrines come into competition with other factors that bear on the making of foreign policy. Consequently, the purity of presidents' initial foreign policy stances has been diminished. Some postulates of party doctrine are tempered; a few may be shelved altogether. But party doctrines are never scrapped completely, and in the case of Barack Obama they have made a reappearance in the second term. The distance separating a Republican and a Democratic foreign policy in the era of partisan polarization remains considerable.

Among the factors that compete with party doctrines, three appear to be most important: personal proclivities, institutional constraints, and perceived imperatives for national security. Presidents may enter office with—or develop once they are there—concerns and objectives that are inconsistent with their own party's doctrine. In seeking to change American foreign policy from the approach of their predecessors in the other party, they may find themselves constrained by the powerful institutions of the national security state. And they may discover, as realist theory in international relations predicts, that the national security of the nation prescribes many of the same actions regardless of party.

The pattern I describe cuts in both directions for presidents. Unplanned deviations from original stances are sometimes experienced as frustration at the inability of presidents to carry out their initial agendas. On the other hand, a loosening of the strictures of pure party doctrines is sometimes experienced as an advance in presidential autonomy. To the extent that a president is an inheritor rather than an inventor of party doctrine, the diminished grip of doctrinal purity allows for greater agency in shaping foreign policy.

In the current era of partisan polarization, presidents must maneuver across highly political terrain in foreign policy making. To illustrate the interplay of pure party doctrines with other factors in foreign policy, I briefly discuss each president from Reagan to Obama. The initial foreign policy approaches of these five chief executives were all partisan, though sometimes more out of conviction (Reagan, the second Bush, and Obama) and sometimes more as a reflection of domestic political forces (the first Bush and Clinton). In tracing the trajectory of their foreign policies, my accounts are necessarily selective in focus and details.

Ronald Reagan

In his first term, Ronald Reagan was highly doctrinaire in his approach to foreign policy. Reagan's characterization of the USSR as an "evil empire" is notorious. Yet a fuller and more revealing statement in his first press conference as president captures even better a Manichean worldview that was a throwback to Goldwater. Questioned about long-range Soviet objectives, he replied that they remained what they had always been since 1917: "the promotion of world revolution and a one-world Socialist or Communist state." Such an enemy was necessarily to be mistrusted: "The only morality they recognize is what will further their cause, meaning they reserve unto themselves the right to commit any crime, to lie, to cheat, in order to attain [their end]."[41]

With such a grim view of the Soviet Union, Reagan in his first four years in office topped all of his Cold War predecessors in building up the American military while downplaying American diplomacy. Even as he slashed taxes in 1981, he increased spending on arms faster than any other president in a time of peace. Between 1981 and 1984, there was scarcely any movement in arms control, in large part because Reagan appointed Cold War stalwarts from CPD as the chief U.S. negotiators. Reagan's wariness toward the Communists, coupled with a succession of infirm Soviet leaders, made him the only president of the Cold War era not to hold a summit with a Soviet premier during his first term in office.[42]

Reagan and his aides viewed the Third World as rife with Soviet proxies who needed to be knocked off rather than contained. The Reagan Doctrine announced a more aggressive American strategy of channeling money and arms to what the president called "freedom fighters" combating Communist regimes. The centerpiece of his "rollback" approach came to be Nicaragua, whose Sandinista regime filled the president with dread. Nicaragua is a tiny country, but its presence in what Reagan considered America's "backyard" made it a supposed behemoth as a domino. Hence he warned the American people that "if we ignore the malignancy of Nicaragua, it will spread and become a mortal threat to the entire New World." Oddly, in view of the poor condition of highways in Central America, he propagated the alarming idea that "the Sandinistas are just two days' drive from Harlingen, Texas."[43] Reagan intervened in Central American affairs through both of his terms, but resistance from Democrats in Congress and indifference on the part of the American public confined him largely to the tactics of covert action.

To round out this picture of the ascendance of pure party doctrine during Reagan's first term, consider his stance toward the United Nations. As his first ambassador to the UN, Reagan appointed Jeane Kirkpatrick. Kirkpatrick was a Cold War Democrat and yet another CPD stalwart. Reagan selected Kirkpatrick for this post because he admired her argument that it was okay for the United States to back non-Communist authoritarian regimes because they might evolve toward democracy but unwise to draw closer to Communist governments because they could never be changed. Predictably, Kirkpatrick's stance in the UN was confrontational toward the Soviet Union and other nations alleged to be in its camp.[44]

What was remarkable about Reagan's second term, of course, was its startling departure from party doctrine. Almost from the moment he became the new Soviet leader in 1985, Mikhail Gorbachev was exempted by Reagan from the category of Communist cheats and liars. The two men quickly became friendly and eager to negotiate with one another. At a Washington summit in December 1987, Reagan, the erstwhile critic of arms-control deals, signed the Intermediate-Range Nuclear Forces Treaty along with Gorbachev. The following May brought their partnership to a symbolic climax, as Reagan, visiting Moscow at Gorbachev's invitation,

strolled with his new Communist friend through the heart of the old "evil empire,"
Red Square.[45]

Reagan's break with the Republicans' pure party doctrine on bilateral relations
with the Soviets (though not on taking the fight to Communists from Afghanistan
to Nicaragua) may have had a number of causes, but one of them surely was his
own preferences. Contrary to the fears of his critics, who thought the Republican
president was alarmingly casual about the risks of global war, Reagan turned out
to be as scared as they of a nuclear holocaust. For one ephemeral moment during
a hasty summit at Reykjavik, Iceland, in October 1986, the president accepted
Gorbachev's proposal to abolish all nuclear weapons within a decade. The deal
collapsed almost immediately due to Reagan's refusal to sacrifice his cherished
Strategic Defense Initiative, but the fact that he was attracted to Gorbachev's vision of a world without nuclear arms was revealing. That their longtime leader was
now cozy with their enemy was bewildering to hard-line adherents of Republican
doctrine. Yet partisan purity was no match in this instance for the force of presidential agency.[46]

George H. W. Bush

George H. W. Bush was not by his nature an adherent of the Republicans' pure
doctrine in foreign affairs. Essentially moderate in his view of the world, and prid-
ing himself on his prudence, Bush surrounded himself with foreign policy advisers like Brent Scowcroft, James Baker, and Colin Powell rather than with the type
of Cold War hawks who had peopled the Reagan administration. Nonetheless,
Bush was Reagan's hand-picked heir and had pledged to continue the Reagan Revolution. He took office under the suspicious glare of his party's conservative base,
which was all too ready to pounce upon departures from orthodoxy and pound
Bush as a heretic.

At first, Bush actually positioned himself to the right of Reagan by cooling
back down the warmer atmosphere that had developed with Reagan's summits
and arms agreement with Gorbachev. In part a reflection of Bush's caution and
belief in prudence, this "Pause" in the emerging détente with the Soviet Union
also allowed him to protect his vulnerable right flank. The Bush administration
even fed the right some well-chewed red-meat language: two days after Bush was
inaugurated, his national security adviser, Brent Scowcroft, warned in a television
appearance that Gorbachev's charm offensive might be a Machiavellian maneuver
to lull the West into complacency.[47]

Throughout nearly all of his initial year in office, Bush continued the Pause
in the teeth of mounting pressure not only from the frustrated Soviets but from

impatient American allies and U.S. public opinion as well. His cautious refusal to depart from Republican orthodoxy seemed increasingly peculiar as one of the key premises of the Republicans' pure doctrine, the imperialist aggressiveness of the Soviets, collapsed with the extraordinary events in Eastern Europe. Finally, during a shipboard summit with Gorbachev in the waters off Malta in December 1989, Bush began to emulate Reagan's cordial relationship with the Soviet leader. From that point on, until the startling demise of the USSR at the end of 1991, Bush acted supportively rather than suspiciously toward Gorbachev. Ideology no longer interfered with prudence, as Bush jettisoned pure party doctrine for what was essentially a partnership with a no-longer evil no-longer empire.[48]

Although relations with the Soviet Union no longer squared with Republican doctrine, there were other areas of foreign policy where Bush stuck more closely to party orthodoxy. While Reagan, secure in his manufactured image as a cowboy, was freed thereby to deploy limited military force mostly for show, his successor, lampooned on both left and right as a "wimp," felt more of a need to flex Republican muscles. He had his first opportunity in Panama shortly after the Malta summit. Sending in American forces, as Reagan had never been able to do in Central America, Bush pulled off the capture of a petty demon figure, the piratical Manuel Noriega. Now Bush could, in effect, say what his Republican hero, Theodore Roosevelt, had in fact said: "I took Panama."[49]

The oscillation of orthodoxy and prudence in the relationship with Gorbachev was paralleled in Bush's conduct during the first Gulf War. In its geostrategic concern to safeguard American oil interests in the Persian Gulf and in its shrewd construction of a multilateral coalition to share the costs of warfare, Bush's strategy to reverse the Iraqi occupation of Kuwait was classic realpolitik. On the other hand, in its military interventionism on the largest scale since the war in Vietnam and in its Manichean rhetorical trope that equated Saddam Hussein with Adolph Hitler, Bush's big war was a spectacular revival of Republican doctrine (and faced significant opposition from Democrats in the Senate). However, the president and his top advisers held back at the climactic moment of the war, halting the American military advance well before it could unseat the Iraqi regime. Bush received considerable criticism for this caution at the time, and the overthrow of Saddam Hussein remained an idée fixe of Republican conservatives until his son did the job. But the second Gulf War cast a retrospective glow on Bush's prudence in the first one: unlike the son, the father perceived the risks of slaughter in the streets of Baghdad, a lengthy American occupation, and a power vacuum tailor-made for more dangerous adversaries than Saddam.[50]

Bill Clinton

Bill Clinton's foreign policy was frequently criticized as incoherent. For a world in which superpower rivalry had been supplanted by a welter of smaller conflicts whose relevance to the United States was often unclear, the lack of overarching strategic doctrine during his presidency was understandable. But Clinton also suffered from an ambiguous background in foreign policy: a McGovern campaign staffer in his youth, the chairman of the centrist Democratic Leadership Council on the eve of his run for the presidency. Further compounding the problem for his foreign policy, Clinton's experience and interest lay in domestic affairs during a brief period in which much of the American public demanded this focus as it lost interest in the world outside national borders.

Despite these complications, Clinton's course in foreign policy over his eight years in office largely followed the dynamic pattern of his immediate Republican predecessors. Consistent with his party's doctrine during his first years in office, Clinton aimed to cut the defense budget, reaping a "peace dividend" from the end of the Cold War; to keep U.S. forces out of the brutal civil wars in the Balkans; to support a greater military capacity for the United Nations in conducting peacekeeping missions; to promote global economic development and a "democratic peace"; and to advance a liberal social agenda by attempting to integrate gays and lesbians into the armed forces. Predictably, these reflections of Democratic doctrine drew accusations of weakness from Republican leaders.

Opposed by the conservative Republicans who took over Congress in 1995, constrained by the institutions of the national security state, and subjected to the sheer force of international events that he could not ignore, Clinton moved some distance away from his party's pure doctrine over the course of his two presidential terms. A sharp critic of President Bush during the 1992 campaign for slighting human rights in dealing with the Chinese government, Clinton himself shelved human-rights issues in favor of economic considerations as he successfully pushed most-favored-nation status for the People's Republic through Congress. The risk-averse Democrat at the outset grew increasingly comfortable with dispatching American armed forces to the Balkans in 1995 and 1999. And by his final two years in office, Clinton reversed his original course and advocated a larger defense budget, urging Congress to fund many holdover weapons systems from the Cold War era. Using traditional terms from the field of international relations, James Mc-Cormick sums up these shifts: "While its initial approach had a strong dose of idealism, the [Clinton] administration moved toward a sense of realism by the end of its term in office."[51]

To be fair to Clinton, his brand of realism was hardly the same as the Republican version. Clinton's military interventions abroad were mounted in the name of democratic or humanitarian objectives—one reason why most Republicans in Congress continued to oppose them. Moreover, Clinton did not send American ground troops into armed conflicts and thus avoided American casualties, although this constraint placed on war fighting had less to do with Clinton's own preferences than with public opposition to deploying Americans forces "in harm's way." Finally, Clinton remained rooted in Democratic doctrine in his proclivity for the role of peacemaker, successfully in the case of Northern Ireland, less so in the Middle East.[52]

However one measures the distance that President Clinton traveled in departing from pure Democratic doctrine in foreign policy, what was most clearly left behind by his administration was the recognition of American shortcomings in behaving virtuously in the world. His secretary of state during his second term, Madeleine Albright, made this plain in a famous remark: "If we have to use force, it is because we are America. We are the indispensable nation. We stand tall. We see further into the future."[53]

George W. Bush

Of the five presidents during the era of partisan polarization in foreign policy, George W. Bush was ultraorthodox. Beginning his first term as an adherent to his party's pure doctrine, he mostly stayed with it to the day he departed from office. Unlike his father, Bush was inexperienced and incurious in the area of international affairs; there was little by way of personal proclivities in his thinking to mitigate the sway of Republican doctrine. As James Mann has written, to become a credible presidential candidate, Bush turned to Republican foreign policy veterans for tutelage. His tutors called themselves the Vulcans, aiming to signal their "sense of power, toughness, resilience, and durability." Their "preferred solution" to America's problems in the world was "ever-greater military power." Reaffirming what the Vulcans taught, the most influential senior figures surrounding candidate Bush were the two men who had orchestrated the birth of Republican orthodoxy in foreign policy a quarter of a century earlier: Dick Cheney and Donald Rumsfeld.[54]

Once Bush took office, the most powerful influences on his approach to the world were Vice President Dick Cheney, Secretary of Defense Donald Rumsfeld, and Deputy Secretary of Defense Paul Wolfowitz. This neoconservative axis restored the pure Republican doctrine that had slipped in Reagan's final years, lapsed under the president's father, and then been rejected by President Clinton.

Thus, even before the terrorist strike against the United States on September 11, 2001, the Bush administration was, in the words of Colin Campbell, "a breeding ground for unrestrained ideological entrepreneurship."[55] Bush's moderate secretary of state, Colin Powell, was no match for the unilateralist doctrinaires who looked on international diplomacy and multilateral agreements with a cold eye. By September 11, 2001, the Bush administration had already rejected the Kyoto Protocol on global warming, the Comprehensive Test Ban Treaty on nuclear weapons, and a Biological Weapons Protocol. In addition, the administration withdrew the United States from the Antiballistic Missile Treaty so that it could develop a national missile defense program. Barry Goldwater's dictum that talking with Communists was contrary to American security was now extended to talking with nearly every other nation.

Al-Qaida's strike at the American homeland brought the U.S. international backing that sat uncomfortably with pure Republican doctrine. However, once the Bush administration quickly moved on from the war against the Taliban regime in Afghanistan that harbored al-Qaida to announce a new security doctrine of "preventive war" and to target Iraq as its first application, the supportive international coalition fell away (with the exception of Britain's Tony Blair). Once the war in Iraq began, Republican conservatives could again indulge in their dislike of nations, such as France, that did not hail American leadership and American rectitude.

Ultraorthodoxy characterized almost every facet of the war in Iraq. The rhetoric was traditionally Manichean, with the United States standing up boldly for the global good against a charter member of the "axis of evil." The president's own posture was combative, as he dared Iraqi insurgents who launched attacks against American troops to "bring 'em on." Bush even decked himself out in military garb and copiloted a navy fighter onto the aircraft carrier *Abraham Lincoln* in his ill-starred "Mission Accomplished" spectacle. Yet if any single feature of Bush's war in Iraq best reflected the sway of the Republicans' pure party doctrine, it was a downplaying of risks worthy of Barry Goldwater more than of Ronald Reagan. On every score—the interpretation of prewar intelligence, the number of American troops required, the response of the Iraqi people, the financial burden, the construction of an American-style democracy in Baghdad—Republican orthodoxy underestimated the risks of disaster yet did not give ground once it materialized.

Bush's ultraorthodoxy also was manifested in the positions for which he picked hard-liner John Bolton. During Bush's first term, Bolton served as under secretary of state for arms control and international security, where his bête noire was the International Criminal Court, which might have the temerity to bring Americans before its dock. Shortly after his reelection, Bush nominated Bolton to be U.S. ambassador to the United Nations. It is hard to imagine another appointee who could express such disdain for the UN. As Ilan Peleg writes, Bolton "repeatedly denigrated international organizations and called for their abolition. In other times he suggested that the United States should simply ignore such organizations."[56] The fact that Bush nominated Bolton in his second term distinguishes this case from Reagan's appointment of Jeane Kirkpatrick: she served during Reagan's hard-line first term, but was replaced in Reagan's second term by the more conciliatory Vernon Walters.[57] Even though the Republicans had majority control in the Senate at the time of Bolton's nomination to the UN post, his views were so extreme that he could not win confirmation and had to leave when his recess appointment ended in December 2006.

Although the pattern of orthodoxy increasingly tempered by other factors is least evident in the presidency of George W. Bush, it is not altogether absent in his case. During Bush's second term, the leading proponents of the orthodox faith were reduced in influence: Wolfowitz departed for the World Bank, Rumsfeld was dumped after electoral defeat in 2006, and Cheney's voice was muted after the embarrassment to Bush of the Valerie Plame affair. Coupled with the growing sense at home and abroad that Bush's foreign policy was damaging U.S. standing in the world, there was now an opening for a modest return to diplomacy, centered in the State Department. Although the record of actual accomplishments was limited, Condoleezza Rice and her aides at least got the Bush administration back into the business of negotiating with other countries. The administration belatedly turned to resuming talks between Israelis and Palestinians and joining multilateral negotiations for a common strategy to contain Iran. To the dismay of hard-liners like Bolton, it engaged in Six-Party talks over North Korea's nuclear capacity and eventually reached an agreement.[58] In the case of Bush's signature foreign policy, the war on terror, his administration's most controversial tactics were moderated during the second term. George W. Bush had nothing comparable to Reagan's liking for Gorbachev and horror at the prospect of nuclear holocaust, much less his father's caution and prudence, but even he could not stand forever on the rock of partisan orthodoxy.

Barack Obama

The course of Barack Obama's foreign policy has, in a sense, been the reverse of his predecessor's trajectory. While Bush stuck faithfully to party doctrine until his last years in office, Obama's Democratic orthodoxy was significantly circumscribed during his first term, only to be revived in his second term when shifts in the contours of international politics created openings for a partial return to the president's original pledge of a more liberal foreign policy.

Because Bush's fidelity to pure Republican doctrine led the United States into disaster in Iraq and diminished the nation's stature around the world, prospects for the pursuit of Democratic doctrine in foreign policy seemed brighter at the moment Obama entered office than at any time since the onset of partisan polarization. Furthermore, he appeared more personally committed to the tenets of his party's pure doctrine than Clinton had been. As James Mann observes, Obama's intention was that the United States "would manage to work out a new, more modest international role."[59]

A partial list of Obama's original international agenda makes plain its Democratic provenance. Among the new president's initial goals were closing the Guantanamo prison, ending the practice of torture, and generally eschewing the high-handed claims of Bush's "neo-imperial presidency"; initiating diplomatic dialogues with American adversaries, especially Iran; establishing a more sympathetic relationship with the Muslim world; responding favorably to forces of change in Latin America; vigorously advancing the cause of nuclear nonproliferation; and closing the book on Bush's war in Iraq. Overall, the ambitiousness of Obama's international agenda was nearly as great as that of his domestic agenda.

Despite the distractions from foreign policy of an economic crisis and a sweeping health-care reform bill, Obama did advance some of this agenda in his first two years. On the broad front of repairing the damaged standing of the United States in the world community, he could claim considerable progress. In December 2009 he accepted a Nobel Peace Prize, awarded not for his accomplishments but for his intentions (most of the global community prefers the Democratic to the Republican doctrine). In many small ways, Obama followed Democratic orthodoxy in its rejection of a Manichean worldview. For example, reaching out to a suspicious Muslim world in a Cairo speech, he acknowledged that the United States had been partly responsible for past breaches when it "played a role in the overthrow of a democratically elected Iranian government." Orthodox Democratic statements like these elicited orthodox Republican responses. Thus Mitt Romney said of Obama: "Never before in American history has its president gone before so many foreign audiences to apologize for so many Americans misdeeds, real and imagined. . . . There are anti-American fires burning all across the globe; President Obama's words are like kindling to them."[60]

Yet much of Obama's agenda went unfulfilled in his first term. American troops left Iraq and torture was banned, but the Guantanamo prison remained open. Iranian leaders scorned dialogue with the United States for years. Hostile foreign leaders elsewhere (for example, President Hugo Chavez in Venezuela) kept up their anti-American verbiage. In keeping with a campaign promise, and under pressure from the military establishment, Obama substantially expanded American involvement in the Afghan War, albeit without Bush's swagger. Although this move reflected his campaign argument that Iraq had from the start been the wrong war and Afghanistan the right war, his party base nonetheless was dismayed: in an *ABC News/Washington Post* survey conducted in December 2010, only 25 percent of Democrats considered the war worth fighting, as compared to 50 percent of

Republicans.[61] Whether it stemmed from Republican adversaries, recalcitrant national-security agencies and their congressional allies, or foreign regimes whose worldview and interests are contrary to those of the United States, opposition to the president's global agenda was more formidable than he had anticipated.[62]

More surprising to Obama's supporters than the obstacles to Democratic orthodoxy were the president's departures from it. Liberal Democrats repeatedly voiced their distress about Obama's counterterrorism policies: warrantless surveillance, rendition of suspected terrorists, and above all an expanded use of "targeted killings" by unmanned drones. The antiwar champion they thought they had elected in 2008 was turning out, they charged, to be little different than his war-mongering predecessor. The continuities with Bush's counterterrorism approach were real enough, but they reflected the same kinds of factors that had tempered partisan orthodoxy in Obama's predecessors. National-security bureaucracies, especially the Pentagon, the National Security Agency, and the CIA, pushed hard against the White House to protect the status quo. The realist imperative that the commander in chief is responsible for safeguarding the lives of Americans weighed heavily on Obama, according to the testimony of his close aides. And he was never fervently antiwar as were many on the Democratic left.[63]

Assessing Obama's foreign policy at the end of his first term, most Republicans charged the president with weakness and many Democrats expressed disappointment. The only praise the president tended to receive came from foreign policy analysts, who decided that Obama was at heart a pragmatist with foreign policy instincts closer to those of George H. W. Bush than to more doctrinaire predecessors.[64] Yet his second term complicated the picture of Obama the pragmatist as it suggested his desire to restore Democratic doctrine in those areas where there had been favorable shifts in the political ground.

Foreign policy difficulties ran as deep in Obama's second term as in his first. The attempt to "reset" relations with Russia, one of his administration's signal foreign policy undertakings, finally collapsed with Russian president Putin's invasion and annexation of the Crimea. Even more frustrating was the return of the American military to Iraq. No goal so marked Obama's initial foreign policy as putting an end to the American military debacle in Iraq; no reversal was thus as painful as the need to redeploy American air power and special forces to combat the shocking advances of the fanatical Islamic State in Iraq and Syria. The Obama administration's response to the new crisis in the Middle East brought opposition from both flanks: surveys showed loss of support from antiwar Democrats, who feared a slippery slope toward a second Iraq war, and massive condemnation from Republicans, who already thought the president was not tough enough.[65] The president faced even more intense criticism of his approach toward the Islamic State after terrorist attacks in Paris and California late in 2015.

More so than in his first term, Obama now was determined to debate critics of his foreign policy, especially those on the right. Responding in a 2014 commencement address at West Point to the accusation that he was a timid president refusing to exercise traditional American leadership in global affairs, he said: "Since World War II, some of our most costly mistakes came not from our restraint, but from our willingness to rush into military adventures without thinking through the consequences, without building international support and legitimacy for our action, without leveling with the American people about the sacrifices required."[66] Critics lambasted the speech for lacking a clarion call to reassert American commitment and strength. Yet Obama's case for restraint in foreign policy was consistent with the original premise of his presidency and articulated a cornerstone of Democratic doctrine.

Obama also seized on new openings during his second term to pursue long-delayed objectives in his original foreign policy. As previously mentioned, during his first run for the presidency he had pledged to seek dialogue with America's customary adversaries. Little progress was made on this front during his first term, but now leadership changes in two nations, Cuba and Iran, created opportunities for bold departures. With Raúl Castro, an economic reformer, in place of his brother Fidel, and with moderate Hassan Rouhani as Iranian president instead of hardliner Mahmoud Ahmadinejad, Obama moved to capitalize on the emergence of new leaders more receptive to American diplomacy. The restoration of official relations with Cuba after a fifty-five-year Cold War rupture was historic but relatively easier to accomplish due to the president's constitutional power to recognize foreign governments.[67] Negotiating a historic agreement to restrict the size and nature of Iran's nuclear program was more difficult and fraught with risk, but the Obama administration's leadership of a broad coalition of global powers to pursue a diplomatic way out of a prospective military catastrophe in the Middle East was a powerful signpost of the president's underlying adherence to Democratic doctrine.[68]

Equally reflective of contemporary partisan polarization in foreign policy was the Republican reaction to the administration's nuclear accord with Iran. Congressional Republicans cast aside the last vestiges of bipartisanship in foreign policy in trying to undermine the negotiations with Iran. House Speaker John Boehner invited Israeli president Benjamin Netanyahu, a vehement opponent of any deal with Iran, to address Congress in defiance of the Obama administration.[69] Freshman senator Tom Cotton of Arkansas drafted a letter to the Iranian government, signed by forty-seven of the fifty-four Republicans (but no Democrats) in the upper house, warning this longstanding American adversary that any agreement with a Democratic president was likely to be undone whenever Republicans had the power to do so.[70] Congressional votes on the Iran accord were not strictly partisan: while no Republicans supported it, fidelity to Israel and mistrust of Iran led a small minority of Democrats to oppose the president. Yet in the main, the struggle over policy toward Iran revealed just how polarized were a Democratic president and a Republican Congress as both stood by core premises of their respective party doctrines.

CONCLUSION

The emergence of rival party doctrines has significantly impacted presidential leadership in foreign policy. The most obvious effect of partisan polarization has been the decline in support for presidential undertakings abroad. Especially compared to the era with which this chapter began—the era of Eisenhower and Kennedy—presidents today can expect that, save for exceptional circumstances, many members of Congress will oppose their foreign policies. Party identifiers from the out party will also be predisposed to disapprove of the president's performance in foreign affairs. It is not only the extent of opposition, but its vehemence, that marks the contemporary politics of foreign policy. On partisan ground, harsh views of a president's motives and maneuvers in foreign affairs will echo through mainstream media and proliferate on the Internet and social media.

Yet if partisan polarization has increased the political costs that presidents incur in foreign policy making, it has not, at least so far, prevented them from prevailing in most contests over America's approach to the world. The field of foreign policy may have become as uncivil as the fields of economic and social policy, but presidents still have constitutional and positional advantages in global affairs that they lack in domestic policy arenas, especially when they wear the cloak of commander in chief.

Ironically, partisan polarization at times may expand a president's room to maneuver in foreign policy making. The Cold War consensus of Eisenhower's and Kennedy's time had relatively rigid parameters: many moves appeared ruled out lest a president of that era open himself to the charge of "soft on Communism." Presidents today who shape their foreign policies in light of party doctrines can move more boldly to the right or left with a supportive political base behind them. Alternatively, they can cut against ideological type and place national security imperatives above partisan values. Barack Obama has experienced plenty of partisan vituperation from Republicans for his foreign policy. Yet Obama has been able to thrill liberal Democrats with an opening to Cuba and a diplomatic deal with Iran, to anger them with an increase in drone strikes, and to sustain a fleeting "rally-round-the flag" consensus of both parties by ordering the killing of Osama bin Laden. Foreign policy making on partisan ground is not necessarily less successful than in the past. But the political forms it assumes have to be recognized as fundamentally different.

The most important consequence of foreign policy making on partisan ground may, in the end, have less to do with presidential power than with the nation's course in global affairs. Prior to World War II, the foreign policies of the two major American parties were sometimes far apart—but the United States was not then a global behemoth. During the early Cold War period, anti-Communism provided the basis for an overlapping consensus between the parties. Since the era of partisan polarization commenced over three decades ago, however, rival partisan doctrines have created something of a split personality in the global leadership of the world's one superpower. Under conditions of partisan polarization, American foreign policy will tend to veer in a different direction with each change in party control of the presidency.

Conclusion

Philopoemen was a model for Machiavelli of a leader who knew how to ask the right questions. Surveying terrain, the Achaean inquired of his companions how the contours of the landscape might suggest stratagems for attack or retreat. Only if the commander of military forces studied the ground upon which battles might be fought would he be prepared for "all the contingencies." The Achaean general's questions are as applicable to political leadership as to military leadership. In the case of the American presidency, it is not only chief executives themselves who need to survey the grounds on which their political battles will take place. Anyone who has a stake in presidents' fates, or who simply wants to understand presidents' actions in their full contexts, needs to pay attention to what this book has called the political ground for presidential leadership.

In the spirit of Machiavelli, I have turned to history in this book for not only insight into recurrent patterns but also an awareness of flux and contingency on political ground. Much of the wisdom that classic scholarship on the presidency produces congeals over time into conventional wisdom, steeped in political realities that no longer hold. A Machiavellian perspective points us toward using the past for clues into new configurations of structure and agency. It requires us continually to reassess the balance between what endures and what is already in motion.

The contours of media ground have periodically shifted for presidents over the course of American history. During the "golden age of presidential television" from Kennedy to Reagan, centralized media offered advantageous terrain for mounting presidential spectacles. Of course talent at using media was still essential for a successful spectacle. Presidents Kennedy and Reagan presented winning spectacles, but Johnson, Ford, and Carter floundered in presenting appealing identities. (Nixon was a special case—relentless and often clever use of media that conveyed strength and willpower but nary a trace of charm or warmth.) By contrast, the combination of increasingly decentralized media and increasingly polarized politics has made for a harsh terrain for presidential spectacles. There are now so many media outlets for covering and commenting on presidents, a sizable number of which are in the hands of partisan foes, that presidential gestures are routinely called into question and presidents' identities themselves are subjected to deconstruction and disparagement. At the fringes of media, where partisan furies run hottest, presidents are denounced as criminals (Bill Clinton alleged to have ordered the murder of aide Vince Foster) or frauds (Barack Obama alleged to be a foreigner by birth).

It is not only lesser talent at presenting spectacles, then, that distinguishes George W. Bush from Ronald Reagan or Barack Obama from John F. Kennedy. Bush and Obama have had to operate on tougher media terrain. Still, the unfavorable changes in the contours of the media ground have not ruled out the possibility of an effective presidential spectacle. President Clinton encountered antagonistic media and vitriolic partisan foes, yet after a shaky start his postmodern spectacle kept him buoyant in the public eye. His shifting political personae may have been opportunistic, and they may not have cut very deep for making policy or creating a legacy, but they were critical for warding off attacks that might have proved fatal to another president.

Unlike media ground, the ground of political economy has been more stable for presidents. One dynamic factor has been the changing character of American capitalism itself, most recently with the decline of industry and the ascendance of finance. Yet the essential features of this ground in political terms have changed little since the New Deal: capital has so many structural and instrumental advantages that presidents, requiring its cooperation in managing the economy, shy away from conflict with it. When some presidents, from the Democratic Party, nonetheless have found themselves in confrontations with "economic royalists," they soon have perceived that the economic risks for taking on the capitalist elite threaten their political fortunes. Retreat has been the pattern for Kennedy, Clinton, and, to a lesser extent, Obama when presidential power has encountered the power of capital on the field of political struggle.

Capital is immensely powerful in the United States, but it is not politically invulnerable. The failures of the capitalist system to live up to its promises at times offer openings for presidents to alter the balance of power. Franklin Roosevelt could record victories over high finance (creation of the Securities and Exchange Commission) and industry (regulation and collective bargaining). Barack Obama scored an important if more modest victory over Wall Street with the Dodd-Frank legislation. In the case of the Democratic Party, the party's base, increasingly liberal today, is a force for pushing its presidents toward taking on capital. As combating economic inequality becomes a passionate cause for American liberalism, a Democratic president may have less of a political incentive than in the past to retreat when "economic royalists" pull out their big guns.

Coalition politics takes place on a swirling battleground and requires presidents and their political aides to attend to multiple fronts at once. A few sectors of this battleground, involving "captured groups" like organized labor for Democrats and evangelical conservatives for Republicans, are relatively secure. On other fronts, presidents go on the attack, as FDR did with African Americans and Nixon did with white workers, launching raids to poach blocs of voters from the opposing party. On still other fronts, presidents and the party that battles them thrust and counterthrust in bids for the support of groups, such as senior citizens, that are rich in electoral resources and politically up for grabs. Many of the maneuvers that determine the shape of electoral coalitions occur outside the limelight, cast into obscurity by rhetorical rituals that present the president as the representative and servant of all the people.

Of all the forms of coalition politics that presidents encounter, the most complex—but sometimes the most fruitful—involves the allied forces of social movements. These difficult partners, whose sense of urgency and overriding commitment to their cause produce tensions with a White House holding different priorities and concerned about alienating other groups in its coalition, can cause political headaches for presidents. Especially when movements employ the tactics of protest politics, dramatizing the gap between the ideals presidents espouse and their inaction in following through on them, the White House wishes they would just quiet down and behave like normal interest groups. Yet it has been the pressure from the likes of the civil rights movement and LGBT movement that has driven presidents to be bolder than they planned. Eventual commitment to movement causes has cost presidents politically, at least in the case of Democratic presidents and the South, but it has also sealed political support among not only adherents of the movement but also those who have been moved by its campaign for social justice. The ultimate payoff for presidents here lies less in electoral support than in legacy, as presidents are celebrated for democratic advances they had not originally championed.

The ground of domestic policy making is tough terrain. Presidents today are often glibly judged for their domestic policy accomplishments by the standards of earlier eras when this terrain was more favorable; compared to the New Deal or the Great Society, the domestic record for a contemporary president is bound to look inferior. The frequency of divided government is only part of the problem. Domestic policy making today is shadowed by looming federal deficits and haunted by loss aversion amid a dense environment of benefits and services that earlier domestic policy landmarks fostered. When recent presidents have pursued policy breakthroughs on domestic ground, the electoral price they have paid has often been immense regardless of whether they failed, as with Clinton on health-care reform and Bush with social-security privatization, or succeeded, as with Obama and the Affordable Care Act.

Nevertheless, extending the timeframe more broadly from FDR to Obama, presidents do rack up some domestic policy victories. Not all of these victories, however, have similar origins, dynamics, or ultimate satisfactions for presidents. It is important to distinguish policy victories where presidents deserve full credit as entrepreneurial innovators from victories where the lion's share of credit belongs to other political actors or groups that have overcome presidential caution and transformed incremental proposals into transformative laws. In yet a third category are domestic policy accomplishments where credit-claiming is the name of the game. Here presidents have stolen the thunder from rivals with actions at odds with their own preferences, using domestic policy simply as a tool of political advantage. Presidents Nixon and Clinton reaped some electoral gains from their respective identifications with environmental protection and the war on crime, but neither expressed any pride for what he had achieved in these policy areas.

Presidents today can still stride most confidently across the ground of foreign policy making. With few exceptions, recent presidents have prevailed in foreign policy despite the hindrance of polarized partisan doctrines. George W. Bush not only kept the war in Iraq going after it became unpopular with the public, but ordered a fresh surge of American forces in defiance of a newly seated Democratic Congress. Barack Obama deepened an increasingly unpopular military engagement in Afghanistan and expanded a disturbing drone war that his own liberal base despised. Later, he turned the tables politically, delighting his base and incensing his opposition with a diplomatic entente with Cuba and nuclear arms accord with Iran.

But if partisan polarization has not disabled presidential leadership in foreign policy, it has raised the political costs for presidents. Even as presidents advance on the ground of foreign policy making, they face constant sniping from partisan foes. Especially when their global initiatives reflect their party's pure doctrines, presidents need to devote more time and effort than in the Cold War years to holding all of their own congressional troops in line as the opposition's legislative contingent routinely puts up a wall of resistance. Excepting events like September 11 or the killing of Osama bin Laden, public support for presidential ventures in foreign policy, breaking down mostly along partisan lines, is weaker overall than when both parties made a show of bipartisanship.

Although presidents from both parties still retain more freedom of action in foreign policy than on domestic ground, the changing contours of international politics affect the relative odds of success for the respective party doctrines. In the aftermath of terrorist strikes in 2001, the tense tenor of that moment favored Republican Party doctrine, boosting President Bush. In the wake of long, bloody, and largely fruitless military campaigns in Iraq and Afghanistan, the advantage shifted to the Democratic doctrine, boosting President Obama. Indeed, in his effort to sell the nuclear deal with Iran to Congress and the public in 2015, Obama eagerly made use of the miscarriages of Republican doctrine, arguing that opposition to the Iran deal "echoes of some of the same mind-set and policies that failed us in the past," now revived by "the same folks who were so quick to go to war in Iraq."[1] However, following terrorist strikes associated with the Islamic State late in 2015, Republican doctrine was positioned for a comeback.

In the five fields of presidential politics that this book has explored, the Machiavellian metaphor has directed attention to the ground—or, if one prefers, cognate terms such as "context" and "structure"—that sets the conditions for presidential agency. That is not the common way in which most Americans understand their presidents. In the realm of the contemporary spectacle, presidents and their critics struggle to define who the president really is through individualistic accounts that are healthy for media revenues and comfortably familiar to public spectators. Yet as I hope this study has repeatedly demonstrated, to explore the political ground for presidential leadership is not to fall into the trap of determinism. Presidential success is shaped in disparate fields of action by the contours of each ground upon which presidents must maneuver. Yet their ability to maneuver successfully is enhanced if they have thoroughly studied that ground and learned the lessons of their predecessors who prevailed or failed on similar terrain. In the introduction, I signaled my dissent from Richard E. Neustadt's landmark study because he slighted context and made individual skill and temperament the crux of successful presidential leadership. Yet my own view of the presidency is at one with Neustadt's in believing that good presidents, under whatever conditions they face, have to be savvy politicians.

Just as Machiavelli had a larger use for the prince—as the agent for unifying a fractured and disconsolate Italy—so does a focus on a Machiavellian concern for studying the ground of executive action point to a larger prospect for the presidency. America's best presidents have been tough-minded politicians at their core, surveying the political terrain they faced without distorted visions or sentimental illusions. Yet their political prowess has been a prerequisite to their most valuable democratic accomplishments. It is notable that three of the greatest politicians who ever occupied the White House—Thomas Jefferson, Abraham Lincoln, and Franklin D. Roosevelt—were also among the greatest of democratic educators, articulating fundamentals of the democratic creed in words that still resonate with Americans.

If presidents need to know what the ground looks like over which they have to tread, so do observers of presidents. When context is obscured and individuality reigns supreme in the perception of observers, shortfalls are quickly assessed and disillusionment often follows. To avoid false hopes and to prevent erroneous assessments, we need to become much more mindful of context. Watching a president, whether in moments of victory or moments of defeat, we need to keep our eyes on both the figure and the ground.

NOTES

INTRODUCTION

1. Niccolo Machiavelli, *The Prince*, in *The Portable Machiavelli*, ed. Peter Bondanella and Mark Musa (New York: Penguin Books, 1979), 124–126.

2. Joseph S. Nye Jr., *The Powers to Lead* (New York: Oxford University Press, 2008), 85–108.

3. Machiavelli, *The Prince*, 159.

4. Ibid., 148.

5. See George C. Edwards III, *At the Margins: Presidential Leadership of Congress* (New Haven, Conn.: Yale University Press, 1989), and George C. Edwards III, *On Deaf Ears: The Limits of the Bully Pulpit* (New Haven, Conn.: Yale University Press, 2003).

6. George C. Edwards III, *The Strategic President: Persuasion and Opportunity in Presidential Leadership* (Princeton, N.J.: Princeton University Press, 2009), 189.

7. Richard E. Neustadt, *Presidential Power and the Modern Presidents: The Politics of Leadership from Roosevelt to Reagan* (New York: Free Press, 1990), 29. The original edition of this book (1960) was titled *Presidential Power*.

8. William G. Howell, *Power without Persuasion: The Politics of Direct Presidential Action* (Princeton, N.J.: Princeton University Press, 2003), 24.

9. William G. Howell, *Thinking about the Presidency: The Primacy of Power* (Princeton, N.J.: Princeton University Press, 2013).

10. In addition to Howell's work, see David E. Lewis and Terry M. Moe, "The Presidency and the Bureaucracy: The Levers of Presidential Control," in *The Presidency and the Political System*, ed. Michael Nelson, 10th ed. (Los Angeles: CQ Press, 2014), 374–405.

11. Edwards, *The Strategic President*, 188–192.

12. Stephen Skowronek, *The Politics Presidents Make: Leadership from John Adams to Bill Clinton* (Cambridge, Mass.: Harvard University Press, 1997).

13. Ibid., xvi.

14. Original versions—for chapter 1: "The Presidential Spectacle," in *The Presidency and the Political System*, ed. Michael Nelson, 10th ed. (Los Angeles: CQ Press, 2014); for chapter 2: "Presidents and Economic Royalists," paper delivered at the American Political Science Association Annual Meeting, Chicago, August 2013; for chapter 3: "Leadership and the Tending of Coalitions," paper for conference on "Political Leadership: Developing a Comparative Framework," Oxford University, Oxford, GB, June 2010; for chapter 4: "Presidential Policy Leadership: Types and Variations," paper delivered at the American Political Science Association Annual Meeting, Toronto, September 2009, and "Domestic Policymaking: Politics and History," in *Governing at Home: The White House and Domestic Policymaking*, ed. Michael Nelson and Russell L. Riley (Lawrence: University Press of Kansas, 2011); for chap-

ter 5: "Partisan Polarization, the Presidency, and U.S. Foreign Policy," paper for conference on "Global Leadership," Yale University, New Haven, Conn., March 2011.

CHAPTER ONE. MEDIA AND THE PRESIDENTIAL SPECTACLE

1. Niccolo Machiavelli, *The Prince*, in *The Portable Machiavelli*, ed. Peter Bondanella and Mark Musa (New York: Penguin Books, 1979), 135–136.

2. Mathew A. Baum and Samuel Kernell, "Has Cable Ended the Golden Age of Presidential Television?" *American Political Science Review* 93, no. 1 (March 1999): 99–114.

3. George C. Edwards III, *On Deaf Ears: The Limits of the Bully Pulpit* (New Haven, Conn.: Yale University Press, 2003), 188.

4. Baum and Kernell, "Has Cable Ended the Golden Age of Presidential Television?"

5. Ibid. Also see Garry Young and William B. Perkins, "Presidential Rhetoric, the Public Agenda, and the End of Presidential Television's 'Golden Age,'" *Journal of Politics* 67, no. 4 (November 2005): 1190–1205.

6. Edwards, *On Deaf* Ears, 190.

7. Jeffrey E. Cohen, *The Presidency in the Era of 24-Hour News* (Princeton, N.J.: Princeton University Press, 2008), 49–70.

8. On the emergence of a media eager to expose the secrets of presidential politicians, see Matt Bai, *All the Truth is Out: The Week Politics Went Tabloid* (New York: Knopf, 2014).

9. Juliet Eilperin, "Here's How the First President of the Social Media Age Has Chosen to Connect with Americans," *Washington Post*, May 27, 2015.

10. See Martha Joynt Kumar, *Managing the President's Message: The White House Communications Operation* (Baltimore: Johns Hopkins University Press, 2007).

11. Daniel Dayan and Elihu Katz, "Electronic Ceremonies: Television Performs a Royal Wedding," in *On Signs*, ed. Marshall Blonsky (Baltimore: Johns Hopkins University Press, 1985), 16.

12. Roland Barthes, *Mythologies* (New York: Hill and Wang, 1972), 15–25.

13. Theodore J. Lowi, *The Personal President* (Ithaca, N.Y.: Cornell University Press, 1985), 96.

14. See Stephen J. Wayne, "Great Expectations: What People Want from Presidents," in *Rethinking the Presidency*, ed. Thomas Cronin (Boston: Little, Brown, 1982), 185–199; and Thomas E. Cronin, *The State of the Presidency*, 2nd ed. (Boston: Little, Brown, 1980), 2–25.

15. Guy Debord, *Society of the Spectacle* (Detroit: Black and Red, 1983), paragraph 60.

16. On the confidence of the public personality and the anxiety of the audience, see Richard Sennett, *The Fall of Public Man* (New York: Knopf, 1977).

17. Erving Goffman, *The Presentation of Self in Everyday Life* (Garden City, N.Y.: Anchor Books, 1959), 104.

18. Prominent students of presidential rhetoric include Mary Stuckey, Karlyn Kohrs Campbell, Martin Medhurst, and David Zarefsky.

19. Edwards, *On Deaf* Ears, 104.

20. Lawrence R. Jacobs, "Irrational Exuberance: Selling Domestic Policy from the White

House," in *Governing at Home: The White House and Domestic Policymaking*, ed. Michael Nelson and Russell L. Riley (Lawrence: University Press of Kansas, 2011), 148. For qualifications to this conclusion, finding certain conditions under which presidents can succeed in moving public opinion in their direction, see Brandon Rottinghaus, *The Provisional Pulpit: Modern Presidential Leadership of Public Opinion* (College Station: Texas A&M University Press, 2010).

21. For an alternative approach to public perceptions of presidents as leaders, relying primarily on survey data, see Jeffrey Cohen, *Presidential Leadership in Public Opinion: Causes and Consequences* (New York: Cambridge University Press, 2015).

22. See Douglass Adair, "Fame and the Founding Fathers," in *Fame and the Founding Fathers: Essays by Douglass Adair*, ed. Trevor Colbourn (New York: W. W. Norton, 1974).

23. On Washington and image-making, see Richard J. Ellis, *Presidential Travel: The Journey from George Washington to George W. Bush* (Lawrence: University Press of Kansas, 2008), 20–25; Bruce Miroff, *Icons of Democracy: American Leaders as Heroes, Aristocrats, Dissenters, and Democrats* (Lawrence: University Press of Kansas, 2000), 33–34.

24. Ellis, *Presidential Travel*, 25–26.

25. On Theodore Roosevelt's image-making, see Miroff, *Icons of Democracy*, 166–175.

26. Franklin D. Roosevelt, Fireside Chat, December 29, 1940, millercenter.org/president /fdroosevelt/speeches/speech-3319.

27. Dan Rather and Gary Paul Gates, *The Palace Guard* (New York: Warner Books, 1975), 285.

28. Patrick Anderson, *The President's Men* (Garden City, N.Y.: Anchor Books, 1969), 239.

29. David Halberstam, *The Best and the Brightest* (Greenwich, Conn.: Fawcett Crest Books, 1973), 57.

30. Anderson, *The President's Men*, 279.

31. See Michael Rogin, *Ronald Reagan, the Movie, and Other Episodes in Political Demonology* (Berkeley: University of California Press, 1987), 1–43.

32. Paul D. Erickson, *Reagan Speaks: The Making of an American Myth* (New York: New York University Press, 1985), 49, 51, 52.

33. Quoted in ibid., 100.

34. Lou Cannon, *Reagan* (New York: Putnam, 1982), 371–401.

35. "Meet David Stockman," *Newsweek*, February 16, 1981.

36. Nicholas Lemann, "The Peacetime War," *Atlantic*, October 1984: 88.

37. "From Bad to Worse for U.S. in Grenada," *U.S. News and World Report*, October 31, 1983.

38. Richard A. Gabriel, *Military Incompetence: Why the American Military Doesn't Win* (New York: Hill and Wang, 1985), 154.

39. Quoted in "Fare Well, Grenada," *Time*, December 26, 1983.

40. *New York Times*, October 26, 1983.

41. Ibid.

42. *New York Times*, October 28, 1983.

43. "Getting Back to Normal," *Time*, November 21, 1983.

44. "'We Will Not Be Intimidated,'" *Newsweek*, November 14, 1983.

45. Gabriel, *Military Incompetence*, 186.

46. Anthony Lewis, "What Was He Hiding?" *New York Times*, October 31, 1983.

47. Maureen Dowd, "Bubba Don't Preach," *New York Times*, February 9, 1997.

48. Howard Fineman and Bill Turque, "How He Got His Groove," *Newsweek*, September 2, 1996; and Garry Wills, "The Clinton Principle," *New York Times Magazine*, January 19, 1997.

49. See Bert A. Rockman, "Leadership Style and the Clinton Presidency," in *The Clinton Presidency: First Appraisals*, ed. Colin Campbell and Bert A. Rockman (Chatham, N.J.: Chatham House, 1996), 325–362.

50. Stephen Skowronek, *The Politics Presidents Make: Leadership from John Adams to Bill Clinton* (Cambridge, Mass.: Harvard University Press, 1997), 447–464.

51. Elizabeth Drew, *Showdown: The Struggle between the Gingrich Congress and the Clinton White House* (New York: Simon and Schuster, 1996).

52. Fineman and Turque, "How He Got His Groove."

53. Evan Thomas et al., "Victory March," *Newsweek*, November 18, 1996.

54. "Bush's 69% Job Disapproval Rating Highest in Gallup History," www.gallup.com /poll, April 22, 2008.

55. Matthew L. Wald, "Bush Relaxes Clinton Rule on Central Air-Conditioners," *New York Times*, April 14, 2001.

56. "George W. Bush: Bullhorn Address to Ground Zero Workers," www.americanrhet oric.com/speeches/gwbush911groundzerobullhorn.htm; Kenneth T. Walsh, "George W. Bush's 'Bullhorn' Moment," *U.S. News and World Report*, April 25, 2013.

57. Quoted in *New York Times*, January 30, 2002.

58. Elisabeth Bumiller, "Keepers of Bush Image Lift Stagecraft to New Heights," *New York Times*, May 16, 2003.

59. Maureen Dowd, *Bushworld: Enter at Your Own Risk* (New York: Putnam's, 2004), 356. For details about the carrier event, see David E. Sanger, "In Full Flight Regalia, the President Enjoys a 'Top Gun' Moment," *New York Times*, May 2, 2003.

60. Paul Krugman, "Man on Horseback," *New York Times*, May 6, 2003.

61. Scott McClellan, *What Happened? Inside the Bush White House and Washington's Culture of Deception* (New York: Public Affairs, 2008), 274.

62. Quoted in Frank Rich, *The Greatest Story Ever Sold: The Decline and Fall of Truth in Bush's America* (New York: Penguin Books, 2007), 77, 156–157.

63. Sudarsan Raghavan and Dan Eggen, "Shoe-Throwing Mars Bush's Baghdad Trip," *Washington Post*, December 15, 2008.

64. Ron Suskind, *Confidence Men: Wall Street, Washington, and the Education of a President* (New York: Harper Collins, 2011), 482.

65. Lindsey Boerma, "Obama Reflects on His Biggest Mistake as President," cbsnews. com, July 12, 2012.

66. "Barack Obama's Inaugural Address" (transcript), *New York Times*, January 20, 2009.

67. Stephen Skowronek, *Presidential Leadership in Political Time: Reprise and Reappraisal*, 2nd ed. (Lawrence: University Press of Kansas, 2011), 185.

68. Sarah Palin, "Statement on the Current Health Care Debate," Palin's Facebook page, August 7, 2009.

69. See Jill Lepore, *The Whites of Their Eyes: The Tea Party's Revolution and the Battle over American History* (Princeton, N.J.: Princeton University Press, 2010).

70. Scott Horsley, "Obama's Backyard Chats Aim to Connect with Voters," npr.org, September 29, 2010.

71. Amy Gardner, "Obama Plays Up Love of Beer to Ferment Coalition of the Swilling," *Washington Post*, August 15, 2012.

72. Jonathan Martin, "Obama, Biden Share Burgers," *Politico*, May 5, 2009.

73. Linda Feldman, "Obama's No-Win Situation on Border Crisis," *CSMonitor.com*, July 10, 2014.

CHAPTER TWO. PRESIDENTS AND ECONOMIC ROYALISTS

1. Samuel I. Rosenman, ed., *The Public Papers and Addresses of Franklin D. Roosevelt*, vol. 5 (New York: Russell and Russell, 1969), 232–234.

2. Niccolo Machiavelli, *The Prince*, in *The Portable Machiavelli*, ed. Peter Bondanella and Mark Musa (New York: Penguin Books, 1979), 107–108.

3. For earlier work on presidents and the political economy, see William F. Grover, *The President as Prisoner: A Structural Critique of the Carter and Reagan Years* (Albany: State University of New York Press, 1989) and two previous books of mine, *Pragmatic Illusions: The Presidential Politics of John F. Kennedy* (New York: David McKay Company, 1976) and *Icons of Democracy: American Leaders as Heroes, Aristocrats, Dissenters, and Democrats* (New York: Basic Books, 1993). For recent works on the subject, see Lawrence R. Jacobs and Desmond King, eds., *Obama at the Crossroads: Politics, Markets, and the Battle for America's Future* (New York: Oxford University Press, 2012) and William F. Grover and Joseph G. Peschek, *The Unsustainable Presidency: Clinton, Bush, Obama and Beyond* (New York: Palgrave Macmillan, 2014).

4. Fred Block, "The Ruling Class Does Not Rule: Notes on the Marxist Theory of the State," in *The Political Economy: Readings in the Politics and Economics of American Public Policy*, ed. Thomas Ferguson and Joel Rogers (Armonk, N.Y.: M. E. Sharpe, 1984), 37.

5. Charles E. Lindblom, *Politics and Markets: The World's Political-Economic Systems* (New York: Basic Books, 1977), 170–188; Lindblom, "The Market as Prison," *Journal of Politics* 44, no. 2 (May 1982): 324–336.

6. Alan Brinkley, *The End of Reform: New Deal Liberalism in Recession and War* (New York: Vintage Books, 1996).

7. Robert Lekachman, *The Age of Keynes* (New York: Vintage Books, 1968), 287, 270.

8. Mark A. Smith, *The Right Talk: How Conservatives Transformed the Great Society Into the Economic Society* (Princeton, N.J.: Princeton University Press, 2007).

9. Richard J. Barnet, *Roots of War: The Men and Institutions behind U.S. Foreign Policy* (New York: Penguin Books, 1973), 179.

10. John Gerring, *Party Ideologies in America, 1828–1996* (New York: Cambridge University Press, 1998), 234.

11. Thomas B. Edsall, *Building Red America: The New Conservative Coalition and the Drive for Permanent Power* (New York: Basic Books, 2006), 107.

12. See Ira Katznelson, *Fear Itself: The New Deal and the Origins of Our Time* (New York: Liveright, 2013), 172–194; and Joseph E. Lowndes, *From the New Deal to the New Right: Race and the Southern Origins of Modern Conservatism* (New Haven, Conn.: Yale University Press, 2008), 11–44.

13. On the Democratic Leadership Council, see Kenneth Baer, *Reinventing Democrats: The Politics of Liberalism from Reagan to Clinton* (Lawrence: University Press of Kansas, 2000); on moderate Northern Democrats, see Jacob S. Hacker and Paul Pierson, *Winner-Take-All Politics: How Washington Made the Rich Richer—and Turned Its Back on the Middle Class* (New York: Simon & Schuster, 2010).

14. Hacker and Pierson, *Winner-Take-All Politics*, 239.

15. Ibid, 113; Thomas Byrne Edsall, *The New Politics of Inequality* (New York: W. W. Norton, 1984), 107–140.

16. Frank R. Baumgartner et al., *Lobbying and Policy Change: Who Wins, Who Loses, and Why* (Chicago: University of Chicago Press, 2009), 208, 202, 241. For broad findings on the power of economic elites and business-oriented interest groups, see Martin Gilens and Benjamin I. Page, "Testing Theories of American Politics: Elites, Interest Groups, and Average Citizens," *Perspectives on Politics* 12, no. 3 (September 2014): 564–581.

17. Noam Scheiber, *The Escape Artists: How Obama's Team Fumbled the Recovery* (New York: Simon & Schuster, 2011), 212–230; Joseph E. Stiglitz, *Freefall: America, Free Markets, and the Sinking of the World Economy* (New York: W. W. Norton, 2010), 335–338; Eric Lipton and Ben Protess, "Banks' Lobbyists Help in Drafting Financial Bills," *New York Times*, May 23, 2013.

18. Edsall, *The New Politics of Inequality*, 105.

19. On presidential travels to fundraisers, see Brendan J. Doherty, *The Rise of the President's Permanent Campaign* (Lawrence: University Press of Kansas, 2012), 13–41.

20. Robert Yoon, "Goldman Sachs was Top Obama Donor," *cnn.com*, April 20, 2010.

21. Harry Bradford, "Goldman Sachs Employees Ditch Obama, Donate $2 Million to Romney," *Huffington Post*, October 9, 2012.

22. On historical variation in the political influence of business, see David Vogel, *Fluctuating Fortunes: The Political Power of Business in America* (New York: Basic Books, 1989). Covering the period from Kennedy through Reagan, Vogel argues that business power grows when the economy is weak and declines with prosperity. His analysis does not fit well with the half century before Kennedy or the quarter century since Reagan.

23. David M. Kennedy, *Freedom from Fear: The American People in Depression and War, 1929–1945* (New York: Oxford University Press, 1999), 136.

24. Ibid., 214.

25. Quoted in ibid., 282.

26. See Thomas Ferguson, "Industrial Conflict and the Coming of the New Deal: The Triumph of Multinational Liberalism in America," in *The Rise and Fall of the New Deal*

Order, 1930–1980, ed. Steve Fraser and Gary Gerstle (Princeton, N.J.: Princeton University Press, 1989), 3–31; and Steve Fraser, "From the 'New Unionism' to the New Deal, *Labor History* (Summer 1984): 405–430.

27. Roosevelt quoted in Bruce Miroff, *Icons of Democracy: American Leaders as Heroes, Aristocrats, Dissenters, and Democrats* (Lawrence: University Press of Kansas, 2000), 268–269.

28. John Morton Blum, *V Was for Victory: Politics and American Culture during World War II* (New York: Harcourt Brace Jovanovich, 1976),117–146.

29. Material on Kennedy is drawn from Bruce Miroff, *Pragmatic Illusions: The Presidential Politics of John F. Kennedy* (New York: David McKay Company, 1976), 167–222, and Miroff, *Icons of Democracy*, 294–300.

30. John F. Kennedy, *Public Papers: 1961* (Washington, D.C.: Government Printing Office, 1962–64), 87.

31. Kennedy, *Public Papers: 1962*, 315–316; Kennedy quoted in Kim McQuaid, *Uneasy Partners: Big Business in American Politics, 1945–1990* (Baltimore, Md.: Johns Hopkins University Press, 1994), 114.

32. Papers of Theodore C. Sorensen, John F. Kennedy Library (JFKL), Boston, Box 29.

33. Papers of Walter W. Heller, JFKL, Box 5.

34. Kennedy, *Public Papers: 1962*, 877; Kennedy, *Public Papers: 1963*, 215; Galbraith quoted in Miroff, *Pragmatic Illusions*, 207.

35. Data on profits and pay in Herb Gebelein, "Economic Policy in Practice: Perspective on the 1960s," in *John F. Kennedy: The Promise Revisited*, ed. Paul Harper and Joann P. Krieg (Westport, Conn.: Greenwood Press, 1988), 186–189; McQuaid, *Uneasy Partners*, 124.

36. Kennedy, *Public Papers: 1963*, 863; Dillon quoted in Theodore C. Sorensen, *Kennedy* (New York: Bantam Books, 1966), 521.

37. On Clinton's pre-presidential career, see David Marannis, *First in His Class: A Biography of Bill Clinton* (New York: Simon & Schuster, 1996).

38. Bob Woodward, *The Agenda: Inside the Clinton White House* (New York: Simon & Schuster, 1994), 68–71, 138–139.

39. Ibid., 84, 91.

40. Ibid., 134.

41. Ibid., 142–143.

42. Ibid., 239.

43. On the 1993 deficit-reduction package, see William C. Berman, *From the Center to the Edge: The Politics and Policies of the Clinton Presidency* (Lanham, Md.: Rowman & Littlefield, 2001), 23–26.

44. Michael Hirsh, *Capital Offense: How Washington's Wise Men Turned America's Future Over to Wall Street* (Hoboken, N.J.: Wiley, 2010), 85–102, 271.

45. Ibid., 1–19.

46. Ibid., 182–184.

47. Berman, *From the Center to the Edge*, 101.

48. Raymond Tatalovich and John Frendreis, "Clinton, Class, and Economic Policy," in *The Postmodern Presidency: Bill Clinton's Legacy in U.S. Politics*, ed. Steven E. Schier (Pittsburgh: University of Pittsburgh Press, 2000), 55–59.

49. Robert Reich, "Why Business Should Love Gore," *American Prospect*, July 31, 2000.

50. Stiglitz, *Freefall*, 62–74; Paul Krugman, numerous *New York Times* op-eds during Obama's first term.

51. Scheiber, *Escape Artists*, 9; Ron Suskind, *Confidence Men: Wall Street, Washington, and the Education of a President* (New York: HarperCollins, 2011), 143–149.

52. Scheiber, *Escape Artists*, 209, 112; Suskind, *Confidence Men*, 202.

53. Suskind, *Confidence* Men, 246–269.

54. Obama quoted in Hirsh, *Capital Offense*, 300; Obama quoted in Elizabeth Williamson, "Obama Slams 'Fat Cat' Bankers," *Wall Street Journal*, December 14, 2009.

55. Material on business hostility to Obama is drawn from: "No Love Lost: Barack Obama and Corporate America," *Economist*, September 23, 2010; Alex MacGillis, "The Big Split: Why the Hedge Fund World Loved Obama in 2008—and Viscerally Despises Him Today," *New Republic*, March 14, 2012; Paul Krugman, "Pathos of the Plutocrat," *New York Times*, July 19, 2012; Nicholas Confessore, "Obama's Not-So-Hot Date with Wall Street," *New York Times Magazine*, May 2, 2012.

56. Chris Cillizza, "What Bill Daley Taught the White House," *Washington Post*, January 9, 2012.

57. Lawrence R. Jacobs and Desmond King, "Varieties of Obamaism: Structure, Agency, and the Obama Presidency," in Jacobs and King, *Obama at the Crossroads*, 3; Suskind, *Confidence Men*, 433.

58. Scheiber, *Escape Artists*, 221–223.

59. For a narrative account of the passage of Dodd-Frank, see Robert G. Kaiser, *Act of Congress: How America's Essential Institution Works, and How It Doesn't* (New York: Knopf, 2013).

60. Suskind, *Confidence Men*, 3–6, 343–345, 443–445.

61. Jonathan Weisman and Eric Lipton, "In New Congress, Wall St. Pushes to Undermine Dodd-Frank Reform," *New York Times*, January 13, 2015.

62. Nathaniel Popper and Peter Eavis, "New Rules Spur a Humbling Overhaul of Wall St. Banks," *New York Times*, February 19, 2015.

63. Ben Protess and Peter Eavis, "Rule That Curbs Bank Risk-Taking Nears Approval," *New York Times*, December 9, 2013.

64. "Full Text of Barack Obama's Speech in Osawatomie Kansas," December 6, 2011, www.guardian.co.uk.

65. Timothy Noah, "Has Income Inequality Lessened under Obama?" *MSNBC*, July 24, 2014.

66. Neil Irwin, "Wall Street Is Back, Almost as Big as Ever," *New York Times*, May 18, 2015.

67. Bruce Springsteen, "Death to My Hometown," *Wrecking Ball* (2012).

68. Arlette Saenz, "Bruce Springsteen Sitting Out 2012 but Backs Obama," *ABC News*, February 17, 2012.

CHAPTER THREE. PRESIDENTS AND COALITION POLITICS

1. Ralph Ketcham, *Presidents above Party: The First American Presidency, 1789–1829* (Chapel Hill: University of North Carolina Press, 1987).

2. Sidney M. Milkis, *The President and the Parties: The Transformation of the American Party System since the New Deal* (New York: Oxford University Press, 1993).

3. B. Dan Wood, *The Myth of Presidential Representation* (New York: Cambridge University Press, 2009), xi.

4. Douglas L. Kriner and Andrew Reeves, *The Particularistic President: Executive Branch Politics and Political Inequality* (New York: Cambridge University Press, 2015). Also see Brendan J. Doherty, *The Rise of the President's Permanent Campaign* (Lawrence: University Press of Kansas, 2012), and John Hudak, *Presidential Pork: White House Influence over the Distribution of Federal Grants* (Washington, D.C.: Brookings Institution Press, 2014).

5. Niccolo Machiavelli, *The Prince*, in *The Portable Machiavelli*, ed. Peter Bondanella and Mark Musa (New York: Penguin Books, 1979), 107–109.

6. Marty Cohen, David Karol, Hans Noel, and John Zaller, *The Party Decides: Presidential Nominations before and after Reform* (Chicago: University of Chicago Press, 2008).

7. James MacGregor Burns, *The Deadlock of Democracy: Four-Party Politics in America* (Englewood Cliffs, N.J.: Prentice-Hall, 1963); Milkis, *The President and the Parties*; Daniel J. Galvin, *Presidential Party Building: Dwight G. Eisenhower to George W. Bush* (Princeton, N.J.: Princeton University Press, 2010). Party factionalism poses yet another potential problem for presidents. On this topic, see Daniel DiSalvo, *Engines of Change: Party Factions in American Politics, 1868–2010* (New York: Oxford University Press, 2012).

8. See Lester G. Seligman and Cary R. Covington, *The Coalitional Presidency* (Chicago: Dorsey Press, 1989), 63–66.

9. Katherine Krimmel, "Special Interest Partisanship: The Transformation of American Political Parties," paper delivered at the American Political Science Association Annual Meeting, Chicago, August 2013.

10. Ibid.

11. Joseph A. Pika, "The White House Transition Project: The White House Office of Public Liaison," Report 2009-03 (2008), whitehousetransitionproject.org.

12. Committee on Oversight and Government Reform, U.S. House of Representatives, "The Activities of the White House Office of Political Affairs," October 2008: 2–4.

13. Edward-Isaac Dovere, "White House to Launch New Political Office," *Politico*, January 24, 2014.

14. See especially Terry M. Moe, "The Politicized Presidency," in *The New Direction in American Politics*, ed. John E. Chubb and Paul E. Peterson (Washington, D.C.: Brookings, 1985).

15. Bert A. Rockman, "The American Presidency in Comparative Perspective: Systems, Situations, and Leaders," in *The Presidency and the Political System*, ed. Michael Nelson, 3rd ed. (Washington, D.C.: CQ Press, 1990), 57–82.

16. Polarization between Republicans and Democrats in Congress is conventionally

measured through DW-NOMINATE, a scaling approach developed by political scientists Keith T. Poole and Howard L. Rosenthal.

17. Jeffrey M. Jones, "Obama Approval Ratings Still Historically Polarized," gallup.com /poll/181490/Obama-approval-ratings-historically-polarized.aspx.

18. Daniel J. Galvin, "The Dynamics of Presidential Policy Choice and Promotion," in *Building Coalitions, Making Policy: The Politics of the Clinton, Bush, and Obama Presidencies*, ed. Martin A. Levin, Daniel DiSalvo, and Martin M. Shapiro (Baltimore, Md.: Johns Hopkins University Press, 2012), 308–331.

19. Anne Farris, Richard Nathan, and David J. Wright, *The Expanding Administrative Presidency: George W. Bush and the Faith-Based Initiative* (Albany, N.Y.: Rockefeller Institute of Government, 2004).

20. Paul Frymer, *Uneasy Alliances: Race and Party Competition in America* (Princeton, N.J.: Princeton University Press, 1999).

21. Zoltan L. Hajnal and Jeremy D. Horowitz, "Racial Winners and Losers in American Party Politics," *Perspectives on Politics* 12, no. 1 (March 2014): 100–118.

22. Daniel Schlozman, *When Movements Anchor Parties: Electoral Alignments in American History* (Princeton, N.J.: Princeton University Press, 2015), 18.

23. Ibid., 198.

24. Frymer, *Uneasy Alliances*, especially 46–48.

25. Bruce Miroff, *Icons of Democracy: American Leaders as Heroes, Aristocrats, Dissenters, and Democrats* (Lawrence: University Press of Kansas, 2000), 298.

26. See Dorian T. Warren, "The Unsurprising Failure of Labor Law Reform and the Turn to Administrative Action," in *Reaching for a New Deal: Ambitious Governance, Economic Meltdown, and Polarized Politics in Obama's First Two Years*, ed. Theda Skocpol and Lawrence R. Jacobs, (New York: Russell Sage Foundation, 2011), 191–229, and Schlozman, *When Movements Anchor Parties*, 159–160, 193.

27. Steven Greenhouse, "Democrats Drop Key Part of Bill to Assist Unions," *New York Times*, July 17, 2009.

28. On Republican cooptation of evangelicals, see Sidney M. Milkis, Daniel J. Tichenor, and Laura Blessing, "'Rallying Force': The Modern Presidency, Social Movements, and the Transformation of American Politics," *Presidential Studies Quarterly* 43, no. 3 (September 2013): 655–665. Also see Schlozman, *When Movements Anchor Parties*, 198–201.

29. See Robert C. Lieberman, *Shifting the Color Line: Race and the American Welfare State* (Cambridge, Mass.: Harvard University Press, 1998).

30. Sean Farhang and Ira Katznelson, "The Southern Imposition: Congress and Labor in the New Deal and Fair Deal," *Studies in American Political Development* 19, no. 1 (April 2005): 1–30.

31. Daniel J. Tichenor, "Splitting the Coalition: The Political Perils and Opportunities of Immigration Reform," in Levin et al., *Building Coalitions, Making Policy*, 104.

32. On social movements as difficult partners, see Bruce Miroff, *Pragmatic Illusions: The Presidential Politics of John F. Kennedy* (New York: Longman, 1976), 223–270, and Daniel J. Tichenor, "Leaders, Citizenship Movements, and the Politics Rivalries Make," in *Formative*

Acts: American Politics in the Making, ed. Stephen Skowronek and Matthew Glassman (Philadelphia: University of Pennsylvania Press, 2007), 241–268.

33. Sally Hunter Graham, "Woodrow Wilson, Alice Paul, and the Woman Suffrage Movement," *Political Science Quarterly* 98, no. 4 (Winter 1983–1984): 665–679.

34. Milkis, Tichenor, and Blessing, "'Rallying Force'": 665.

35. Bruce Miroff, *The Liberals' Moment: The McGovern Insurgency and the Identity Crisis of the Democratic Party* (Lawrence: University Press of Kansas, 2007), 215–218.

36. Jo Becker, "How the President Got to 'I Do' on Same-Sex Marriage," *New York Times Magazine*, April 20, 2014.

37. Sidney M. Milkis and Boris Heersink, "Through Seneca Falls, and Selma, and Stonewall: Barack Obama and the Gay Rights Movement," paper delivered at the American Political Science Association Annual Meeting, San Francisco, September 2015.

38. "Gay Rights Protestors Interrupt Obama speech at Fundraiser," *Hill*, April 20, 2010.

39. Suzanne Malveaux, "Gay Rights Protestors Demand Obama Help End 'Don't Ask, Don't Tell,'" *CNN Politics*, November 15, 2010.

40. Milkis and Heersink, "Through Seneca Falls, and Selma, and Stonewall," 28.

41. Simone Wilson, "Obama Totally Screws up Gay Activists' Plans to Protest His L.A. Visit Tomorrow," *LAWEEKLY*, May 9, 2012.

42. See Becker, "How the President Got to 'I Do.'"

43. See Harvard Sitkoff, *A New Deal for Blacks: The Emergence of Civil Rights as a National Issue* (New York: Oxford University Press, 1978), and Nancy J. Weiss, *Farewell to the Party of Lincoln: Black Politics in the Age of FDR* (Princeton, N.J.: Princeton University Press, 1983).

44. Figures on black voting percentages for Eisenhower and Nixon from "Blacks and the Democratic Party," *FactCheck.org*, April 18, 2008.

45. Robert Mason, *Richard Nixon and the Quest for a New Majority* (Chapel Hill: University of North Carolina Press, 2004).

46. Jefferson Cowie, "Nixon's Class Struggle: Romancing the New Right Worker, 1969–1973," *Labor History* 43, no. 3 (2002): 257–283; Miroff, *Liberals' Moment*, 184–194, 255–256.

47. Gary R. Orren, "Candidate Style and Voter Alignment in 1976," in *Emerging Coalitions in American Politics*, ed. Seymour Martin Lipset (San Francisco: Institute for Contemporary Studies, 1978), 164.

48. Benjamin Ginsburg and Martin Shefter, "The Presidency, Interest Groups, and Social Forces: Creating a Republican Coalition," in *The Presidency and the Political System*, ed. Michael Nelson, 3rd ed. (Washington, D.C.: CQ Press, 1990), 335–352.

49. Jonathan Oberlander, "The Bush Administration and the Politics of Medicare Reform," in Levin et al., *Building Coalitions, Making Policy*, 153–154.

50. Jeffrey M. Jones, "U.S. Seniors Have Realigned with the Republican Party," gallup .com/poll/168083/seniors-realigned-republican-party.aspx.

51. Oberlander, "The Bush Administration," 154.

52. Ibid., 154–165.

53. Jackie Calmes, "Challenged on Medicare, G.O.P. Loses Ground," *New York Times*, September 15, 2012.

54. Jones, "U.S. Seniors Have Realigned."

55. Elections.nytimes.com/2012/results/presidential exit-polls.

56. Stephen Skowronek, *The Politics Presidents Make: Leadership from John Adams to Bill Clinton* (Cambridge, Mass.: Harvard University Press, 1997).

57. See Ira Katznelson, *Fear Itself: The New Deal and the Origins of Our Time* (New York: Liveright, 2014).

58. James MacGregor Burns, *Roosevelt: The Soldier of Freedom* (New York: Harcourt Brace Jovanovich, 1970), 503–506.

59. See Timothy Stanley, *Kennedy vs. Carter: The 1980 Battle for the Democratic Party's Soul* (Lawrence: University Press of Kansas, 2010).

60. Roy Basler, ed., *Collected Works of Abraham Lincoln*, vol. 2 (New Brunswick, N.J.: Rutgers University Press, 1953), 468.

CHAPTER FOUR. TOUGH TERRAIN: MAKING DOMESTIC POLICY

1. Niccolo Machiavelli, *The Prince*, in *The Portable Machiavelli*, ed. Peter Bondanella and Mark Musa (New York: Penguin Books, 1979), 136.

2. See the discussions by former White House domestic policy aides in Michael Nelson and Russell L. Riley, eds., *Governing at Home: The White House and Domestic Policymaking* (Lawrence: University Press of Kansas, 2011).

3. For the logic of "loss aversion," see Daniel Kahneman, *Thinking, Fast and Slow* (New York: Farrar, Straus and Giroux, 2011), 278–288. For an application of the concept to the presidency, see George C. Edwards III, *On Deaf Ears: The Limits of the Bully Pulpit* (New Haven, Conn.: Yale University Press, 2003), 227–228.

4. William G. Howell, *Power without Persuasion: The Politics of Direct Presidential Action* (Princeton, N.J.: Princeton University Press, 2003), 26. Also see Kenneth R. Mayer, *With the Stroke of a Pen: Executive Orders and Presidential Power* (Princeton, N.J.: Princeton University Press, 2001).

5. Ricardo Rodrigues shows that when presidents decide to issue executive orders, they are also constrained by anticipated reactions from public opinion and from groups that are important to their coalitions. Ricardo Jose Pereira Rodrigues, *The Preeminence of Politics: Executive Orders from Eisenhower to Clinton* (New York: LFB Scholarly Publishing, 2007).

6. David M. Kennedy, *Freedom from Fear: The American People in Depression and War, 1929–1945* (New York: Oxford University Press, 1999), 261.

7. Frances Perkins, *The Roosevelt I Knew* (New York: Harper & Row, 1964), 278.

8. Ibid.

9. Edwin E. Witte, *The Development of the Social Security Act* (Madison: University of Wisconsin Press, 1962), 3–75.

10. Ibid., 78–79.

11. Ibid., 79–108.

12. Ibid., 85–86; Robert C. Lieberman, *Shifting the Color Line: Race and the American Welfare State* (Cambridge, Mass.: Harvard University Press, 1998), 59–60.

13. Perkins, *The Roosevelt I Knew*, 282.

14. Lieberman, *Shifting the Color Line*, 23–66.

15. Perkins, *The Roosevelt I Knew*, 281.

16. Ibid., 283.

17. George W. Bush, *Decision Points* (New York: Crown Publishers, 2010), 325.

18. See Jesse H. Rhodes, *An Education in Politics: The Origin and Evolution of No Child Left Behind* (Ithaca, N.Y.: Cornell University Press, 2012).

19. On "A Nation at Risk" and the Charlottesville Summit, see Patrick J. McGuinn, *No Child Left Behind and the Transformation of Federal Education Policy, 1965–2005* (Lawrence: University Press of Kansas, 2006), 42–44, 60–63.

20. Rhodes, *An Education in Politics*, 114–125.

21. McGuinn, *No Child Left Behind*, 123.

22. Ibid., 125.

23. Ethan Bronner, "Governor Bush and Education: Turnaround in Texas Schools Looks Good for Bush in 2000," *New York Times*, May 28, 1999.

24. Bush, *Decision Points*, 325.

25. Frederick M. Hess, "Why LBJ Is Smiling: The Bush Administration, 'Compassionate Conservatism,' and No Child Left Behind," in *Building Coalitions, Making Policy: The Politics of the Clinton, Bush, and Obama Presidencies*, ed. Martin A. Levin, Daniel DiSalvo, and Martin M. Shapiro (Baltimore, Md.: Johns Hopkins University Press, 2012), 44.

26. McGuinn, *No Child Left Behind*, 158.

27. Ibid., 165–172.

28. Andrew Rudalevige, "No Child Left Behind: Forging a Congressional Compromise," in *No Child Left Behind?: The Politics and Practice of School Accountability*, ed. Paul E. Peterson and Martin R. West (Washington, D.C.: Brookings Institution Press, 2003), 36.

29. McGuinn, *No Child Left Behind*, 173–175.

30. Ibid., 177.

31. Tom Loveless, "The Peculiar Politics of No Child Left Behind," Brookings Institution paper, August 2006, 4.

32. Lydia Saud, "No Child Left Bbehind Rated More Negatively than Positively," www.gallup.com, August 20, 2012.

33. Rhodes, *An Education in Politics*, 174–176. For Obama's prepresidential views on education policy, see Barack Obama, *The Audacity of Hope: Thoughts on Reclaiming the American Dream* (New York: Crown Publishers, 2006), 159–163.

34. Hess, "Why LBJ Is Smiling," 59–64; Rhodes, *An Education in Politics*, 159–162, 174–178.

35. James MacGregor Burns, *Roosevelt: The Lion and the Fox, 1882–1940* (New York: Harcourt, Brace & World, 1956), 218.

36. Michael Goldfield, "Worker Insurgency, Radical Organization, and New Deal Labor Legislation," *American Political Science Review* 83, no. 4 (December 1989): 1257–1282.

37. Theda Skocpol and Kenneth Finegold, "Explaining New Deal Labor Policy, *American Political Science Review* 84, no. 4 (December 1990): 1297–1304.

38. David Plotke, *Building a Democratic Political Order: Reshaping American Liberalism in the 1930s and 1940s* (New York: Cambridge University Press, 1996), 92.

39. Steven Fraser, *Labor Will Rule: Sidney Hillman and the Rise of American Labor* (New York: Free Press, 1991), 286–289.

40. Burns, *Roosevelt*, 215–216; Kennedy, *Freedom from Fear*, 291–296.

41. Burns, *Roosevelt*, 217.

42. Ibid., 216–217; Kennedy, *Freedom from Fear*, 297.

43. Plotke, *Building a Democratic Political Order*, 93–94, 101.

44. Ibid., 96–99.

45. Burns, *Roosevelt*, 219–220.

46. Kennedy, *Freedom from Fear*, 291.

47. Carl M. Brauer, *John F. Kennedy and the Second Reconstruction* (New York: Columbia University Press, 1977).

48. John Lewis, *Walking with the Wind: A Memoir of the Movement* (New York: Harcourt Brace & Company, 1999), 245.

49. Bruce Miroff, *Pragmatic Illusions: The Presidential Politics of John F. Kennedy* (New York: Longman, 1976), 228–230.

50. Nick Bryant, *The Bystander: John F. Kennedy and the Struggle for Black Equality* (New York: Basic Books, 2006), 209–260.

51. Miroff, *Pragmatic Illusions*, 233–250.

52. Arthur M. Schlesinger Jr., *A Thousand Days: John F. Kennedy in the White House* (Greenwich, Conn.: Fawcett Crest Books, 1967), 867.

53. Quoted in Bryant, *The Bystander*, 371.

54. Schlesinger, *A Thousand Days*, 868.

55. Bryant, *The Bystander*, 376.

56. Ibid., 381–411.

57. Quoted in ibid., 423.

58. Miroff, *Pragmatic Illusions*, 260–267.

59. J. Brooks Flippen, *Nixon and the Environment* (Albuquerque: University of New Mexico Press, 2000), 133.

60. Melvin Small, *The Presidency of Richard Nixon* (Lawrence: University Press of Kansas, 1999), 309.

61. Quoted in Jonathan Schell, *The Time of Illusion* (New York: Vintage Books, 1976), 78.

62. Quoted in ibid., 143.

63. Joan Hoff, *Nixon Reconsidered* (New York: Basic Books, 1994), 21.

64. Small, *The Presidency of Richard Nixon*, 196.

65. Flippen, *Nixon and the Environment*, 27, 46–47.

66. Ibid., 28.

67. Ibid., 50–51.

68. Ibid., 85–89.

69. Ibid., 115–116, 132–134.

70. Ibid., 135.

71. Quoted in Hoff, *Nixon Reconsidered*, 23.

72. Quoted in Rick Perlstein, *Nixonland: The Rise of a President and the Fracturing of America* (New York: Scribner, 2008), 460.

73. Quoted in Small, *The Presidency of Richard Nixon*, 197.

74. Quoted in ibid.

75. Quoted in Flippen, *Nixon and the Environment*, 142.

76. Quoted in Small, 197.

77. Stanley I. Kutler, *The Wars of Watergate: The Last Crisis of Richard Nixon* (New York: Alfred A. Knopf, 1990), 135–136; Flippen, *Nixon and the Environment*, 179–183.

78. Quoted in Flippen, *Nixon and the Environment*, 214.

79. Kutler, *The Wars of Watergate*, 545.

80. For Clinton's prepresidential political career, see David Maraniss, *First in His Class: A Biography of Bill Clinton* (New York: Simon and Schuster, 1995).

81. Kenneth S. Baer, *Reinventing Democrats: The Politics of Liberalism from Reagan to Clinton* (Lawrence: University Press of Kansas, 2000), 170–171, 181, 200.

82. See Randall Kennedy, *Race, Crime, and the Law* (New York: Vintage Books, 1997), 345–348.

83. Katherine Q. Seelye, "White House Offers Compromise to Free Logjam on Crime Measure," *New York Times*, July 21, 1994.

84. Baer, *Reinventing Democrats*, 217.

85. On Heston, see Ted Gest, *Crime and Politics: Big Government's Erratic Campaign for Law and Order* (New York: Oxford University Press, 2003), 237.

86. David B. Holian, "He's Stealing My Issue! Clinton's Crime Rhetoric and the Dynamics of Issue Ownership," *Political Behavior* 26, no. 2 (June 2004): 95–124.

87. David Johnston and Tim Weiner, "Seizing the Crime Issue, Clinton Blurs Party Lines," *New York Times*, August 1, 1996.

88. Holian, "He's Stealing My Issue," 103.

89. Bill Clinton, *My Life* (New York: Knopf, 2004), 558.

90. See Carrie Johnson, "20 Years Later, Parts of Major Crime Bill Viewed as Terrible Mistake," *National Public Radio*, September 12, 2014.

91. Clinton quoted in Andrew Cohen, "Bill Clinton and Mass Incarceration," Brennan Center for Justice, October 14, 2014.

92. Jonathan Alter, *The Promise: President Obama, Year One* (New York: Simon and Schuster, 2010), 244–246.

CHAPTER FIVE. FOREIGN POLICY MAKING ON PARTISAN GROUND

1. Journalists routinely refer to the polarized features of the two parties on foreign policy. But substantive analyses of partisan polarization in foreign policy are hard to find, especially in scholarly literature. For an important exception, see Peter Beinart, "When Politics No Longer Stops at the Water's Edge: Partisan Polarization and Foreign Policy," in *Red and Blue Nation: Consequences and Correction of America's Polarized Politics*, ed. Pietro S. Nivola and David W. Brady (Washington, D.C.: Brookings Institution, 2008), 151–167. The impact of polarization on presidential leadership in foreign policy has received scant attention. For example, Robert C. Smith and Richard A. Seltzer, *Polarization and the Presidency: From*

FDR to Barack Obama (Boulder, Colo.: Lynne Reiner Publishers, 2015), focuses entirely on domestic politics.

2. Niccolo Machiavelli, *The History of Florence*, in *Machiavelli: The Chief Works and Others*, vol. 3, trans. Allan Gilbert (Durham, N.C.: Duke University Press, 1965), 1336–1337.

3. David G. Lawrence, *The Collapse of the Democratic Presidential Majority: Realignment, Dealignment, and Electoral Change from Franklin Roosevelt to Bill Clinton* (Boulder, Colo.: Westview Press, 1996), 97–99.

4. Eisenhower quoted in Blanche Wiesen Cook, *The Declassified Eisenhower: A Startling Reappraisal of the Eisenhower Presidency* (New York: Penguin Books, 1984), 179–180.

5. Bruce Miroff, *The Liberals' Moment: The McGovern Insurgency and the Identity Crisis of the Democratic Party* (Lawrence: University Press of Kansas, 2007), 133.

6. John F. Kennedy, *The Strategy of Peace* (New York: Popular Library, 1961), 32.

7. Theodore C. Sorensen, *Kennedy* (New York: Bantam Books, 1966), 686.

8. Kennedy, *Strategy of Peace*, 85.

9. Kennedy quoted in Robert Dallek, *An Unfinished Life: John F. Kennedy, 1917–1963* (Boston: Little, Brown, 2003), 325

10. John F. Kennedy, *Public Papers: 1961* (Washington, D.C.: Government Printing Office, 1962), 306.

11. See John Kane, *Between Virtue and Power: The Persistent Moral Dilemma of U.S. Foreign Policy* (New Haven, Conn.: Yale University Press, 2008).

12. Barry Goldwater, *The Conscience of a Conservative* (New York: MacFadden Books, 1964), 4; Barry Goldwater, *Where I Stand* (New York: McGraw-Hill, 1964), 28.

13. Goldwater, *Where I Stand*, 53, 10.

14. See David Karol, *Party Position Change in American Politics: Coalition Management* (New York: Cambridge University Press, 2009), 136–142.

15. Goldwater, *Where I Stand*, 51; *Conscience*, 111; *Where I Stand*, 80.

16. Goldwater, *Conscience*, 122, 124, 125.

17. Ibid., 112, 113.

18. Ibid., 102–107.

19. Ibid., 114–118.

20. McGovern quoted in Miroff, *Liberals' Moment*, 131, 127.

21. McGovern quoted in ibid., 127; Miroff, *Liberals' Moment*, 132–133.

22. McGovern quoted in Miroff, *Liberals' Moment*, 38, 130.

23. Miroff, *Liberals' Moment*, 37–38; McGovern quoted in ibid., 132.

24. Walter Isaacson, *Kissinger: A Biography* (New York: Simon & Schuster, 1992), 657–665, 669–672.

25. James Mann, *Rise of the Vulcans: The History of Bush's War Cabinet* (New York: Viking, 2004), 57–72.

26. Mann, *Rise of the Vulcans*, 71–73; "1976 Republican Platform: Morality in Foreign Policy," www.ford.utexas/library/document/platform/morality.

27. Lawrence J. Korb, "It's Time to Bench 'Team B,'" www.americanprogress.org/issues /2004.

28. Jerry W. Sanders, *Peddlers of Crisis: The Committee on the Present Danger and the Politics of Containment* (Boston: South End Press, 1983), 149–233.

29. Reagan quoted in Dinesh D'Souza, *Ronald Reagan: How an Ordinary Man Became an Extraordinary Leader* (New York: Free Press, 1997), 78.

30. Burton I. Kaufman and Scott Kaufman, *The Presidency of James Earl Carter*, 2nd ed., rev. (Lawrence: University Press of Kansas, 2006), 187–189, 197.

31. See Miroff, *Liberals' Moment*, 265–267.

32. On Kennedy's Georgetown University speech, see Timothy Stanley, *Kennedy vs. Carter: The 1980 Battle for the Democratic Party's Soul* (Lawrence: University Press of Kansas, 2010), 132–133.

33. Miroff, *Liberals' Moment*, 267–271.

34. "Democratic Party Platform of 1984," www. presidency.ucsb.edu/ws/index.

35. For a different view of congressional checks on presidents in foreign affairs than is presented here, see William G. Howell and Jon C. Pevehouse, *While Dangers Gather: Congressional Checks on Presidential War Powers* (Princeton, N.J.: Princeton University Press, 2007).

36. "Obama Stands by Plan to Talk with Iran," *CNN Politics*, July 23, 2008.

37. For the Nancy Reagan ad, see livingroomcandidate.org/commercials/1980/nancy-reagan.

38. Bush quoted in John Feffer, "Bush's Path from 'Humility' to 'Bring it On,'" www .ipsnews.net/news, January 16, 2009.

39. Miroff, *Liberals' Moment*, 273.

40. Ibid., 276.

41. Ronald Reagan, *The President's News Conference*, January 29, 1981, www.presidency .ucsb/ws/index.

42. Dov S. Zakheim, "The Military Buildup," in *President Reagan and the World*, ed. Eric J. Schmertz, Natalie Datlof, and Alexej Ugrinksky (Westport, Conn.: Greenwood Press, 1997), 205–215; John Lewis Gaddis, "The Reagan Administration and Soviet-American Relations," in *Reagan and the World*, ed. David E. Kyvig (Westport, Conn.: Greenwood Press, 1990), 17–38.

43. Reagan quoted in Jonathan Power, "This Time, Stay out of Nicaragua's Affairs," *Los Angeles Times*, November 2, 2001.

44. Seymour Maxwell Finger, "Ronald Reagan and the United Nations: His Policies and His Representatives," in Schmertz, Datlof, and Ugrinsky, *President Reagan and the World*, 11–18.

45. Gaddis, "The Reagan Administration and Soviet-American Relations," 27–32.

46. On the importance of the Strategic Defense Initiative at Reykjavik, see I. M. Destler, "Reagan and the World: An 'Awesome Stubborness,'" in *The Reagan Legacy: Promise and Performance*, ed. Charles O. Jones (Chatham, N.J.: Chatham House Publishers, 1988), 252.

47. On Scowcroft's statement, see Michael R. Beschloss and Strobe Talbott, *At the Highest Levels: The Inside Story of the End of the Cold War* (Boston: Little, Brown, 1994), 17. On the Pause, see ibid., 19–150.

48. Ibid., 468–472.

49. Larry Berman and Bruce W. Jentleson, "Bush and the Post-Cold-War World: New Challenges for American Leadership," in *The Bush Presidency: First Appraisals*, ed. Colin Campbell and Bert A. Rockman (Chatham, N.J.: Chatham House Publishers, 1991), 98, 110.

50. On Bush's prudence during the war's endgame, see John Robert Greene, *The Presidency of George Bush* (Lawrence: University Press of Kansas, 2000), 135–139.

51. James M. McCormick, "Clinton and Foreign Policy: Some Legacies for a New Century," in *The Postmodern Presidency: Bill Clinton's Legacy in U.S. Politics*, ed. Steven E. Schier (Pittsburgh: University of Pittsburgh Press, 2000), 81. On Clinton and China, see William C. Berman, *From the Center to the Edge: The Politics and Policies of the Clinton Presidency* (Lanham, Md.: Rowman & Littlefield Publishers, 2001), 37–38. On Clinton and the defense budget, see Emily O. Goldman and Larry Berman, "Engaging the World: First Impressions of the Clinton Foreign Policy Legacy," in *The Clinton Legacy*, ed. Colin Campbell and Bert A. Rockman (New York: Chatham House Publishers, 2000), 231, 249–250.

52. Goldman and Berman dub Clinton "Peacemaker in Chief." See their "Engaging the World," 231.

53. "Madeleine Albright Quotes," www.brainyquote.com/quotes/authors/m/madeleine_albright.

54. See Mann, *Rise of the Vulcans*, ix–xix, 234–260.

55. Colin Campbell, "Ideology Meets Reality: Managing Regime Change in Iraq and the Transformation of the Military," in *The George W. Bush Legacy*, ed. Colin Campbell, Bert A. Rockman, and Andrew Rudalevige (Washington, D.C.: CQ Press, 2008), 259.

56. Ilan Peleg, *The Legacy of George W. Bush's Foreign Policy: Moving beyond Neoconservatism* (Boulder, Colo.: Westview Press, 2009), 70.

57. On Walters, see Finger, "Ronald Reagan and the United Nations," 14–17.

58. Peleg, *The Legacy of George W. Bush's Foreign Policy*, 151–152.

59. James Mann, *The Obamians: The Struggle inside the White House to Redefine American Power* (New York: Penguin Books, 2012), 251.

60. Obama and Romney quoted in "Obama Remarks Never a True 'Apology,'" *PolitiFact*, www.politifact.com/truth-o-meter/statements/2010/mar/15/mitt-romney/obama-remarks.

61. ABC News/*Washington Post* Poll: The War in Afghanistan, December 16, 2010.

62. Robert S. Singh, "Continuity and Change in Obama's Foreign Policy," in *The Obama Presidency: Appraisals and Prospects*, ed. Bert A. Rockman, Andrew Rudalevige, and Colin Campbell (Los Angeles: CQ Press, 2012), 268–294.

63. See Mann, *Obamians*, 100–116, 336–337; Peter Baker, "A Legacy in the Balance on Surveillance Policies," *New York Times*, December 19, 2013; Peter Baker, "Obama's Path from Critic to Overseer of Spying," *New York Times*, January 15, 2014.

64. See, for example, Joseph S. Nye Jr., *Presidential Leadership and the Creation of the American Era* (Princeton, N.J.: Princeton University Press, 2013), 144–148.

65. Michael D. Shear and Dalia Sussman, "Poll Finds Dissatisfaction Over Iraq," *New York Times*, June 23, 2014.

66. "Transcript of President Obama's Commencement Address at West Point," *New York Times*, May 28, 2014.

67. Karen DeYoung and Nick Miroff, "Obama, Castro Hold Historic Meeting, Agree to Foster a 'New Relationship,'" *Washington Post*, April 11, 2015.

68. Peter Baker, "President Obama Calls Preliminary Iran Deal 'Our Best Bet,'" *New York Times*, April 5, 2015.

69. Jake Sherman, "John Boehner's Bibi Invite Sets up Showdown with White House," *Politico*, January 22, 2015.

70. Peter Baker, "G.O.P. Senators' Letter to Iran about Nuclear Deal Angers White House," *New York Times*, March 9, 2015.

CONCLUSION

1. Obama quoted in Michael D. Shear, "Obama Compares Critics of Iran Deal to Iraq War Hawks," *New York Times*, July 21, 2015.

INDEX